FROM NORMANDY TO THE NORTH SEA 1944-45

ALLIES in BATTLEDRESS

FRENCH, BELGIANS, DUTCH, POLISH, CZECHS, NORWEGIANS AND DANISH

JEAN BOUCHERY

Computer graphics by Jean-Marie & Jean-Baptiste MONGIN, André JOUINEAU

Translated from the French by Lawrence BROWN

Histoire & Collections - Paris

By the same author, published by *Histoire & Collections*

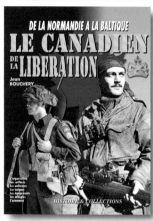
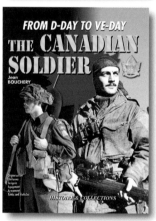

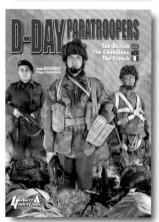

INTRODUCTION

As with my previous books, *'The British soldier'* (2 volumes), and the *'Canadian soldier* (1 volume), this volume will conclude a sweeping trilogy dedicated to the various Allied formations and units that were engaged in the north-west Europe campaign under the command of the Anglo-Canadian 21st Army Group.

Although many of these soldiers had already seen action against the German army since 1939, thousands of volunteers gathered in Great Britain under their national colours and wore the same battledress as their British brothers in arms alongside whom they would fight. Preceded by the heroic French parachutists of the 2e RCP (4th SAS) dropped into the heart of Brittany in the last hours of 5 June 1944, foreign volunteers saw action in Normandy, along the coast of the English Channel, in Belgium, Holland and finally into Germany in the spring of 1945. What were the specific characteristics of these soldiers so ardently motivated by the hope of taking part in the liberation of their motherland? It is the ambition of this book to help the reader discover the answer to this question with a whole host of previously unpublished details such as could only be found in a plethora of books available from specialist bookshops. Whether an amateur historian, collector, modeller or a member of a re-enactment group, the reader will find something of interest in what is, in the end, a 'text book', the fruit of long and painstaking work that makes possible the acquisition of in-depth knowledge of the 'Allies in Battledress'.

Jean BOUCHERY

Note that throughout the book, the adjective 'foreign' will be used for all French, Belgian, etc. contingents, to differentiate them from other 'Allied' soldiers, such as the Canadians or Americans.

This photograph was taken on 4 September 1944 during the liberation of Brussels by men of the 21st Army Group (Guards Armoured Division) who entered the city the previous day. It symbolises perfectly the odyssey of the foreign volunteers clothed with British Battledress. The volunteers seen here are Belgian infantry of the Piron Brigade back in their homeland. Assault platoon commander Lieutenant Rogge, standing on the running board, was killed in Holland on 11 September.
(Private collection)

ACKNOWLEDGEMENTS

Naturally, a great part of my gratitude firstly goes to the team at Histoire & Collections that put together the layout of this book: Jean-Marie Mongin played the greatest role, alongside management assistant Sandrine Régat who patiently typed out my manuscript. Philippe Charbonnier, chief editor of *Militaria Magazine* and *Dossiers Militaria* for his expert advice, translations of my English archives and his photographic talents.

Putting together a book such as this cannot be done without countless contacts of all types, that lead to the involveme of a whole host of people. The following list of names bears testimony to this
and if I have left anyone out may they please accept my apologies.
My heartiest thanks go to:
Mr. Nicolas Fournier and William Maufroy of the Archive department of the town of Dunkirk, the archivists of the Service Historique de la Défense, Château de Vincennes (94). Mr. Pierre Lernieux, Musée Royal de l'Armée, Brussels. Mr. Stéphane Jonot, Mémorial Polonais du Mont Ormel. Marc Jacquinot and Mark Worthington, Mémorial Pegasus de Ranville (14). Mrs. Anna Lebbel, Assistant Curator, Royal Marines Museum, Southsea, UK. Mr. Michael Taylor, my correspondent with the War Department archives at Kew who kindly gave me the detailed organisation tables of the various formations and units mentioned in the book. Mr. J.-M. Michaud, curator of the Musée de la Résistance Bretonne & des SAS de Saint-Marcel (56)

I cannot omit the names of two glorious veterans of the 1er Bataillon de Fusiliers Marins Commando:
Maurice Chauvet (†) who kindly allowed me to use his wonderful sketches,
and Léon Gautier for his valuable information concerning weapons and equipment.

Thanks also to Mr. Daniel Blanchard, Damien Cierpisz for their translations, the loan of items in their collections and documents concerning the Polish chapter. Claude Hélias and Jiri Trogan (translator for the Czech chapter) Stefania Figuière, one of my Dutch relations, Jean-Louis Marichal, Vincent Billiet, Christophe Deschodt, Patrick Lengrand, Patrick Nonzerville, Robert Le Chantoux, Yves Sacleux, Laurent Taveau, Jean-Paul Pace, Denis Lassu Patrick Beaufigeau, Jordan Gaspin, Mike Van Dobbelsteen, Arjen Bosman, Jacques Sicard, J. B. Favier, Alain Sala, Doctor Marc Landry, Jean-Yves Nasse, Nicolas Gohin and Stéphane Hadjadje.

I would like to make a special mention for the historian Eddy Florentin who recently passed away, my mentor and friend for forty years and who opened the doors to his fantastic library and without whom none of this would hav been possible. Special thanks also to Stéphane Brière with whom I exchanged an incredible amount of correspondence concerning the 1st Polish Armoured division.

Thanks also are due to two Parisian militaria shops and their managers,
Frédéric Finel at "Overlord", 96 rue de la Folie Méricourt, Paris XIe,
Pierre Besnard and Patrice Bouchery at "Le Poilu", 18 rue Emile Duclos, Paris XVe.

CONTENTS

THE ALLIES RESIST

Europe in July 1940

All European nations, apart from neutral Sweden and Switzerland, were either occupied by the German army, had signed bilateral agreements (USSR), or were led by political regimes favourable to the Third Reich. In July 1940, the major part of continental Europe was under the domination of the Third Reich. Standing alone against this threat, Great Britain, via the voice of its prime minister Winston Churchill, launched an appeal as early as August 1940 to all the nations that had been at war with Germany and its allies, whatever their size and whatever they cou contribute to the struggle, in order to join the United Kingdo where they would be armed and equipped to carry on the figh Politicians and governments that refused to collaborate with th enemy also chose exile in London and exhorted their compatrio to join them and continue the struggle alongside the British ar contribute to the resistance in occupied countries. The amount volunteers from occupied countries was relatively low in 1940 b gradually grew stronger over the years as others joined them fro overseas territories or continental Europe.

A political map of Europe from the 1930s before the Anschluss and the annexation of the Sudetenland in October 1938.
(Private collection)

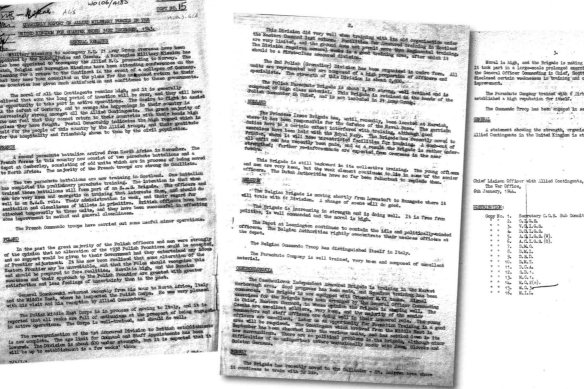

Extracts from a British General Staff report, dated 31 December 1943, concerning the condition of Allied troops fighting under British command. *(Private collection)*

In November 1940 the Allied strength in Great Britain and overseas territories was as follows:

FORCE	Navy	Army	Air	TOTAL
Free French	2750	1080	350	**4180**
Polish	1750	17450	8500	**27700**
Dutch	2400	1570	270	**4240**
Czechoslovak	0	3470	1250	**4720**
Norwegian	1000	1410	324	**2734**
Belgian	0	780	165	**945**

This amounted to, only for the army, a total of 25,760 officers and other ranks.

By 1 January 1944 there were no less than 42,886 service personnel organised into an armoured division, 3 brigades and 3 battalions that would join the Anglo – Canadian 21st Army Group in order to take part in the north-west European campaign due to begin in the spring of 1944. For a year in which manpower was chronically insufficient, the contribution made by Allied contingents was far from negligible.

The opinion of the British host in 1944:

Secret Copy No 15, War Office No 106/4 185. Three-monthly report on Allied forces in Great Britain for the period ending 31 December 1943, made for the future large scale operations planned for the continent in 1944.

"Liaison missions were formed by the Dutch, Belgians, Poles and Czechs to assist the staff officers of the 21st Army Group. The Norwegians also created a similar mission for the Allied general staff for Norway. The Belgian, Dutch and Norwegian missions took part in several conferences concerning their return to the continent in the event of a German collapse. The fact that they were consulted on this subject strengthened the satisfaction and trust of these governments.

The morale of these contingents remained high, with the hope that the long period of inaction was soon to end and that they would play an active role in operations.

The desire to fight and contribute to the defeat of Germany and avenge the suffering endured by their compatriots appears to have been particularly strong. The great majority of these men believed that they would not be able to return home with their heads held high unless they had been involved in the fighting. Analysing correspondence shows the great esteem that they held for the British population, as well as their gratitude for the hospitality and friendship given by these civilians.

France

A second parachutist battalion arrived from North Africa in November. French forces in Great Britain now comprised of two parachutist battalions and a depot in Camberley where various units were gathered whilst awaiting their departure for North Africa (this movement order was later cancelled).

The majority of these men were followers of De Gaulle. The two parachutist battalions were for the time being undergoing training in Scotland. One battalion had completed its basic jump training. It was planned that these two units, once fully trained, would be attached to a SAS Brigade. The officers and men were enthusiastic and energetic when the training concerned a subject that motivated them and they would, therefore, be good for SAS type missions. They were not interested in paperwork and little attention was paid to smartness and cleanliness in barracks. British officers were temporarily attached to these units and improvements in this domain were soon made. French commando units had already taken part in some minor, but useful operations (units not mentioned in the table as they were attached to the Royal Navy).

Poland

Up to 1944, most of the officers and other ranks considered that no modification of the 1938 Polish borders was possible and that they would not support a government ready to accept a compromise on the subject. It now appears that they had understood the necessity of a readjustment of the country's eastern border, a reality that the Poles had to take into account.

Morale was high and the Russian victories were greeted with much satisfaction, rather than the previous feelings of incertitude. General Sosnkowski (commander-in-chief of western Polish forces) returned

As for the French contingent, a later report submitted by the same inspectors considered that the leadership was globally too old and suggested that it be replaced by younger British officers. This sort of appraisal was not, however, limited to the Free French units. It can also be seen with the other Allied units formed in Great Britain, notably the Polish. As an example, we can mention Commandant Philippe Kieffer commanding the 1er Bataillon de Fusiliers-Marins Commando, aged 42 in 1944, whereas Brigadier Lord Lovat, commanding the 1st Special Service Brigade to which Kieffer's unit was attached, was only 32 years of age.

from a trip to North Africa, Italy and the Middle East, where he had inspected the Polish Corps. He was very satisfied with his tour and the way in which the Allied commanders welcomed him.

The Polish Corps was in the process of being transferred to Italy and the men were full of enthusiasm at the idea of taking part soon in operations. The Corps was well trained and ought to perform well. The reorganisation of the 1st Armoured Division according to the British set-up was now complete. The age limit for command and staff positions was increased.

The division had a sub-strength of 600 men and would receive its full complement a few weeks later. This formation had obtained good results, in its old structure, during the Eastern Command manoeuvres the previous autumn. Terrain suitable for training armoured formations was rare in Scotland and the area did not allow for exercises beyond regimental level. The division, therefore, had to carry out a further few weeks of training on more suitable terrain, after which it became a first rate formation.

The 2nd Division (grenadiers) was formed on paper. All the units were represented, with a high proportion of officers and specialists for a total strength of approximately 2,500 men. The Polish Parachute Brigade had approximately 2,500 well-trained and high quality men. The Brigade remained under the command of the Polish commander-in-chief and did not belong to the 21st Army Group for the time being.

Holland

The Princes Irene Brigade had, up to this point in time, been stationed at Harwich where it ensured the protection of the naval base.

These barrack missions had to some extent slowed down the trainin[g] even though satisfactory exercises had been undertaken with the Roy[al] Navy.

The Brigade found itself now in Frinton where it had everything th[at] it required for training. Unsatisfactory personnel had been weeded-o[ut] and as a consequence, this formation was slightly understrength, wi[th] reinforcements due to arrive from abroad shortly. The Brigade s[till] suffered from an important delay in its collective training. The you[ng] officers and men were often volunteers, but personnel of lesser qual[ity] were still present amongst the officers and the Dutch authorities we[re] reticent to replace them.

Belgium

The Belgian Brigade would soon leave Lowestoft for Ramsga[te] where it was to train with the 61st Division.

This move would be beneficial and the Brigade saw its strength i[n]crease and it behave well. It was not contaminated by politics and [its] command structure and morale were satisfactory.

The Leamington depot received politically motivated or idle office[rs] as the Belgian authorities sent them there on purpose. The Belgi[an] commandos distinguished themselves in Italy. The parachutist com[any] was high quality, extremely willing and made up of excelle[nt] soldiers.

Czechoslovakia

The Czechoslovak Independent Armoured Brigade was undergoi[ng] training in the region of Market Harborough. Progress was noticeab[le] and squadron level manoeuvres were in the process of being learn[t]. The Brigade was now equipped with Crusader Mk VI tanks whi[le] awaiting for Cromwell tanks due for the beginning of 1944.

Signalling exercises were carried out on the initiative of the GO[C] Eastern Command, who reported back that the unit was making goo[d] progress.

The unit commanders and staff officers had adapted well to tan[k] warfare. Junior officers were very competent. Large scale briga[de] scale manoeuvres had to organised as quickly as possible however.

The contingent that arrived from the Middle East in September wa[s] shared out amongst the various units and was integrated without an[y] difficulties. The unit did not suffer from political rivalries, althoug[h] some minor problems were encountered with the Jews, Slovaks an[d] Sudden Germans.

Norway

The Brigade had recently moved towards Callender/St. Andrews (Sco[t]land) and was continuing its training with the 52nd Division. Morale w[as] high and the unit was progressing in a satisfactory manner. It had take[n] part in lengthy manoeuvres that were led by the GOC Scottish Comman[d] these had revealed some training weaknesses that would need to be rec[ti]fied.

The parachute company was trained by the 6th Airborne Division, an[d] had an excellent reputation.

The Norwegian commandos had seen action in several minor oper[a]tions."

The history of Allied contingents is succinctly summed-up hereafter with maps. The history enthusiast is referred to the extensive bibliography at the end of the book for further reading.

Prime Minister Winston Churchill, without whom the contribution of Allied contingents would have been impossible, visiting 21st Army Group commander Field Marshal Montgomery's headquarters, 21 June 1944. (Imperial War Museum)

THE 21st ARMY GROUP

Except for the 2nd and 3rd French parachute regiments (4th and 3rd SAS) attached to the SAS Brigade, all of the Foreign formations and units attached to the 21st Army Group were committed within the 1st Canadian Army. Commanded by General HDG Crerar, it was operationally activated from 23 July 1944 onwards. It comprised I British Corps, II Canadian Corps and various reserve units. The sector allocated to the 1st Canadian Army, after the fighting around Falaise, was situated along the coast of the English Channel and the North Sea, to the left of the 2nd British Army.

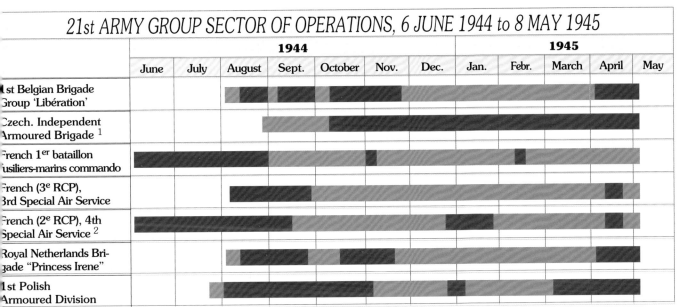

21st ARMY GROUP SECTOR OF OPERATIONS, 6 JUNE 1944 to 8 MAY 1945

	1944							1945				
	June	July	August	Sept.	October	Nov.	Dec.	Jan.	Febr.	March	April	May
1st Belgian Brigade Group 'Libération'												
Czech. Independent Armoured Brigade [1]												
French 1er bataillon fusiliers-marins commando												
French (3e RCP), 3rd Special Air Service												
French (2e RCP), 4th Special Air Service [2]												
Royal Netherlands Brigade "Princess Irene"												
1st Polish Armoured Division												

With attached French units, see relevant chapters. 2. Operations in December 1944 and January 1945 under American command.

Period of concentration, rest or reorganisation.　　Combat operations

PREMIÈRE
ARMÉE CANADIENNE
DE LA NORMANDIE À L'ESCAUT
1944

Lieutenant General Henry DG Crerar (1889-1965), Commanding the 1st Canadian Army.

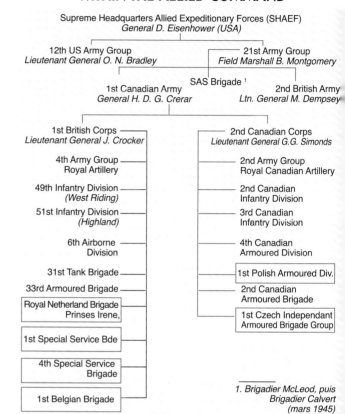

THE 1st CANADIAN ARMY, 1944-45

General officer commanding (as of 20 March 1944):
General HDG Crerar, CH, CB, DSO. Established (staff) 6 April 1942 in Great Britain. Operational beginning 23 July in Normandy with the attachment of the British I Corps to the II Canadian Corps.

THE 21st ARMY GROUP
WITHIN THE ALLIED COMMAND

Supreme Headquarters Allied Expeditionary Forces (SHAEF)
General D. Eisenhower (USA)

12th US Army Group
Lieutenant General O. N. Bradley

21st Army Group
Field Marshall B. Montgomery

SAS Brigade [1]

1st Canadian Army
General H. D. G. Crerar

2nd British Army
Ltn. General M. Dempsey

1st British Corps
Lieutenant General J. Crocker

2nd Canadian Corps
Lieutenant General G.G. Simonds

4th Army Group
Royal Artillery

2nd Army Group
Royal Canadian Artillery

49th Infantry Division
(West Riding)

2nd Canadian
Infantry Division

51st Infantry Division
(Highland)

3rd Canadian
Infantry Division

6th Airborne
Division

4th Canadian
Armoured Division

31st Tank Brigade

1st Polish Armoured Div.

33rd Armoured Brigade

2nd Canadian
Armoured Brigade

Royal Netherland Brigade
Prinses Irene,

1st Czech Independant
Armoured Brigade Group

1st Special Service Bde

4th Special Service
Brigade

1st Belgian Brigade

1. Brigadier McLeod, puis
   Brigadier Calvert
   (mars 1945)

Directly committed to action by the 21st Army Group, the French parachutists of the 3rd and 4th SAS operated independently, and after a brief period under American command during the Battle of the Bulge (December 1944-January 1945) rejoined the 1st Canadian Army in April 1945 in Holland.

At first attached to the 2nd British Army for landing operations on

6 June 1944, the 1st Special Service Brigade – with the French 1er Bataillon de Fusiliers Marins Commando – also joined the 1st Canadian Army in August 1944.

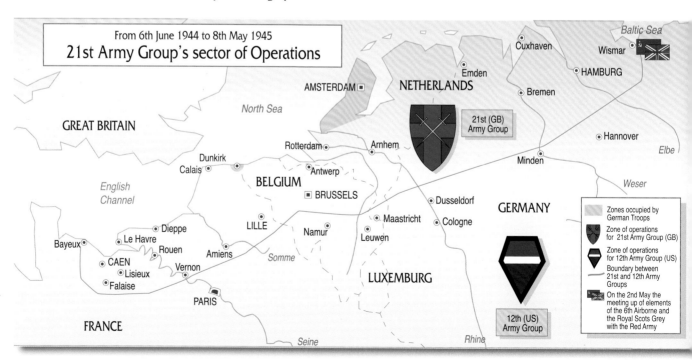

From 6th June 1944 to 8th May 1945
21st Army Group's sector of Operations

Baltic Sea

Cuxhaven
Wismar
Emden
• HAMBURG
AMSTERDAM ■
NETHERLANDS
• Bremen

North Sea

GREAT BRITAIN

21st (GB)
Army Group

• Hannover

Rotterdam
Arnhem
Elbe

Dunkirk
Calais
• Antwerp
Minden
English Channel
BELGIUM
Weser

■ BRUSSELS

• Dieppe
LILLE
• Dusseldorf
GERMANY

Bayeux •
Le Havre
Namur
• Maastricht
• Cologne
Rouen
Amiens
Leuwen

CAEN
Vernon
Somme
• Lisieux
Falaise
LUXEMBURG

PARIS
12th (US)
Army Group

FRANCE

Seine
Rhine

Zones occupied by
German Troops

Zone of operations
for 21st Army Group (GB)

Zone of operations
for 12th Army Group (US)

Boundary between
21st and 12th Army
Groups

On the 2nd May the
meeting up of elements
of the 6th Airborne and
the Royal Scots Grey
with the Red Army

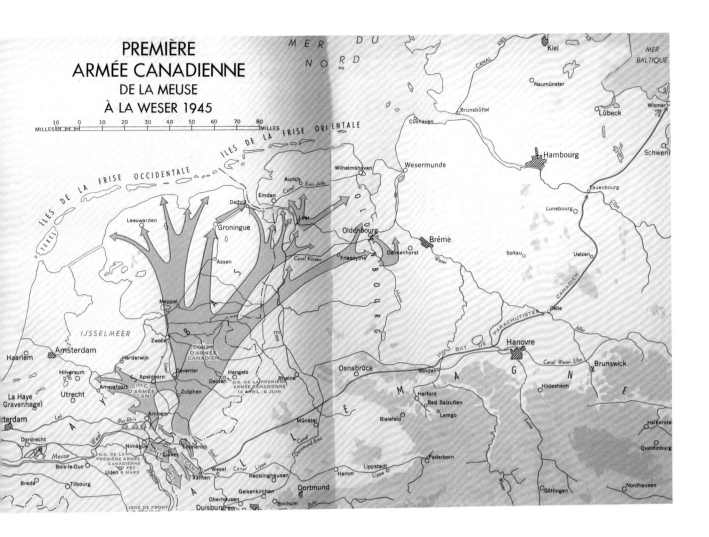

PREMIÈRE
ARMÉE CANADIENNE
DE LA MEUSE
À LA WESER 1945

column of tactical and transport vehicles of the 1st Polish Armoured Division in Great Britain before embarking for
ormandy. From right to left: 3 Ton, 4 x 4, General Service Fordson WOT; Car 4 x 4, Heavy Utility, Humber FWD;
ep (4 x 4, 5-cwt); Trucks, 3 Ton, 4 x 2, General Service Dodge Canada D 60L, two Jeeps and three 15-cwt, 4 x 2,
eneral Service Ford WOT 2.
korski Institute Museum)

UNIT AND FORMATION ORGANISATION

The distribution of personnel, weapons and materiel, as well as unit organisation was laid down by the official War Establishment Tables issued by the War Office.

But, except for the 1st Polish Armoured Division that used exactly the War Establishment of the equivalent British formation, all other foreign

Arm of service strips sewn under the jacket or greatco formation. These cloth strips measured 51 mm x 6.5 mm a had been in use within the British Army since 1940. Th allowed the identification of arm of service. They were n adopted by French units, the 1st Polish Armoured division a the Czech Armoured briga

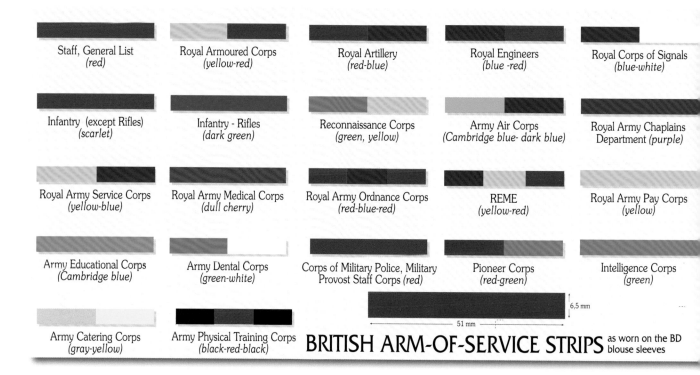

Staff, General List (red)
Royal Armoured Corps (yellow-red)
Royal Artillery (red-blue)
Royal Engineers (blue -red)
Royal Corps of Signals (blue-white)

Infantry (except Rifles) (scarlet)
Infantry - Rifles (dark green)
Reconnaissance Corps (green, yellow)
Army Air Corps (Cambridge blue- dark blue)
Royal Army Chaplains Department (purple)

Royal Army Service Corps (yellow-blue)
Royal Army Medical Corps (dull cherry)
Royal Army Ordnance Corps (red-blue-red)
REME (yellow-red)
Royal Army Pay Corps (yellow)

Army Educational Corps (Cambridge blue)
Army Dental Corps (green-white)
Corps of Military Police, Military Provost Staff Corps (red)
Pioneer Corps (red-green)
Intelligence Corps (green)

Army Catering Corps (gray-yellow)
Army Physical Training Corps (black-red-black)

6,5 mm
51 mm

BRITISH ARM-OF-SERVICE STRIPS
as worn on the BD blouse sleeves

STRENGTH, UNITS, BILLETING OF FOREIGN TROOPS IN THE UNITED KINGDOM, 1944

Nationality	Establishment (a)		Total strength (b)		Units	Billeting localities
	Officers	OR	Officers	OR		
French			394	1960	Semi-Brigade Headquarters 4th SAS (2e RCP) 3rd SAS (3e RCP), Depot	Cupar Comrie Camberley
			14	136	1er Bataillon de Fusiliers-Marins Commando	Bexhill-on-Sea (May 1944
Polish	2257	24098	5141	22241	— Corps Headquarters — Armoured Division — Cadre Armoured Division — Parachute Brigade — Corps Troops, Training Units, Static Units	Kinnaird, Falkirk HQ Melrose Div. HQ ALLOA Armd, Bde Catterick HQ Leven Scotland
Dutch	209	2115	268	2198	— Brigade Headquarters, Signal Section, Reconnaissance Unit, Field Artillery Troop, 3 Independent Companies, Independent Parachute Company (b), Ancillary Services — Depot and Training Establishment	Dovercurt to Frinton (02.01.1944) Tettenhall
Belgian	196	2647	323	2922	— **1st Group.** Headquarters, Signal Section, 3 Independent Coys, Field Battery, Engineer Unit, Armoured Car Squadron, Ancillary Services, Independent Parachute Company — **2nd Group.** Administrative Company, Instruction Company, Provost Section, Gendarmerie Unit	Lowestoft moving to Ramsgate (09.01.1944) Fritz Hill, Leamington area Leamington
Czechoslovakian	361	4286	649	4158	**Independent Armoured Brigade Group** **Brigade Headquarters.** 2 Armoured Regiments, Field Regiment (less one battery), Anti-Tank Battery, Light Anti-Aircraft Troop, Field Company (less one section), Motor Battalion (less one company), Armoured Reconnaissance Squadron, Signals, Ancillary Serv., Depot and Training Centre	Northampton Area Southend
Norwegian	242	2062	587	2045	**Brigade Headquarters.** 4 Independent Mountain Coys, (3 formed), Field Battery, Brigade Train, Signal Training Coy — Independent Parachute Coy, Training Camp and Schools	Callander St. Andrews
			7362	35660		Total OF/OR = 4288

(a) Including London Headquarters and miscellaneous establishments. French depot has no fixed establishment. (b) Personnel dispersed amongst Independent Companies.

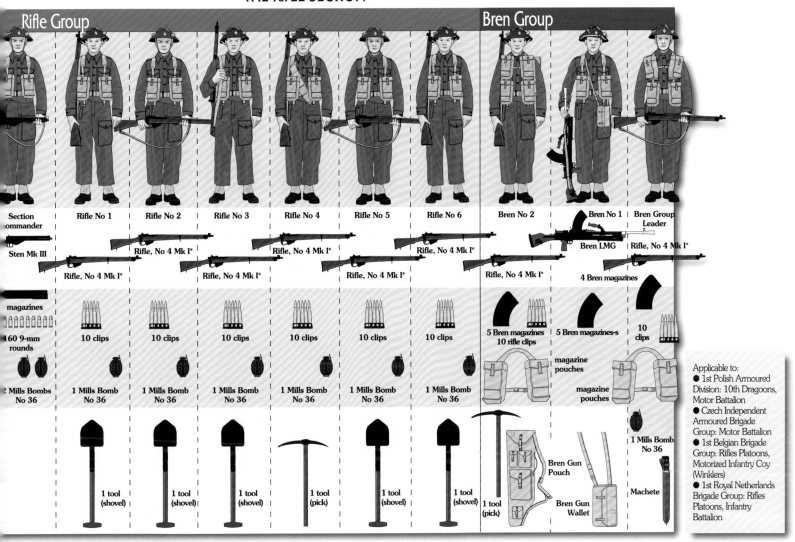

Rifle Group

Section Commander	Rifle No 1	Rifle No 2	Rifle No 3	Rifle No 4	Rifle No 5	Rifle No 6
Sten Mk III	Rifle, No 4 Mk I*	Rifle, No 4 Mk I*	Rifle, No 4 Mk I*	Rifle, No 4 Mk I*	Rifle, No 4 Mk I*	Rifle, No 4 Mk I*
	Rifle, No 4 Mk I*	Rifle, No 4 Mk I*	Rifle, No 4 Mk I*			
magazines / 160 9-mm rounds	10 clips	10 clips	10 clips	10 clips	10 clips	10 clips
2 Mills Bombs No 36	1 Mills Bomb No 36	1 Mills Bomb No 36	1 Mills Bomb No 36	1 Mills Bomb No 36	1 Mills Bomb No 36	1 Mills Bomb No 36
	1 tool (shovel)	1 tool (shovel)	1 tool (shovel)	1 tool (pick)	1 tool (shovel)	1 tool (shovel)

Bren Group

Bren No 2	Bren No 1	Bren Group Leader
	Bren LMG	Rifle, No 4 Mk I*
	4 Bren magazines	
5 Bren magazines / 10 rifle clips	5 Bren magazines-s	10 clips
magazine pouches	magazine pouches	
Bren Gun Pouch / Bren Gun Wallet		1 Mills Bomb No 36 / Machete
1 tool (pick)		

Applicable to:
- 1st Polish Armoured Division: 10th Dragoons, Motor Battalion
- Czech Independent Armoured Brigade Group: Motor Battalion
- 1st Belgian Brigade Group: Rifles Platoons, Motorized Infantry Coy (Winklers)
- 1st Royal Netherlands Brigade Group: Rifles Platoons, Infantry Battalion

---

War Office War Establishment. The following 10 pages gave precise ...tails of strength and their respective roles, personal and collective ...eapons, as well as the vehicle park.

...nits and formations were formed depending on the limitations of avail-...ble manpower.

Therefore, 'Brigade Group' is only a generic term that does not corre-...pond to a rigid order of battle. We can see, for instance, that the Czech. ...rmoured Brigade had 3,500 men, whereas the 1st Nederland Brigade ...nly amounted to 1,500. The War Office, however, retained the founda-...ons of the British structure and thus the foreign brigades were a mixture ...f combat and organic support units.

NB. In all subsequent chapters, the unit organisation charts (see ...xample page 23) are combined with the unit serial numbers vis-...ble on all vehicles, as defined on page 15.

For further reading, see 'British Army of WWII War Establishment Tables' by ...ary Kennedy.

Status of Foreign ground forces present in Great Britain on 1 January 1944, as ...awn from the Quarterly report on Allied Military Forces, 31 December 1943

Apart from a few variations, this was the manpower engaged in Europe begin-...ng in June 1944. Although it was part of the French Air Force (Armée de l'air), ...e Chasseurs Parachutistes were listed along with ground forces in order to be on a ...r with British Airborne Forces. The 1er Bataillon de Fusiliers Marins Commando ...rench Navy) was attached to the Royal Marines and is not, therefore, on this chart. ...e relevant chapter).

II/154/2
Notified in ACIs 29th December 1943
Effective date 30th November 1943

Date	30 Nov '43
Officers	38
ORs	670
Total	708
MCs	10
Vehicles	187
Trailers	6

A TANK BATTALION

WAR ESTABLISHMENT

(As agreed by Standardization Conference (1943))

Consisting of –

Battalion headquarters (4 infantry tanks and 2 tank observation posts)

Headquarter squadron of –
Squadron headquarters
AA troop (6 AA tanks)
Reconnaissance troop (11 light tanks)
Intercommunication troop (9 scout cars); and
Administrative troop

Three squadrons (each) –
Squadron headquarters, divided into fighting portion (1 infantry tank; 2 close support infantry tanks; 1 scout car) and administrative portion; and

Five troops, each of three infantry tanks.

VEHICLE AND COMBAT VEHICLE MARKINGS

Lettering and the identification Prefix Letters

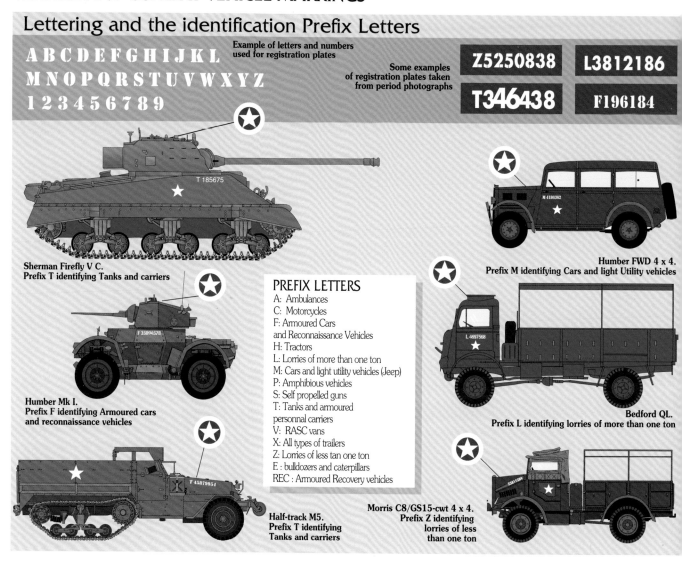

ABCDEFGHIJKL
MNOPQRSTUVWXYZ
1234567890

Example of letters and numbers used for registration plates

Some examples of registration plates taken from period photographs

Z5250838   L3812186
T346438   F196184

Sherman Firefly V C.
Prefix T identifying Tanks and carriers

T 185675

Humber Mk I.
Prefix F identifying Armoured cars and reconnaissance vehicles

F 33894578

Half-track M5.
Prefix T identifying Tanks and carriers

T 45879054

PREFIX LETTERS
A: Ambulances
C: Motorcycles
F: Armoured Cars
and Reconnaissance Vehicles
H: Tractors
L: Lorries of more than one ton
M: Cars and light utility vehicles (Jeep)
P: Amphibious vehicles
S: Self propelled guns
T: Tanks and armoured
personnal carriers
V: RASC vans
X: All types of trailers
Z: Lorries of less tan one ton
E: bulldozers and caterpillars
REC: Armoured Recovery vehicles

Humber FWD 4 x 4.
Prefix M identifying Cars and light Utility vehicles

M 4186362

Bedford QL.
Prefix L identifying lorries of more than one ton

L 4697568

Morris C8/GS15-cwt 4 x 4.
Prefix Z identifying lorries of less than one ton

Z5A1728A

When visible on photographs, these elements are of the utmost importance when making an exact identification of a precise unit in a given area (during the occupation of France by the German army, Allied intelligence systematically asked the resistance movements to pass on sketches of vehicle and tank markings). These 'Unit Ser Numbers' were figures placed on a colour rectangle and specific each unit within a larger formation (division, brigade...).

The Unit Serial Number was placed at the front right-hand si

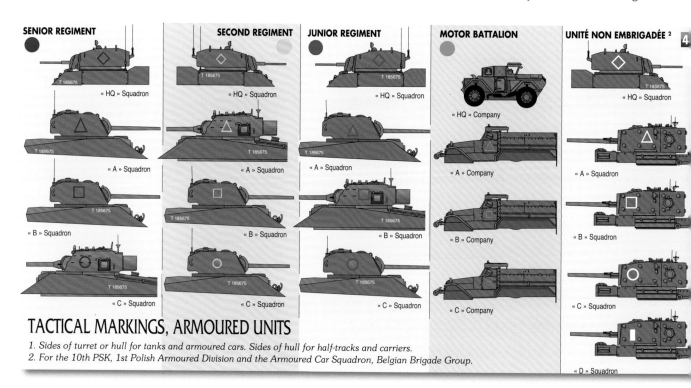

SENIOR REGIMENT	SECOND REGIMENT	JUNIOR REGIMENT	MOTOR BATTALION	UNITÉ NON EMBRIGADÉE [2]
« HQ » Squadron	« HQ » Squadron	« HQ » Squadron	« HQ » Company	« HQ » Squadron
« A » Squadron	« A » Squadron	« A » Squadron	« A » Company	« A » Squadron
« B » Squadron	« B » Squadron	« B » Squadron	« B » Company	« B » Squadron
« C » Squadron	« C » Squadron	« C » Squadron	« C » Company	« C » Squadron
				« D » Squadron

TACTICAL MARKINGS, ARMOURED UNITS
1. Sides of turret or hull for tanks and armoured cars. Sides of hull for half-tracks and carriers.
2. For the 10th PSK, 1st Polish Armoured Division and the Armoured Car Squadron, Belgian Brigade Group.

CAMOUFLAGE SCHEMES

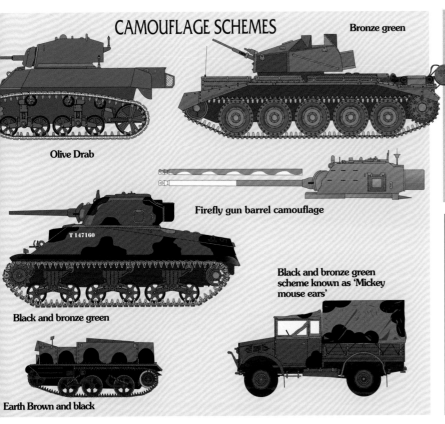

Bronze green

Olive Drab

Firefly gun barrel camouflage

T 147160

Black and bronze green

Black and bronze green scheme known as 'Mickey mouse ears'

Earth Brown and black

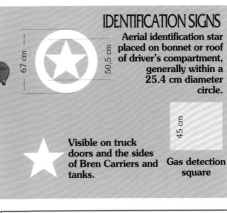

IDENTIFICATION SIGNS

67 cm

50,5 cm

Aerial identification star placed on bonnet or roof of driver's compartment, generally within a 25.4 cm diameter circle.

45 cm

Visible on truck doors and the sides of Bren Carriers and tanks.

Gas detection square

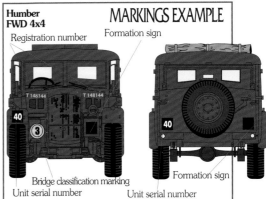

MARKINGS EXAMPLE

Humber FWD 4x4

Registration number

Formation sign

T 148144   T 148144

40

3

40

Bridge classification marking

Unit serial number

Formation sign

Unit serial number

BRIDGE CLASSIFICATION MARKINGS

22.8 cm diameter disk positioned at the front of the vehicle. The number indicates the vehicle total all-up weight, that must be equal or less than that shown on the identical sign placed before engineer-constructed expedient bridges.

2	2/3	5	7	9	15	27	30	27
Jeep	Jeep with trailer	Scout car, Humber	Truck, 3-Ton	Armoured car, Daimler	Armoured car, Staghound	Cromwell tank	Sherman tank	Variant, Cromwell CIABG

nd the rear left-hand side of a vehicle or tank. The
serial numbers (such as '51', right) bear no relation
whatsoever with the actual number of the unit, the
ase colour (or colours) is specific to the role of a reg-

51

15,4 cm

21,6 cm

24,14 cm

iment, battalion or company. The formation badge was positioned on the opposite side in an area measuring 21.6 cm x 24.10 cm.

Unit Serial Numbers colours

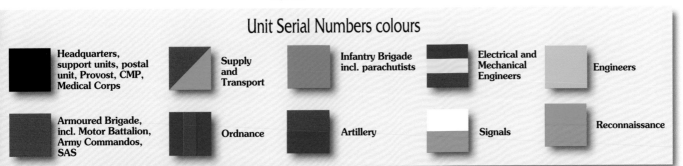

Headquarters, support units, postal unit, Provost, CMP, Medical Corps

Supply and Transport

Infantry Brigade incl. parachutists

Electrical and Mechanical Engineers

Engineers

Armoured Brigade, incl. Motor Battalion, Army Commandos, SAS

Ordnance

Artillery

Signals

Reconnaissance

Example of Polish tank markings

463

53

53

48

Sherman Mk V (M4A4) from A Squadron, 24th Uhlans, August 1944.

SYNOPTIC TABLE OF THE MAIN VEHICLES AND GUNS USED BY THE FORMATIONS CITED IN THIS PUBLICATION

Vehicle payloads:

5-cwt: 250 kg (Jeep)
10-cwt: 500 kg
15-cwt: 750 kg (Half-Track in British nomenclature)
30-cwt: 1,500 kg

Heavier payload is in tons, the approximate equivalent of the continental 'tonne'.

Observations

American half-tracks used by the 21st Army groups were made by the International Harvester Co, White Motor Co.-made half-tracks being reserved for the US Army. In an identical payload category, tactical or utility vehicles could come from various manufacturers. For example, the 3-ton Ford Canada could be substituted to the British 3-Ton, GS Bedford. T[ ] Challenger tank was issued to the 1st Polish Armoured Division in N[ ] vember 1944 and to the Czech. Armoured Independent Brigade Gro[ ] in May 1945. Most of the Shermans issued to the 1st Polish Armd. D[ ] were the M4A4 type (Mk V). The M4A1-76 (Mark II A) was supplied [ ] of October 1944. The M4A3 was reserved for the US Army and w[ ] not present in the 21st AGp. The units shown on the following tab[ ] are, from left to right: 1st Belgian Independent Brigade Group ('Briga[ ] Piron'), French 2e and 3e Régiments de chasseurs parachutistes (4th a[ ] 3rd SAS); 1er Bataillon de Fusiliers Marins Commando[1], Royal Neth[ ] lands Brigade ('Prinses Irene'); 1st Polish Armoured Division; and Czec[ ] Independent Armoured Brigade Group.

1. Vehicles organic to No 4 Commando, and the SAS Brigade for the 2e and 3e RCP.

Lights Tanks, Cruisers Tanks

1. Light Tank M3A3 (USA)
1. Light Tank M5A1 (USA)
2. Cromwell A27 Mk IV
3. Cromwell Howitzer 95 mm A27 Mk VI close support
4. Challenger
5. Sherman M4A4 (USA)
6. Sherman M4A1 76 (USA)
7. Sherman M4A4 'Firefly' (USA-UK)
8. Sherman ARV (USA)
9. Cromwell A27 Armoured Recovery Vehicle

Transport and command

10. Universal carrier or Windsor Carrier (Canada)
11. Loyd Carrier
12. Half-Track M5/M9 (USA)

13. Armoured Command vehicle, AEC Matador HP 4x4

Reconnaissance

14. Scout Car Humber Mk I
15. White M3A1 Scout Car (USA)
16. Daimler Mk I
17. Armored Car T17E1 (Staghound I) (USA)
18. Humber Mk III A
19. Scout Car Daimler

Anti-tank guns

20. 6-Pounder (57-mm) Anti-Tank Gun
21. 17-Pounder (76,2-mm) Anti-Tank Gun
22. Tank Destroyer M10 (USA)
23. Tank Destroyer Mk IIC "Achilles" (USA-UK)

Anti-aircraft guns

24. Bofors 40 mm (towed)
25. Centaur AA Mk II 20-mm Polsten-Oerlikon x2
26. T17-E2 (USA)
27. Half-Track M14 (USA)
28. Self-Propelled Bofors vehicle

Field artillery

29. 75-mm Pack howitzer M1A1 (USA)
30. Morris C8 4-wheel Tractor
31. 25-Pounder Howitzer
32. 25-Pounder Howitzer, self-propelled, 'Sexton' (USA-UK)

Light cars, tactical and service vehicles

33. Car, 5-cwt 4x4, Jeep (USA)
34. Humber FWD, 4x4, Heavy Utility

35. Hillman 'Minx' 5-cwt, 4x2
36. Motorcycle, BSA, Triumph, Roya[ ] Enfield, Matchless, Velocette, Welbike
37. 15-cwt 4x2 Water Tank, Bedford
38. 15-cwt 4 wheel Wireless, Morris
39. Latest Type 15-cwt 4x4 Wheel G[ ] Body Bedford
40. 30-cwt FWD GS Body Ford
41. Studebaker 2,5-Ton 6x6 (USA)
42. 3-Ton 4x2 Bedford
43. Truck 3-Ton 4x4 GS, Bedford QLD
44. Ambulance, Austin K2
45. Scammell 30-Ton Recovery
46. Truck 3-Ton
47. 3-Ton 6 wheel Breakdown
48. Scammell 6-wheel heavy breakdown

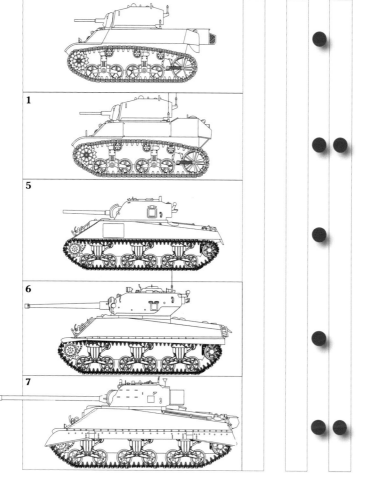

TANKS AND VEHICLES

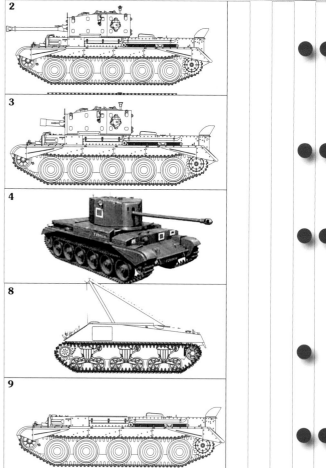

TANKS AND VEHICLES

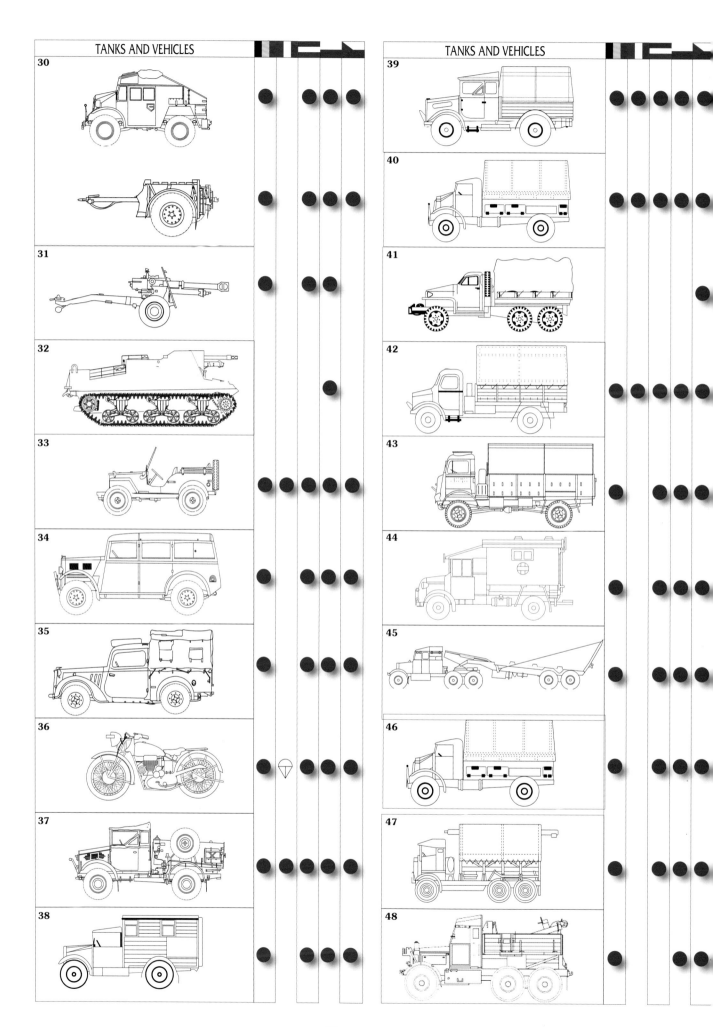

UNIFORMS AND INDIDIVUAL EQUIPMENT

There was not, apart the specific national insignia shown through-out this book, any difference in the outline of the British soldiers and that of Foreign troops in British Battledress.

Clothing and individual equipment was stipulated by War Dress regulations and some brief extracts are shown in the following pages.

More generic information can be found in another volume by the author, 'The British Soldier' volume 1, covering headdress, berets, helmets, uniforms and equipment, field rations, optical equipment, signalling and cartography.

Volume 2 deals with armament, artillery, vehicles and armour. Another book, 'D-Day Paratroopers', covers the British, Canadian and French airborne units, red berets, helmets, jump uniforms, the X-Type parachute, individual and collective equipment, vehicles and their markings, aerial transport.

British Battledress

1937 Pattern Battledress was the standard field uniform for all Army personnel. It was first worn by the British Army during the 1939-40 campaign and comprised of a blouse and trousers, two sets of which were issued to each serviceman, one for combat and one for ceremonial purposes and for walking out. A denim uniform in an identical cut was provided for training and daily chores.

From 1943 onwards, the regulation head wear was the General Service Cap (except for Royal Armoured Corps personnel: Black Beret, Airborne Forces: Maroon Beret, Commandos: Green Beret, Scottish Regiments: Tam O' Shanter).

The Battledress was worn with black leather ankle boots and short anklets. Officers wore the blouse with the collar tailored open, as to expose the shirt and tie. As was the case with all of their kit, officers had to purchase their own uniforms.

Battledress types were the following, as illustrated below:

1. 1937/40 Pattern, issued throughout the war.
2. 1940 'Austerity' Pattern, issued from 1943.
3. 'War Aid' Battledress, made in the USA. Seen in units transferred from Italy in 1945 as well as within the 2e and 3e Régiments de Chasseurs Parachutistes in Holland. Within the same unit, a mix of

Battledress patterns can be frequently seen.

As an exception, the Polish government in exile placed an order for a specific Polish Battledress, notably worn by officers. The jacket was of the same design as the Pattern 1940 'Austerity' but the breast pockets had visible buttons and vertical pleats, as would be seen on the British 1946 Pattern (see chapter concerning the 1st Polish Armoured Division). Canadian Battledress was not worn by Foreign units during the war. Some regular army personnel wore it in a non-regulation way post-war. However, French regiments raised from September 1944 onwards – but not serving with 21 AGp – with men that had served with the Forces Françaises de l'Intérieur (FFI) were issued with Canadian uniforms purchased by the French government [1].

---

1. See 'Réorganisation & réarmement de l'Armée Française', by Chef de bataillon Vernet, SHAT (French Army Historical Service) 1980.

Other issued British Army clothing

Denim Overalls
Leather Jerkin
Groundsheet cape
Rubber proofed coat (for motorcyclists)
Winter tank suit and Denim Tank suit (tank crews)
Denison Smock (airborne troops, commandos)
Smock, Windproof camouflage
Snow camouflage suit

PATTERN 1937 INDIVIDUAL EQUIPMENT

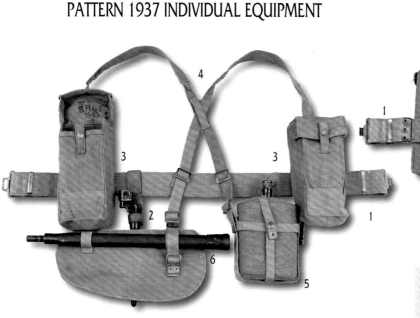

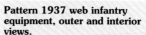

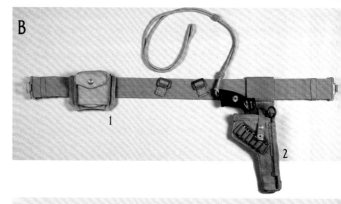

Pattern 1937 web infantry equipment, outer and interior views.

1. Belt. Available in three sizes:
Small: 1.11 m
Large: 1.27 m
Extra Large: 1.42 m.
Adjustable via two double end hooks each mounted on brass tabs (1a).

2. Bayonet and frog
3. Pouches.
4. Braces.
5. Two-pint water bottle and carrier
6. Entrenching tool and helve carrier

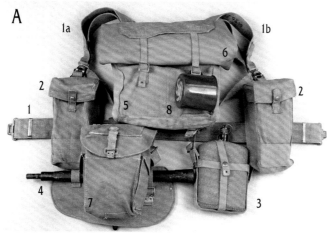

A. THE INFANTRY BATTLE ORDER
1. Belt.
1a & 1b. Shoulder braces and haversack straps.
2. Pouches.
3. Water Bottle.
4. Entrenching tool.
5. Haversack
6. Groundsheet.
7. Respirator bag.
8. Mug.

B. ROYAL ARMOURED CORPS EQUIPMENT SET
1. Pistol ammunition pouch
2. Royal Armoured Corps Pattern 1942 holster and issue No 2 Mk I* revolver, worn on right side.

C AND D. OFFICER'S WEBBING SET (INFANTRY)
1. Belt and braces.
2. Side arm holster (revolver).
3. Ammunition pouch.
4. Officer's valise.
5. Binocular case.
6. Compass case.
The water bottle could be carried on the right hand side by attaching its carrier buckles to the ends of the braces.

E and F. PERSONNEL ARMED WITH THE REVOLVER OR AUTOMATIC PISTOL (except RAC)
1. Sidearm holster.
2. 12-round ammunition case for the revolver.
3. Case for the American M1911 and Browning HP 35 pistol magazines.

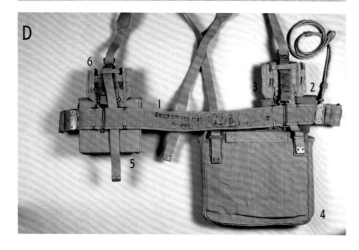

As soon as foreign troops arrived and were rmed into units in the United Kingdom, e British authorities, in agreement with the epresentatives of these units, laid down the gulations concerning the wearing of insignia, hatever the nationality.

As an example, the protocol established on 5 October 1940 between the Foreign Sec- tary Lord Halifax, and Ian Masaryk repre- enting Czechoslovakia. Its Appendix II, con- erning ground forces, stipulated that British rganisation would be adopted, but that the zech units and formations would remain nder the command of Czech officers. Also, ational colours, insignia and badges of rank ould be retained[1].

Thus, all foreign military personnel issued ith British Battledress could be told apart by ational symbols.

The date of approval of a particular insignia d not necessarily mean that this was the date f its first being worn and could be more a case f officially accepting a badge already worn ith the agreement of the unit commander. Some of these insignia uld even be approved but never worn at all, for various reasons.

ank insignia

In the charts within each chapter, ranks designation are indicated the original language and the same applies to the text. The Brit- h equivalent ranks given do not systematically imply an equivalent nction.

In foreign armies, unless stated otherwise, a regiment was com- anded by a colonel, whereas in the British Army this role is under- ken by a lieutenant-colonel. In the following chapters, depending on e subject, the British officer and other ranks system is used with the bbreviations of OF/OR.

___

This applied naturally to all other Foreign contingents.
Some disks bore 'FFF' for 'Free French Forces'.

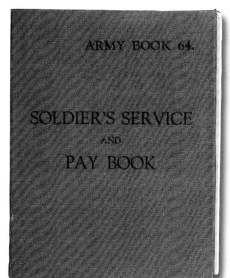

Army Book 64 issued to other ranks.

Personal identification documents

Foreign military personnel were issued with identity documents identical to those used by the British Army.

1. Fibre identification tags attached to a lace and worn around the neck.

2. Army Book 64 with Soldier's Ser- vice and Pay Book. Apart from bearer's unit, it contained all entries concerning identi- ty. This document had to carried by the soldier in all circumstances. Parachutists of the 2e and 3e RCP were issued with same pay book issued to British ground forces, as were the men of the 1er Bataillon de Fusiliers Marins Comman- do who relinquished their French navy identity card when they joined their new unit.

Officers were issued with a Military Identity Card (Army Form B-2606, yellow coloured stock with a red horizontal stripe.) bearing the inscription *Foreign Officer* together with the bearer's photograph

Examples of identity disks markings:

FRANCE [2]
1er Bat. FM Cdo. Christian name or initials, surname, service number; let- ters FN (Forces Navales), 43 (year of enlistment), religion.
2e and 3e RCP: Christian name or ini- tials, service number, religion.

HOLLAND
Royal Netherlands Brigade. Christian name or initials, surname, date of birth, RDA (Royal Dutch Army), religion: (such as 'RK' for 'Rooms Katholiek'), service number.

POLAND
1st Polish Armoured Division. Christian name or initials, surname, service number, 'AP' ('Armia Polska'), religion, such as 'RZ- KAT': Roman Catholic.

Blood group was not always indicated but could entered in the Army Book 64.

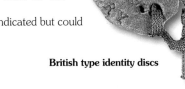

British type identity discs

Decorations

Medal ribbons: Whatever the nationality of the bearer, medal rib- bons worn on uniforms were displayed according to very precise regu- lations. Whatever their importance, national decorations always held precedence over foreign medals.

For example, from left to right and top to bottom, on the left hand side of the blouse:

1	2	3
4	5	6

National awards
1. Gallantry award
2. Commemorative medal

Foreign awards
3. Gallantry award
4, 5, 6. Commemorative medals

The Allied Victory Medal was established in 1919 and awarded to all military personnel (apart from the neutral Dutch) who had taken part in the Great
War and concerned all of the nations covered in this publication, and all military personnel whose age allowed them to serve in the armies of 1939, 1940 or 1944.

E

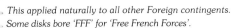

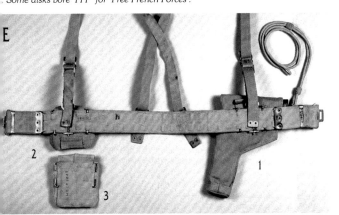

2

3

1

F

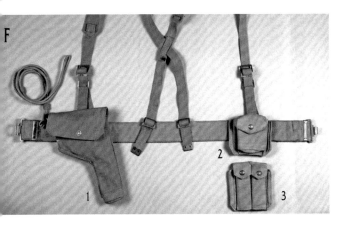

2

1

3

THE BELGIAN VOLUNTEERS

Despite having declared its neutrality in 1936, Belgium was invaded by the armies of the Third Reich on 10 May 1940. After 18 days of fighting, King Leopold III, commander-in-chief, decreed the capitulation of his country's forces on 28 May and handed himself over to the Germans.

On 21 June, ministers Jaspar and Cartier de Marchienne, who had fled to London, made an appeal to all Belgians to carry on the fight and in October, a government in exile was formed under the authority of Prime Minister Hubert Pierlot. General Van Strijdonck de Burkel took command of all Belgian forces in Great Britain, its ground units being gathered in Wales. In October 1940 there were enough men to form an infantry battalion under the command of Major Cumont. Recruits came from men who had escaped from Europe, Belgian residents abroad or from the colonies.

The 1st Belgian Brigade Group

On 12 December 1940, command of this infantry battalion was taken over by Major Jean-Baptiste Piron who had escaped from captivity. After the arrival of reinforcements and equipment, the unit was named the 1st independent Belgian Brigade Group. 1943 and the first months of 1944 were used for training and the integration of new modern equipment for the coming battles in Europe in the Spring of 1944. On 4 August, the brigade embarked at Tilbury on board the Liberty Ships *Gladstone, Paul Benjamin, Henry Austen* and *Finlay*. The brigade landed on 7 August at Courseulles then rallied at Douvres-la-Délivrande. Attached to I British Corps (1st Canadian Army), the brigade was attached to the 6th British Airborne Division and took up positions in the Plumetot-Ranville sector. The

first contact with the enemy took place on the 13th near Sallenelles.

Thursday 17 August saw the start of Operation 'Paddle,' toward the river Seine. Progression was as follows:

The infantry advanced along the Channel coast (La Côte Fleurie) and liberated:

on **17 August**, Sallenelles Franceville

20 August, Home Varaville

21 August, Cabourg Dives, Houlgate,

22 August, Villers-sur Mer,

23 August, Deauville,

24 August, Trouville Villerville, Honfleur,

25 August, Berville.

The Armoured Car Squadron was used by the 6th British Airborne as a reconnaissance unit and liberated:

on **17 August**, Sallenelles; Franceville, **21 August**, Dozulé, Annebault, **22 August**, Beaumont

Top
1943 in Great Britain
Manoeuvres of the 1st Motorised Infantry Company
(Photo Louis Maricha

Above.
War Office document giving the go ahead to form a brigade along British lines replacing the Brigade Group engaged in operations from August to November 1944. It also mentions the formation of six rifle brigades.

6 August 1944. A church parade on board the Liberty Ship *Henry Austen* before landing on the Normandy coastline. In the background one can see two of the Brigade Workshops 3-Ton Leyland trucks. They are equipped with a lifting beam.
(Photo Louis Marichal)

en-Auge, and Pont l'Evêque; on **25 August**, Beuzeville and Pont-Audemer and finally on **30 August**, Tancarville and Harfleur.

After the 6th Airborne Division was sent back to Great Britain, the Belgian brigade was temporarily placed under the command of the 49th Infantry Division (West Riding) before being attached to the Guards Armoured Division (XXX Corps) that was advancing towards the north. At 15.00 hrs on 4 September, the Belgian Brigade Group entered Brussels after crossing the border the previous day at 16.36 hrs. In the following week, the brigade refitted and rested before leaving Brussels and resuming combat operations in the canal area of Belgian and Dutch Limburg. The brigade was retired from operations on 18 November and remained in the Louvain-Saint-Nicolas sector.

The 1st Infantry Brigade 'Liberation'

Thanks to the incorporation of 2,400 'wartime volunteers' in freed Belgium, the formation adopted the structure of a British infantry brigade of three battalions of 850 men. The Field Artillery battery and Armoured Car Squadron left the brigade to form regiments, also along British army lines. Beginning on 5 April 1945, the new Brigade returned to the front line in Holland under the command of the I Canadian Corps.

After the cessation of hostilities, the brigade took part in the occupation duties in Germany, in the British sector, until December 1945 when it was disbanded.

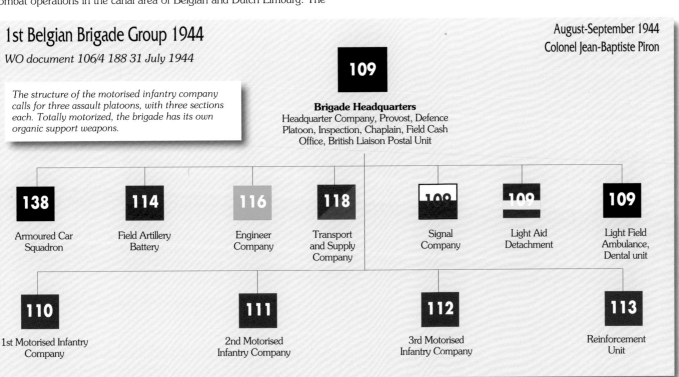

1st Belgian Brigade Group 1944

WO document 106/4 188 31 July 1944

August-September 1944
Colonel Jean-Baptiste Piron

The structure of the motorised infantry company calls for three assault platoons, with three sections each. Totally motorized, the brigade has its own organic support weapons.

109

Brigade Headquarters
Headquarter Company, Provost, Defence Platoon, Inspection, Chaplain, Field Cash Office, British Liaison Postal Unit

138
Armoured Car Squadron

114
Field Artillery Battery

116
Engineer Company

118
Transport and Supply Company

109
Signal Company

109
Light Aid Detachment

109
Light Field Ambulance, Dental unit

110
1st Motorised Infantry Company

111
2nd Motorised Infantry Company

112
3rd Motorised Infantry Company

113
Reinforcement Unit

The Belgian Armoured Car Squadron

In Wales at the end of 1942, the squadron was attached for training purposes to the 49th Reconnaissance Regt, 49th Infantry Division 'West Riding' for a three month period.

As the 1st Belgian Brigade Group insignia had not yet been created, the squadron bore, during this period, the formation badge of the 49th Div. (pre-April 1943 pattern). On 2 September 1944, the squadron found itself on operations with the 49th Recce Regt on the right bank of the Seine.

The 5th Special Air Service Regiment

Following a request by British authorities, the Belgian contingent supplied volunteers to undergo special training for future missions in territory occupied by German forces.

In January 1941, the first volunteers gained their parachute wings and in May 1942, the D Parachute Company was formed comprising of 120 men. Having become a squadron in February 1944, it was attached to the SAS Brigade commanded by Brigadier Mc Leod. 60 men of the Belgian

2 August 1944. A Jeep of the Brigade's Engineers Company crosses the river Touques between the seaside towns of Trouville and Deauville, the latter being liberated in the evening of 22 August by the Brigades' infantry. As the bridges over the river had been destroyed, the Engineers Company had to make crossing points using folding boats and parts of pontoon bridges. Trouville was not liberated until the 24th.
(Photo Louis Marichal)

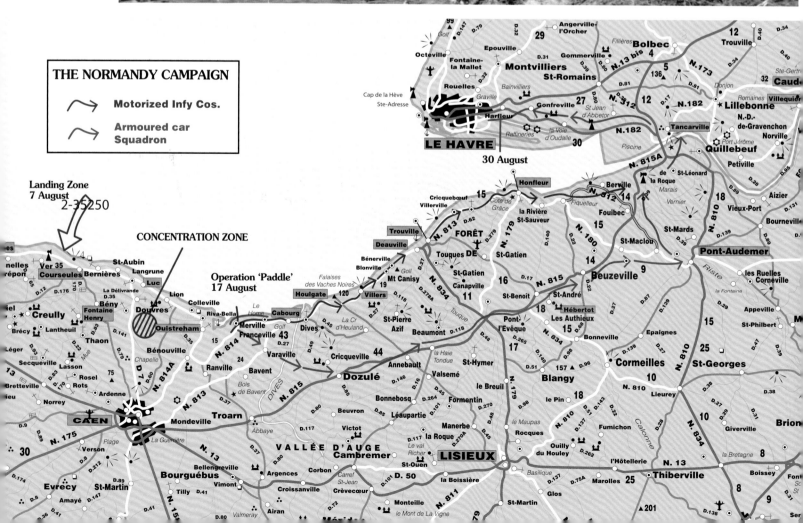

S were sent on operations in France at the end of July in the Perche (operation 'Chaucer'), then between the Eure and Seine rivers as part Operation 'Trueform' (80 men).
These missions were to gather intelligence on enemy positions, to give stance to FFI units, and sabotage.
Starting on 27 August, the SAS were parachuted into the Belgian Ardennes and Limburg where they used armoured Jeeps, the first Belgians operate in uniform on their home soil since 1939.
In March 1945, the squadron was transformed into an SAS regiment which first operated in Holland (operation 'Larkswood'), then in Germany under the command of the 2nd British Army.

Holland 17 October 1944: The brigade is visited by the Minister for National Defence, M. Desmet, and General Chevalier Van Strydonck de Burkel, Commander-in-Chief of Belgian forces in Great Britain.
On the right is Colonel Jean Piron in front of his Car, Heavy Utility 4x4 Humber FWD. The national B sign on the rear left-hand side is above the first pattern of brigade badge.
(Photo Louis Marichal)

SHAEF Belgian infantry battalions, 1944-45

At the end of 1944, the Allied advance had ground to a halt against the Siegfried Line, the Meuse, Holland and Alsace.

1st BELGIAN BRIGADE GROUP – STRENGTH

	OF	OR
Headquarters	3	8
Postal unit		3
Signal Company	2	62
Armoured Car Sqn.	13	207
Field Artillery Bty	20	292
Engineer Company	4	102
Transport/Supply	1	51
Light Aid detachment		
A - Armd Car Sqn.	1	13
B -	1	15
Light Field Ambulance	4	40
Blood Transfusion Unit	1	3
Field Surgical Unit	2	9
Belgian Section 2nd echelon	1	4
1st Mot. Inf. Coy	12	313
2nd Mot. Inf. Coy	12	313
3rd Mot. Inf. Coy	12	313
Total	**102** [2]	**1835**

War Office document No 106/4 188, dated 31 July 1944
Plus six British liaison officers

1st BELGIAN BRIGADE GROUP – LOSSES

	Killed	Wounded [1]	Wounded [2]	POW
Formation, Great Britain (1940-45 [3])	38			
1st Bde Group, Normandy (17 August – 3 Sept. 44)	27	65	88	1 (escaped)
Belgium (3 - 21 Sept. 1944)	7	9	56	35
1st Dutch campaign (21 sept. - 17 Nov. 44)	27	79	42	
1st Brigade 'Libération' (18 Nov. 44 – 2 Apr. 45)	9		42	
2nd Dutch campaign (3 April – 8 May 45)	19	48	174	4
Occupation of Germany (May-December 1945 [4])	30			
Total	**157**	**291**	**402**	**39**

1. Evacuated. 2. Wounded or sick, rejoined at later date. 3. Accidents, air raids, illness. 4. Accidents, mines.

The Headquarters of the 1st Belgian Brigade Group on a Liberty Ship heading for Normandy on 7 August 1944. Colonel Piron, the Brigade commander, is standing in the middle.
On his left is Lieutenant-Colonel McAlistair (Argyll and Sutherland Highlanders) commander of the British liaison group.

1st BELGIAN INFANTRY BRIGADE COMMANDERS

BRIGADE HEADQUARTERS

Brigade Commander
Colonel Jean-Baptiste Piron
(promoted on 4 August 1944)
Brigade Major
Major Poncelet
Intelligence Officer
Capitaine Didisheim
Staff Captain
Capitaine Van Hover
Signal Officer
Capitaine Commandant Richir
Medical Officer
Capitaine médecin Vermeylen
Chaplain
Aumônier Nobels
Provost Officer
Lieutenant Jacques (killed 1 Oct. 1944) replaced by lt. Courmont
Field Cash Officer
Capitaine Richard
　　1st Motorised Unit
Major Wintergroen
　　2nd Motorised Unit
Major Waterloos
　　3rd Motorised Unit
Major Nowe

Field Artillery Battery
Lieutenant colonel de Ridder
Armoured Car Squadron
Major de Selliers de Moranville
Engineer Company
Capitaine Smekens
Transport/Supply
Capitaine Bero
Light Aid Detachment
Lieutenant de Cock
Light Field Ambulance
Lieutenant médecin Petre
Field Surgical unit
Major médecin Dumont
Blood Transfusion unit
Lieutenant médecin Linz
British Liaison
Lieutenant-Colonel McAlistair,
Major Fortescue,
Captain Fairbairn,
Captain Limebeer,
Captain Rush,
1st Lieutenant Warburg
Belgian Liaison
Lieutenant Van Cauwelaert,
Lieutenant Courmont,
Lt. du Monceau de Bergendael

5th (Belgian) SAS insignia

Right sleeve

Left sleeve

The Belgian parachutists adopted the maroon beret in November 1942. The Belgian lion badge was soon replaced by the SAS badge when they were attached to it in February 1944.

Placed on the shoulder straps, the officers' rank insignia were scarlet coloured for the infantry.

1st BELGIAN INFANTRY BRIGADE 'LIBÉRATION'

2109

Strength: 4,420 OF/OR of which 2,150 were wartime volunteers. Note: The infantry battalions adopted the British table of organisation as described in vol. two of 'The British Soldier'

Headquarters
Headquarter Company, Defence Platoon, British Liaison, chaplain, Postal Unit, Inspection, Field Cash Office

- **2109** Brigade Workshop
- **2118** Supply and Transport
- **2113** Medium MG Company
- **2109** Provost Company
- **2109** Signal Company
- **2109** Field Ambulance

- **2114** 1st Field Artillery Regiment
- **2110** 1st Infantry Battalion
- **2111** 2nd Infantry Battalion
- **2112** 3rd Infantry Battalion
- **2113** Reinforcement Unit

THE 5th SAS, 24 JULY 1944

Squadron Headquarters
?7 officers, NCOs and privates
Headquarters Company
?4 officers, NCOs and privates
A Troop
?0 officers, NCOs and privates
Transport section
? officers, NCOs and privates
B Troop
?6 officers, NCOs and private
Quartermaster section
?7 officers, NCOs and privates

STANDARD RIFLE BATTALION, JANUARY 1945

- **HQ**
- **HQ Company**
  - Anti-aircraft platoon
  - Pioneer platoon
  - Administrative platoon
- **Rifle company**

Rifle company

Strength: 24 officers, 34 'elite NCOs', 70 NCOs and 669 corporals and privates

Armament: Enfield No 2 Mk I Revolver, No 4 Mk I* Rifle, Sten Machine-Carbine Mk II/III, Bren Light Machine Gun.

Faced with a serious infantry manpower deficit in the Autumn, the Al-
?d command requested the Belgian government to provide troops for
?arding lines of communications, thus freeing up men for combat units.
? plan for the formation of these units was made straight away and a force
? 75,000 men was raised, with most of these men coming from the Bel-
?an resistance movements. The British Army was to provide armaments,
?othing, equipment and vehicles.

From January 1945, 57 infantry battalions were formed and organised
?o 16 brigades: 42 were attached to the 21st British Army Group and 15
? the 12th US Army Group.

The mission of these battalions consisted of ensuring the guard of lines
? communications, pipelines, fuel and ammunition dumps as well as POW
?mps.

However, 12 of these battalions also took on a non-static role and par-
?ipated in combat operations alongside the British and American armies.
?ansport, railway troops, bomb disposal and workshop and salvage units
?ere also formed.

?67 officers and other ranks were killed during the course of these opera-
?ns.

As the rifle battalions had been hastily formed, initially no provision
?as made for distinctive insignia; the formation badge of the Allied unit
? which they were attached to was most often adopted, along with the
?elgium' shoulder titles for Dutch speakers, and 'Belgique' titles for the
?ench speakers.

Although some commanders wished to develop an esprit de corps
?thin their units and had had distinctive insignia made, the majority of
?attalions were never issued with their own badges.

Colonel Piron (1896-1974)

Born in Couvin, Jean-Baptiste Piron joined the military academy at the age of 17. During the Great War
he was promoted to lieutenant in 1916 and served as an
aerial artillery observer. At the end of the war he carried
on with his military studies and reached the rank of major
in 1936.

He saw action in 1940 during the German invasion.
Interned at Antwerpen along with other Belgian officers, he soon escaped but was captured again and sent
to Aachen where he managed to escape once more
in 1941. After crossing France, he reached Spain and
set sail for Great Britain.

In December 1942, he became the commander of
what was at that time the '1st Belgian Group' which
became the 1st Belgian Brigade Group in 1943. He
was promoted to full colonel on 29 July just before
his unit landed in France in early August 1944. He
remained in the Belgian army after the war, eventually reaching the rank of lieutenant-general. Jean-
Baptiste Piron died at the age of 78.

**Major-General Jean Piron, DSO,
Commander of Belgian Expeditionary
Forces in Western Europe**

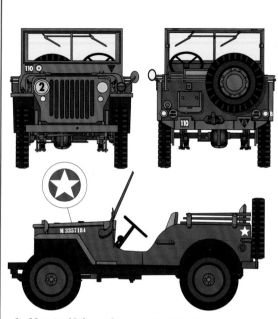

1st Motorized Infantry Company, 1st Rifle Platoon

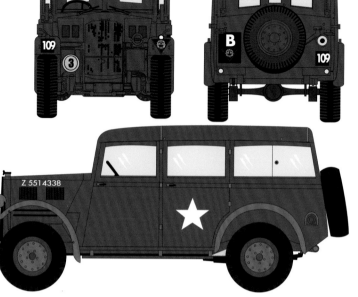

Humber FWD 4x4. Heavy Utility, Brigade Headquarters.

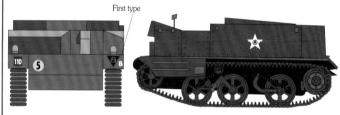

Universal Carrier, 1st Motorized Infantry Company.

Universal Carrier, Brigade 'Libération', Medium Machine Gun Company.

Above.
A Daimler Dingo scout car fitted with a windshield by the Brigade Workshop in November 1944.
Above right.
Brigade Libération, Holland, April 1945. Universal carrier of the Medium Machine Gun Company. Queen Astrid (the vehicle's name here), wife of King Léopold, died in a tragic car accident in August 1935.
(DR)

Belgian national roundel. Regulation type for vehicles and tanks.

1st BELGIAN BRIGADE GROUP - TRANSPORT

BRIGADE HQ
Headquarters Company
— 15 Motorcycles
— 11 light cars
— 2 Jeeps,
— 20 x 15-cwt trucks,
— 2 x 3-Ton trucks,
— 1 Scout Car,
— 2 tlr 10-cwt trucks,
— 4 tlr light trucks
Workshop LAD Type B
— 1 Motorcycle
— 1 x 15-cwt truck,
— 4 x 3-Ton trucks
— 1 Recovery 6 x 4
Signal Company
— 8 Motorcycles
— 2 light cars

— 1 Jeep
— 10 x 15-cwt trucks
— 4 x 3-Ton trucks
— 1 Staghound armoured car
LIGHT FIELD AMBULANCE
— 6 Ambulances
— 2 Motorcycles
— 2 light cars
— 1 x15-cwt truck
— 1 x 15-cwt water bowser
— 3 x 3-Ton trucks
FSU & FTU
— 1 light car
— 3 x 3-Ton trucks
TRANSPORT COMPANY
— 4 Motorcycles
— 1 x car,
— 1 x 15-cwt truck

— 16 x 3-Ton
— 1 x 15-cwt Water bowser
— 1 Recovery
ENGINEER COMPANY
Coy Headquarters
— 2 Motorcycles + 1 Jeep
— 2 x 15-cwt trucks
— 6 x 3-Ton truck
— 1 White Scout Car
Two Troops (for each:)
— 3 Motorcycles
— 3 x 15-cwt trucks
— 2 x 3-Ton trucks
— 1 Scout Car
— 1 White Scout Car

Note. Motorcycles, various vehicles and armour not mentioned in the charts pages 16 to 18.

MOTORISED INFANTRY COMPANY 1944 (X3)

Company Headquarters

Commanding officer
Major

Austin Ambulance

motorcycles (despatch riders)

15-cwt Radio

Water bowser

Baggage

Mechanic

Shoemaker – Tailor

Stores

Kitchen

Clerk

Gun Fitter

Ammunition

Ammunition

Battery charge

Petrol (jerrycans)

Troop carrier

Troop carrier

Troop carrier

SUPPORT GROUP

Medium Machine Gun Platoon

Universal carrier, .303 Vickers MG

110

Unit Serial Number

Mortar Platoon

Motorcycle

15-cwt

Wireless

2-In Mortar

2-In Mortar

Anti-Tank Platoon

Sergeant

Motorcycle

15-cwt

Loyd carrier + 6-pounder

Loyd carrier + 6-pounder

Loyd ammunition

Anti Aircraft section

15-cwt, 2 x .303 MG (AA)

Scout Section

Sergeant

Universal Carrier

Universal Carrier

Universal Carrier

RIFLE PLATOONS (X3)

No 1
15-cwt, 2-in Mortars
90 OF/OR

No 2
15-cwt, 2-in Mortars
90 OF/OR

No 3
15-cwt, 2-in Mortars
90 OF/OR

After the war in Dinan, October 1945. Colonel Piron was promoted to the rank of Major-Général, the badges of which he wears on his shoulder straps and colla
The photo shows him at an official reception accompanied by his aide-de-camp Major Georges Houbion, the latter wearing the metal insignia of Belgian forces i
Great Britain on the right pocket of his blouse. The Major is the grandfather of our friend JL Marichal who has written this chapter.

3   EN ALLEMAGNE OCCUPEE.   En attendant le train des permissionnaires.
     IN BEZET DUITSCHLAND.   Wachtend op den verlofgangerstrein.
     IN GERMANY.   Let's get cracking.

eat Britain, March 1942. The Armoured Car Squadron has
t received its Humber Mk Is, which were used for training until
ril 1943 when they were equipped with the Daimler Mk I that
Squadron used during the 1944 campaign. The red, yellow and
ck Belgian roundel was present on all vehicles.

Inset.
Formation badge of the 49th Div. (type in use prior to 1943)
worn during the Belgian Armoured Car Squadron's
training period in 1942.

elgian Armoured Car Squadron, 1944

The emblem of the Belgian Armoured Car Squadron was that of
e 1er Régiment de Chasseurs à cheval, transported to Great Britain
er the capitulation of the Belgian army in May 1940.

aimler Armoured Car

quadron Headquarters

Front

16 August 1944, on the main road in Sallenelles before the start
of operation 'Paddle' the following day: Daimler Mk I armoured
car 'Enragé' from Troop 4. Lieutenant Pelsmackers, the troop
commander, is sitting and talking to Major Poncelet, the Brigade
Group chief of staff. The man in the turret is Caporal Snoeck. The
War Correspondent on the left is wearing a Mk III helmet.

taghound Armoured Car

Rear

Front

Commander: Sous-Lieutenant Totelin
Radio: Brigadier Van de Putte
Driver: Cavalier Houbleu

**Squadron Headquarters
Radio liaison armoured car.**

No 1. 'Amarante', Major
Selliers de Morainville

No 2. ' Amazone ',
capitaine Lancksweert

No 3. 'As de Pique',
adjudant de Potter

'Ajax', lieutenant
Dulait

' Achille',
lt. d'Andrimont

'Ardent'
sous-lieutenant Totelin

Anti Aircraft No 1,
maréchal des logis Billiet

Anti Aircraft No 2,
maréchal des logis Lemoine

138

2 White Scout Cars (one ambulance)

2 Cars Light Utility 4x2 Hillman, Austin
or Morris (1 assigned to the Chaplain)

2 Cars Heavy Utility Humber FWD 4x42c

3 Trucks 15-cwt (Bedford): 2 General Service + 1 Water Duty (Trailer)

Unit strength was
235 officers, NCOs
and privates. From
the time of landing
in Normandy on
7 August to the end
of the campaign
on 15 November,
the squadron lost 6
killed, 34 wounded
and three prisoner.

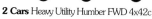

8 Trucks 3-Ton (Ford) (1 Store, 1 Bulk Petrol, 3 General Service, 1 Kitchen, 1 Workshop, 1 Battery Charge)

Squadron radio equipment
Set 19 radio on Daimlers
Set 19 HP for HQ Staghound 'Rearlink', allowing communica-

tions on the brigade network to a range of 35 miles (55 km).

Note: on 15 November 1944, after Normandy, Belgium and

Netherlands campaigns, the Squadron was removed from operations in order to form an armoured car regiment with the arrival
of 900 war volunteers.

No 1. 'Boute en Train',
lieutenant Sauvage

No 2. 'Branle-bas',
maréchal des logis Noël

No 3. 'Burkel',
mdl Putzeys

'Blisken', maréchal
des logis Equeter

'Blackswan', maréchal
des logis Daneau

3 scouts (Winklers) armes with a Bren
LMG or 2 in. Mortar.

No 1. 'Calamity',
lieutenant Dewandre

No 2. 'Corsaire',
mdl Solman

No 3. 'Casse-cou',
mdl Lienard

'Cycloon', maréchal
des logis Matagne

'Cobra', maréchal des
logis Harrewyns

No 1. 'D'Artagnan',
lieutenant Verharghe

No 2. 'Dynamite',
mdl Roelants

No 3. 'Dur à cuire',
mdl Bihay

'Dandermonde',
mdl Chougol

'Diksmuide',
maréchal des logis Collet

No 1. 'Enragé',
lieutenant Peelsmaekers

No 2. 'Effronté',
mdl Flasschoen

No 3. 'Entêté',
mdl Trelachaud

'Eekhoorn',
mdl Gabelle

'Egel', maréchal des
logis Corbeels

No 1. 'Franchimont',
lt. d'Oultremont de
Wégimont de Warfusée

No 2. 'Flandria',
mdl Van Praet

No 3. 'Fear Naught',
mdl Wagemans

'Furet', maréchal des
logis Leleu

'Féroce', maréchal
des logis Maitrejean

LIGHT AID DETACHMENT « A »

Electrician   Squadron Leader   Assistant

Assistant

Mechanics   Recovery

Above.
Daimler Mk I of the Armoured Car Squadron near Sallenelles on 16 August 1944. Whereas the infantry companies advanced along the Channel coast, this unit, attached to the 6th British Airborne, carried out reconnaissance missions inland. *(Photo Louis Marichal)*

Above, right.
Tuesday 22 August 1944 – operation 'Paddle.' Attached to the 6th Airlanding Brigade, a platoon of Daimler Mk I armoured cars of the 1st Belgian Brigade Group entered into the seaside town of Villers-sur-Mer. Rue de la Mer, the Bras d'Or hôtel-restaurant (advertised on the wall) closed down in the post-war years. *(NAC)*

Above, inset.
Ariel 350cc bike of the Armoured Car Squadron. The Belgian roundel is painted on the fuel tank. It is ridden here by Dispatch Rider Jules Gillemot in 1942. *(Photo Louis Marichal)*

HOTEL DU BRA

BONNE TABLE . BONNE CAVE

F207881 138

GLOIRE à la BELGIQUE!

VRIJ BELGIE

BELGIQUE LIBRE

JOYEUX RETOUR
VROO...

PA...
BRÜSSEL

FINIES LES VACANCES !
OH, RATTEN EN MUIZEN, WIJ MOETEN VERHUIZEN !
GOOD TIMES ARE OVER !

Postcards published after the liberation. Even in this humorous format, the similarity of the Belgian soldier's uniform with that of their British brothers in arms is striking.

Oppo...
The Field Battery was armed with twelve 25-Pounder Field Gun Howitz...
Muzzle brakes were fitted to the guns in March 19...

THE ARTILLERY
Normandy, Belgium and first Netherlands campaigns
Commander: Lieutenant Colonel Bennett de Rider

FIELD ARTILLERY BATTERY - Battery Headquarters
— 1 x Motorcycle, 2 x cars,
— 5 x 15-cwt, 1 x 3-Ton,
— 2 x White Scout Cars
— 1 x AOP Carrier, Tlr

3 Troops (A, B, C), each:
— 3 x Motorcycles
— 3 x Jeeps
— 5 x 15-cwt truck,
— 3 x 3-Ton truck,
— 1 x White Scout Car,
— 1 x AOP Carrier
— 6 x Artillery tractors
— 8 x Artillery limbers
— 4 x 25-pdr Field Guns

In December 1944, the battery was withdrawn from operation... in order to be strengthened and reorganised to form a British typ... Field Artillery Regiment. Manpower was brought up to strength b... a draft of 284 'war volunteers' and some of the officers and NCC... were sent to artillery schools in Great Britain.

Given the time needed to train new personnel and the induction... new equipment, the Belgian Field Artillery Regiment did not return... the front line until April 1945.

Normandy 16 August 1944. Prior to operation... 'Paddle', the Field Artillery Battery support... the 6th British Airborne Division. The 25-pounder gun... crew wears the Mk III helmet
(Photo Louis Marichal...

HE LUXEMBURG CONTRIBUTION

When Germany invaded Luxembourg on 10 May 1940 in viola-
on of its neutrality, the Grand Duchess Charlotte, accompanied
y her family and husband, Prince Felix de Bourbon-Parme, chose
o go into exile in the United States. In 1942 she joined her gov-
rnment in London where she played a role in the resistance.

Her eldest son, Prince Jean, the future Grand Duke, joined up
ith his father in the Guards Armoured Division. On 14 April
945, the royal family returned to their country, which had been
nnexed by the Third Reich and where compulsory military service
n the Wehrmacht had been decreed (mobilised: 12,000, killed:
,450, wounded: 1,500, escaped: 3,500).

Volunteers from Luxemburg also formed C Troop of the Belgian
rigade's artillery. Its commanding officer was Lieutenant Pierre
aquet and its strength 80 officers and other ranks. Considered as
eserters by the German authorities, these men wore no national
nsignia and in general adopted false names to avoid reprisals in the
vent of their being taken prisoner.

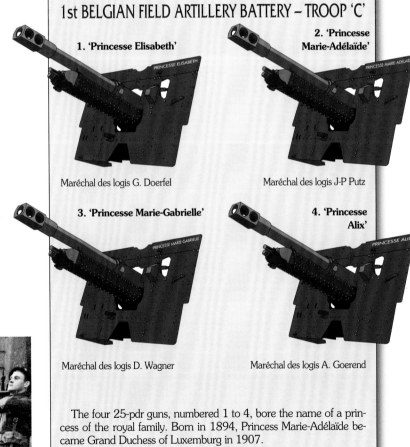

1st BELGIAN FIELD ARTILLERY BATTERY – TROOP 'C'

1. 'Princesse Elisabeth'

Maréchal des logis G. Doerfel

2. 'Princesse Marie-Adélaïde'

Maréchal des logis J-P Putz

3. 'Princesse Marie-Gabrielle'

Maréchal des logis D. Wagner

4. 'Princesse Alix'

Maréchal des logis A. Goerend

The four 25-pdr guns, numbered 1 to 4, bore the name of a princess of the royal family. Born in 1894, Princess Marie-Adélaïde became Grand Duchess of Luxemburg in 1907.

**London, 23 January 1944. Accompanied by her husband Prince Felix, HRH
Grand Duchess Charlotte of Luxemburg inspects the artillerymen of Troop
C/1st Belgian Field Artillery Battery. Like British gunners, the men are
equipped with the cartridge carriers issued to personnel armed with the rifle
but not part of an infantry unit.**

A Luxemburg volunteer training in Great Britain. He wears 'Luxembourg' titles in white letters on brown at the top of the sleeves. These titles were removed when the Luxemburgers were assigned to the 1st Belgian Brigade and were not, therefore, worn during the NW Europe campaign.
(British Official Photograph, Ministry of Information)

Belgian 'Fourragère' in 1940 Croix de Guerre colours.

CAMPAIGN MEDALS AND GALLANTRY DECORATIONS

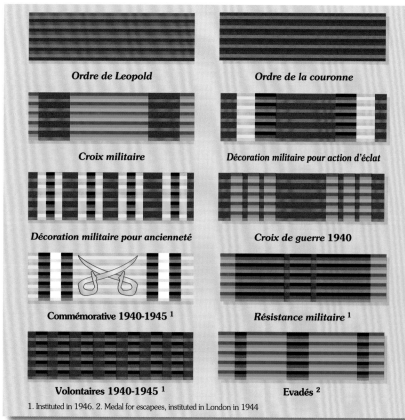

Ordre de Leopold

Ordre de la couronne

Croix militaire

Décoration militaire pour action d'éclat

Décoration militaire pour ancienneté

Croix de guerre 1940

Commémorative 1940-1945 [1]

Résistance militaire [1]

Volontaires 1940-1945 [1]

Evadés [2]

1. Instituted in 1946. 2. Medal for escapees, instituted in London in 1944

THE 1940 CROIX DE GUERRE

Decree No 363 dated 13 April 1945 (excerpts):
"Charles, Prince of Belgium [1], Regent of the Kingdom,

Upon the proposal of the Minister for National Defence:

Are cited and mentioned in army orders with the (collective) award of the fourragère of the 1940 croix de guerre: the 1st Infantry Brigade 'Liberation', the Regiment's 1st Artillery Battery 'Clerken', the 1st Armoured Squadron 'Liberation', the 1st Engineers Battalion 'Yser'.

These units are authorised to add the battle honours 'Normandy' and 'Wessen Canal' to their flags.

1. Brother of King Leopold III

Croix de guerre instituted by the Belgian government in exile in London on 20 July 1940.

HEAD DRESS INSIGNIA

The placing of head dress insignia was identical to that of the British Army, i.e. vertically over the left eye and with the beret slanted to the right.

1. Blackened metal lion on an SAS maroon beret.
2. White metal lion on the Royal Armoured Corps black beret adopted by the Armoured car squadron.
3. Other ranks insignia on a General Service Cap, worn by all Belgian arms and services except the Armoured Car Squadron.

The lion passant (Nov. 1942) is the symbol of the provinces that inspired the national flag colours. 4. Blackened bronze: officers. 5. Silvered metal: NCOs and cavalry (Armoured Car Squadron). 6. Bronze: privates.

Mk II and Mk III helmets with the Belgian flag. The Mk III is mainly seen in infantry companies and the artillery battery.

Helmet, steel, Despatch Rider's (specified in 1943) bearing the characteristic markings of the Military Police and the Belgian flag.

Helmet Crash, Despatch Rider's, 1941 pattern.

(Overlord Collection)

37

The insignia of Belgian forces in Great Britain was created by the Minister for National Defence of the Belgian government in exile on 24 November 1942. It was authorized for all active Belgian military personnel present in Great Britain before 3 September 1944. The insignia was worn on the right hand side of the Battledress blouse.

The symbolism of the Belgian flag

The colours are found in the coat of arms of the Brabant, Flander and Hainaut provinces. Previously placed horizontally, the three co ours were set vertically upon Belgian independence in 1830.

Belgian made shoulder title, end of 1944 – beginning of 1945.

Arm-of-service strips

Staff	Infantry	Armour
RASC	Artillery	RAMC
Chaplains	Pay Corps	Signals

BADGES ON BATTLEDRESS

Right sleeve   Left sleeve

1940 'Austerity' pattern Battledress blouse with the 1st type triangular formation sign, worn until September 1944. The scarlet strip is that of the infantry. Smaller sized enamelled versions of the sign were issued at the end of hostilities for veterans to wear with their civilian clothing.
(Le Poilu collection)

RANK EQUIVALENTS

BELGIUM	GREAT BRITAIN
Général Major	Major General
Brigadier	Brigadier
Colonel	Colonel
Lieutenant-colonel	Lieutenant-colonel
Major	Major [1]
Capitaine commandant [2]	
Capitaine	Captain
Lieutenant	First Lieutenant
Sous-lieutenant	Second Lieutenant
Adjudant de 1re classe	Warrant Officer Class I
Adjudant	Warrant Officer Class II
1er Sergent major	Staff sergeant
1er Sergent	Sergeant
Sergent [3]	Lance Sergeant
Caporal, 2 ans de service	Corporal
Soldat d'élite	Lance Corporal

1. Held the rank of Major except if commanding a regiment in which case he held the British rank of colonel.
2. Intermediate rank between that of captain and major.
3. Section leader, a role undertaken by a corporal in the British Army. The Caporal (or soldat d'élite) was the leader of a Bren group, 2-in. Mortar group, etc.
The backing or rank badges was in the arm of service colour from the rank of colonel and under (Decree No 1161/3 dated 28 September 1943). Note: in cavalry and artillery units, sergeants were called 'Maréchal des Logis' and corporals, 'Brigadier'.

Right sleeve   Left sleeve

1940 'Austerity' pattern Battledress blouse with a second type formation sign worn from September 1944 onwards. The general positioning of the badges remained consistent with British regulations.
(Le Poilu collection)

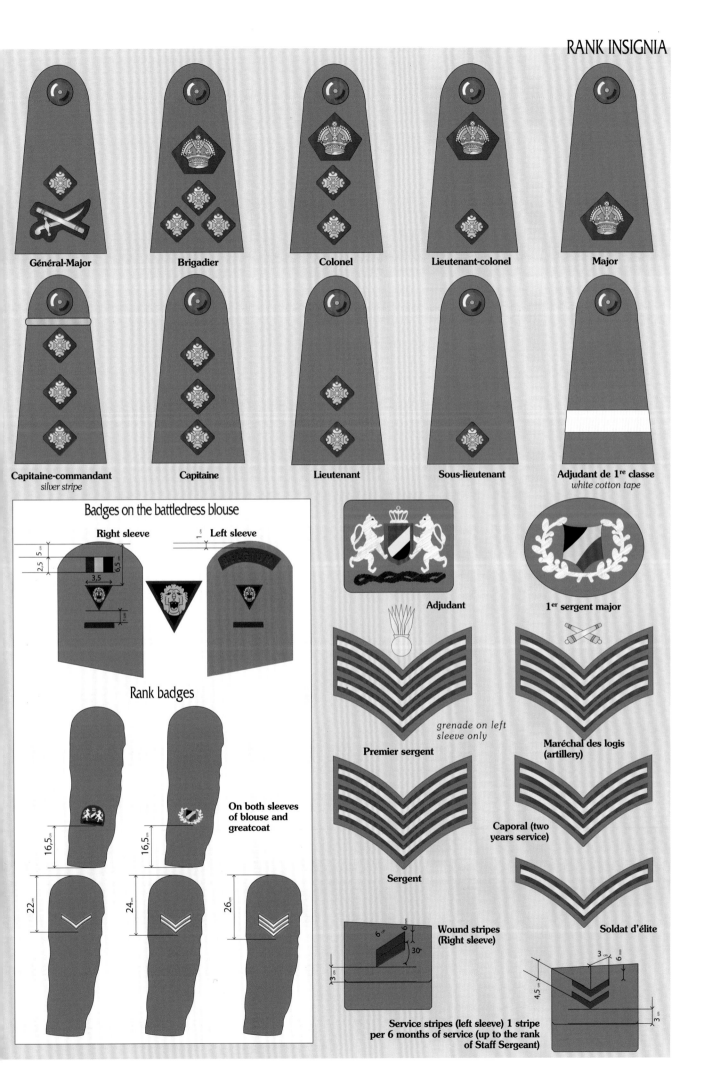

Général-Major

Brigadier

Colonel

Lieutenant-colonel

Major

Capitaine-commandant
silver stripe

Capitaine

Lieutenant

Sous-lieutenant

Adjudant de 1ʳᵉ classe
white cotton tape

Badges on the battledress blouse

Right sleeve

1 ᶜᵐ **Left sleeve**

5 ᶜᵐ

2,5 ᶜᵐ

6,5 ᶜᵐ

3,5 ᶜᵐ

1 ᶜᵐ

Rank badges

16,5 ᶜᵐ

16,5 ᶜᵐ

On both sleeves of blouse and greatcoat

22 ᶜᵐ

24 ᶜᵐ

26 ᶜᵐ

Adjudant

1ᵉʳ sergent major

Premier sergent

grenade on left sleeve only

Maréchal des logis (artillery)

Sergent

Caporal (two years service)

Soldat d'élite

Wound stripes (Right sleeve)

6 ᶜᵐ   6 ᵐᵐ

30°

3 ᶜᵐ

3 ᶜᵐ   6 ᵐᵐ

4,5 ᶜᵐ

3 ᶜᵐ

Service stripes (left sleeve) 1 stripe per 6 months of service (up to the rank of Staff Sergeant)

1. Bronze type cap badge worn by privates and corporals.

2. Belgian made shoulder title, 1945.[1]

3. Machine embroidered Belgian made shoulder title, worn from Sept. 1944 to 1945.[1]

4. Belgian made shoulder title indicating language spoken, 1945 (a 'Belgie' version existed for Dutch speaking personnel). [1]

5. British made shoulder title introduced in July 1941. [1]

6. British made variant. [1]

7. National flag, March 1942, worn at the top of the right sleeve, with the black facing forwards [2] (see blouses on page 38).

8. Insignia of the Brigade Group created in 1943 from a design by Capitaine Paternotte and Didisheim and authorized by Major Piron. In September 1944, following the liberation of Brussels, it appeared that this badge was exactly the same as that worn by members of the Secret army. Indeed, these badges had been parachuted into occupied Belgium.
The Secret army retained this badge and a new insignia was issued to the Brigade. [3]

9. The new badge replacing fig. 8. It retained the lion's head, although it was now placed on the shield of the British 21st Army Group. The first versions were printed (1944), the second embroidered pattern was introduced in 1945 and worn beyond this date. [3]

10. Infantry arm of service strip. Based on the British system, these strips were used until 1946. [3]

11. Lanyard (on the right shoulder) of the wartime volunteers, displayed for parade and walking out.

12. The main motif of the formation sign was the lion's head, which already featured on the WW1 Belgian steel helmet, and which was also retained on the 1931 pattern helmet.

---

1. Worn on the left sleeve of the blouse and greatcoat.

2. Right sleeve of the blouse and greatcoat.

3. On both sleeves.

1940 Pattern 'Austerity' Battledress blouse with a first pattern formation sign worn until September 1944. The scarlet strip denotes the infantry.
(Le Poilu collection)

Gorget patches for Colonels and Brigadiers

Brigadiers, colonels, Artillery, Provost.

Infantry

Armoured, Supply, Field Cash Office

Engineers, Signals

Chaplains

Medical Corps

Coloured arm-of-service backings for officers' rank insignia

All arms of service, possibly for field uniform.

Pattern 1940 Austerity blouse with the second pattern formation sign of September 1944.

Général de Gaulle on board a Free French corvette off Weymouth during sea exercises. Photograph taken in 1943 by the Navy photographer Lucien Guy-Mas.

THE FIGHTIN[G]

The French units mentioned in this chapter and engaged in operations within the 21st British Army Group fought unde[r] under the flag of 'La France Combattante'. This den[o]mination was made official on 1 August 1943 after hav[v]ing been created in Algeria in July 1943 by the Comit[é] Français de la Libération Nationale (CFLN), led by genera[ls] de Gaulle and Giraud. This was confirmed by General de Gaulle o[n] 22 August during a proclamation made to troops stating that the unit[y] of French armies was No w at last a reality.

The France Combattante rallies…

The France Combattante consisted of the following:
– personnel or units that had joined General de Gaulle following his BBC broad[cast] cast on 18 June 1940, and immediately engaged in combat against the Axi[s] under the name of 'Forces Françaises Libres' (FFL),
– units stationed in North Africa or any other overseas territory at the time the armistice was signed in June 1940 by Pétain's government. Uncommitted until the Allied landings of November 1942 in Morocco and Algeria, they entered into the war in 1943 after having been equipped and armed by the United States. [1]

These units continued wearing their respective insignia.

Above, left.
Metallic breast insignia of the Free French ground forces. Designed in London by Caporal Louvier in December 1940.
The first badges were made by a Birmingham manufacturer in 1941, copies being locally made in Cairo and the Lebanon. This British made badge is numbered 42856, the wearer's enrolment number in the FFL. The badge was worn on the right breast.

Above[.]
Adopted on 2 July 1940 following an idea of vice-amiral Muselier, the Cross o[f] Lorraine became the symbol of Free France, the Resistance, and finally the 'Franc[e] Combattante'. It was flown on the ships of the Forces Navales Françaises Libre[s] (FNFL) something that was made official in June 1941[.] This three-colour format, inspired by the French consular flag of 1804[,] was used by numerous units of the France Combattante, No t only in their insignia[,] but also vehicle and tank markings[.]

Brigadier Charles de Gaulle, 1890-1970

As State Under Secretary for War, he left by plane for London on 17 June 1940, convinced that the new government led by Maréchal Pétain would request an armistice. The very next day, he launched an appeal over the BBC airwaves calling on all French people to carry on the fight against Germany and its allies. He thus became the creator and leader of the 'France Libre'. After four years of exile, he returned to mainland France on 14 June 1944, landing on the beach at Courseulles. At the end of August, he announced that only the provisional government (*Gouvernement Provisoire de la République Française* GPRF) of which he was president, held legitimate power. After the legislative elections in October 1945, he resigned on 20 January 1946.

---

1. The history of these units is described in detail in the four volumes of "L'armée de la Victoire" by Colonel Paul Gaujac.

RENCH

sistance within France

Active since June 1940, the Résistance had begun with psychological ions aimed at the population (posters, leaflets), then sabotage, formation intelligence networks and helping Allied military personnel, and civilians ject to racial persecution. From 1943 onwards there was an increase in ned action and the Resistance played an important role in harassing Ger- n troops during the Allied landing in Normandy on 6 June 1944 and in vence on 15 August 1944.

On 2 February 1944, unified within the Forces Françaises de l'Intérieur I), the various resistance elements were the *Armée Secrète* (AS), *Maquis*, ncs-Tireurs and Partisans Français (PTPF) and the *Organisation de la sistance de l'Armée* (ORA). After the liberation of most of France, these urgents, levied into regular army units, joined the 1st French army or intained the siege of the Atlantic or North Sea ports where the German ny still held large garrisons (see chapter covering the French units besieg- the Dunkirk stronghold).

Right.

Fourragères awarded to units mentioned in dispatches, displayed on the left shoulder, as well as on the unit flag pole or pennant.

Award requirements:
1. **Légion d'honneur: 6 army level citations (2e RCP).**
2. **Médaille militaire: 4 army level citations (1er BFMC).**
3. **Croix de guerre: 2 army level citations (3e RCP).**

ow.

e principal French decorations that could be worn in 1944-45. bbons were placed 1 cm above the left uniform pocket in the correct der. Other medals that could also be worn were the Croix de Guerre 14-1918, Croix de Guerre TOE (for overseas theatres of operations).1. gion d'Honneur (3rd Republic model, November 1870).
Ordre de la Libération (created on 16 November 1940 and awarded up 23 January 1946). 1,059 were awarded of which 18 were to units d 5 to towns.
Médaille militaire (3rd Republic model, November 1870).
Croix de guerre 1939-45 (26 September 1939).
Croix du combattant (28 June 1930).
Médailles des évadés (20 August 1926), worn here with a Cross of rraine.
Médaille de la Résistance (9 February 1943).
Médaille coloniale (26 July 1893) worn here with the 'Bir-Hakeim' bar.
e wearing of British campaign medals was No t authorized.

1   2   3

4   5   6   7   8

THE 1ᵉʳ BATAILLON DE FUS

A small group of French Marines under the command of Enseigne de vaisseau (sub-lieutenant) Philippe Kieffer began training in Great Britain in April 1941. Although seconded to the army, most of the volunteers were from the French navy. Following training at the Royal Marines camp and commando school, the unit was given the name of *1ʳᵉ Compagnie de Fusiliers Marins Commandos* in July 1942. It then joined No 10 (Inter-Allied) commando.

During this period, small groups carried out numerous actions on the coast of western Europe. With the influx of new volunteers in June 1943, the company became the *1ᵉʳ Bataillon de Fusiliers Marins Commandos*. The following winter, from November 1943 to March 1944, raids continued along the coastline in order to test the enemy defences. In March 1944, the Battalion left No 10 Commando and was attached

to the British No 4. On 6 June, it landed at the Brèche d'Hermanville and captured the Ouistreham Casino that had been transformed into a strongpoint. Given its strength (177 OF/OR), Lieutenant de vaisseau Kieffer's unit was actually a strengthened company. War Establishment instruction VIII/527/1 dated 8 September 1943 set the strength of a commando battalion (Royal Marines or Army) at 458 men.

In the evening of June 6 they had established positions in the Amfreville sector and were at Bavent woods between 27 July and 16 August. Operation 'Paddle' was launched on 17 August with the objective of capturing the mouth of the river Seine. The campaign ended at Beuzeville on the 25th and on 7 September, the battalion boarded a ship at Arromanches and sailed f Great Britain.

Capitaine de corvette Philippe Kieffer is seen here in Paris in 1945 when he was awarded the Croix de l'Ordre de la Libération.
(Photo Eric Le Penven)

Capitaine de corvette Philippe Kieffer, 1899-1962

A bank executive, Philippe Kieffer[1] was mobilised with the French navy in 1939 as an administrative petty officer. Following the June 1940 armistice, he made his way to Great Britain and signed up for the Free French forces on 1 July. After having served as an interpreter on the battleship *Courbet*, he became a fusilier marin officer and gathered volunteers in order to form the *1ᵉʳ Bataillon de Fusiliers Marins Commando*. Led by Kieffer, the small unit took part in the Normandy landings and the ensuing battle, and then in Holland late 1944 and in 1945.

1. Claude Kieffer, a member of the Resistance and the son of Philippe Kieffer was killed on 25 August during the liberation of Paris.

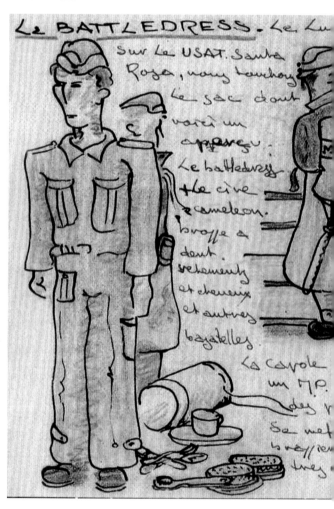

The arrival of foreign volunteers in Great Britain.
After security controls and medical examination, the men were issued with Battledress before joining their designated unit.
(Travel diary, Maurice Chauvet Archives)

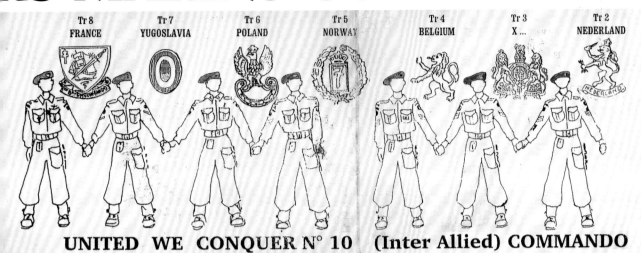

Tr 8	Tr 7	Tr 6	Tr 5	Tr 4	Tr 3	Tr 2
FRANCE	YUGOSLAVIA	POLAND	NORWAY	BELGIUM	X...	NEDERLAND

UNITED WE CONQUER N° 10 (Inter Allied) COMMANDO

e first unit to which Capitaine de corvette Kieffer's Compagnie de Fusilier Marins was
ached to was No 10 (Inter-Allied) Commando. Formed in June 1942 and placed under
command of Lieutenant- Colonel Dudley Lister, it consisted of approximately 450 volunteers
m various nations. The illustration above was drawn by Maurice Chauvet in 1994 and
resents the Allied volunteers and their cap badges. Troop 'X' comprised of anti-Nazi Germans
d Jews that had fled racial persecution. Its insignia was the British General Service Corps cap
dge (1st pattern). The badge worn by Troop 5 'Norge' (Norway) was King Haakon VII's (the
gning sovereign exiled in the United Kingdom) monogram.

IEPPE
SARK
ERSEY
STREHAM
FREVILLE
de BAVENT
ME de LEPINE
ESSINGUE

FUSILIERS
MARINS
COMMANDO

Flag of the 1er Bataillon de Fusiliers
Marins Commando. The battle honours
are: *DIEPPE, SARK, JERSEY,
OUISTREHAM, AMFREVILLE, BOIS
de BAVENT, FERME de LEPINE,
FLESSINGUE.*
For the first two citations (mention in
Navy despatches), the Bataillon was
authorized to wear a fourragère in the
colours of the Croix de guerre ribbon.
The two additional citations were
rewarded by the fourragère in the
colurs of the Médaille militaire. The red
fourragère of the Légion d'honneur
was worn since 1919 by all Fusiliers
marins units since 1919 for the heroic
fighting of Amiral Ronarch's brigade
at Dixmude in 1914.

40
Group Headquarters

2
Armoured
Support Reg.
(Royal Marines)

4
Armoured
Support Reg.
(Royal Marines)

52
Signals

40
Light Aid
Detachment REME

79
Provost

80
Postal
Unit

41
Special Boat
Unit

49
1st Royal Marines
Engineers Commando

81
1st Special Service
Brigade HQ

81
Brigade Light
Aid Detachment

81
Brigade Signals

100
Brigade Light
Aid Detachment

100
4th Special Service
Brigade HQ

100
Brigade Signals

55
3. Army
Commando

56
4. Army
Commando

57
6. Army
Commando

58
45. Royal Marines
Commando

92
41. Royal Marines
Commando

93
46. Royal Marines
Commando

95
47. Royal Marines
Commando

96
48. Royal Marines
Commando

THE SPECIAL SERVICE GROUP UNIT SERIAL NUMBERS

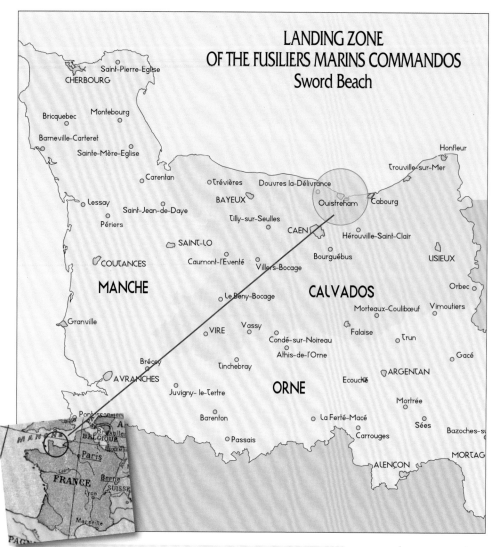

LANDING ZONE OF THE FUSILIERS MARINS COMMANDOS
Sword Beach

(Map of Normandy region showing: CHERBOURG, Saint-Pierre-Eglise, Montebourg, Bricquebec, Barneville-Carteret, Sainte-Mère-Eglise, Carentan, Trévières, Douvres-la-Délivrance, Honfleur, Trouville-sur-Mer, Ouistreham, Cabourg, Lessay, Saint-Jean-de-Daye, BAYEUX, Tilly-sur-Seulles, Périers, CAEN, Hérouville-Saint-Clair, SAINT-LO, Caumont-l'Eventé, Villers-Bocage, Bourguébus, LISIEUX, COUTANCES, MANCHE, Le Beny-Bocage, CALVADOS, Orbec, Morteaux-Coulibœuf, Vimoutiers, Granville, VIRE, Vassy, Falaise, Trun, Condé-sur-Noireau, Gacé, Athis-de-l'Orne, Brécey, ARGENTAN, AVRANCHES, Ecouché, Juvigny-le-Tertre, ORNE, Mortrée, Barenton, La Ferté-Macé, Sées, Bazoches-s..., Passais, Carrouges, MORTAG..., ALENÇON; inset map of FRANCE showing MANCHE, BELGIQUE, Paris, FRANCE, Berne, SUISSE, Lyon, Marseille)

On 5 June 1944, the 1er BFMC was loaded onto 2 Landing Craft, Infantry (Small):
– **LCI 523:**
Troop 8 + 12 men (K-Gun section)
– **LCI 527:**
Headquarters, Troop 1, + 12 men (K-Gun section)

Landing Cra[ft]
Infantry (small) LCI (S[)

**British troop transporter fo[r]
seaborne landings. Wooden hul[l]
Troops disembarked via four ramp[s]
placed at the bow[.]**

Capacity: 6 officers and 96 men with their equipment.
Crew: 2 officers, 15 ratings.
Dimensions: length 26.67 m, width 5.43 m.
Armament: 2 x 20 mm Polsten-Oerlikon guns.
Propulsion: 2 x 1120 hp petrol engines.
Captained by, on 6 June:
LCI (S) 523.
Lieutenant Jack Berry, Royal Navy
LCI (S) 527.
Lieutenant Charles Craven, Royal Navy

Strength of the 1er BFMC, June 6 1944

● Personnel present on D-Day

Headquarters
(Administration, Medical Service, Signals, British Liaison)
— Capitaine de corvette Philippe Kieffer
— Capitaine médecin de 1re classe Robert Lion (KIA 6 June)
— Capitaine aumônier René de Naurois
— 13 officers, petty officers and ratings

Troop 1
— Enseigne de vaisseau de 1re classe Guy Vourch
— 69 officers, petty officers and ratings

Troop 8
— Enseigne de vaisseau de 2e classe Alexandre Lofi
— 71 officers, petty officers and ratings

K-gun section
— Enseigne de vaisseau de 1re classe Pierre Armaury
— 24 officers, petty officers and ratings
TOTAL
177 officers, petty officers and ratings

● Reinforcement and British personnel
— 6 Other ranks

● Losses 6 June 1944
Headquarters
— 1 killed, 2 wounded evacuated, 1 wounded non-evacuated.
Troop 1
— 5 killed, 17 wounded evacuated.
Troop 8
— 1 killed, 11 wounded evacuated, 2 wounded non-evacuated.
K-gun Section
3 KIA, 2 wounded evacuated.

TOTAL
10 killed, 32 wounded evacuated, 3 wounded

● Personnel present on 7 September 1944
following the fighting in Normandy: 55 officers, petty officers and ratings (men hospitalized in Great Britain rejoined later).

LCI (S)

Round CDL tower amidships is to be removed, as in the LCS(L).

The D-Day landings on Sword Beach

● Assault formations

— 13/18 Hussars
(Sherman Duplex Drive)
— Assault Companies
– 2 East Yorkshire
– 1 South Lancashire
– 5 Assault Regt. Royal Eng
– 22 Dragoons (Flails)
– Royal Marine 5 Armoured Support Group (Centaurs).
– 33,76 Field Regts Royal Artillery (105 mm self-propelled)

● Follow up

— Assault Companies
– 2 East Yorkshire,
– 1 South Lancashire,
– No 4 commando (French Cdo).
— 8th Infantry Brigade
– 13/18 Hussars
– 1 Suffolk Regiment
– 1st Commando Brigade HQ
– 41 Royal Marine Commando
– No 3 Commando
– 45 Royal Marine Commando

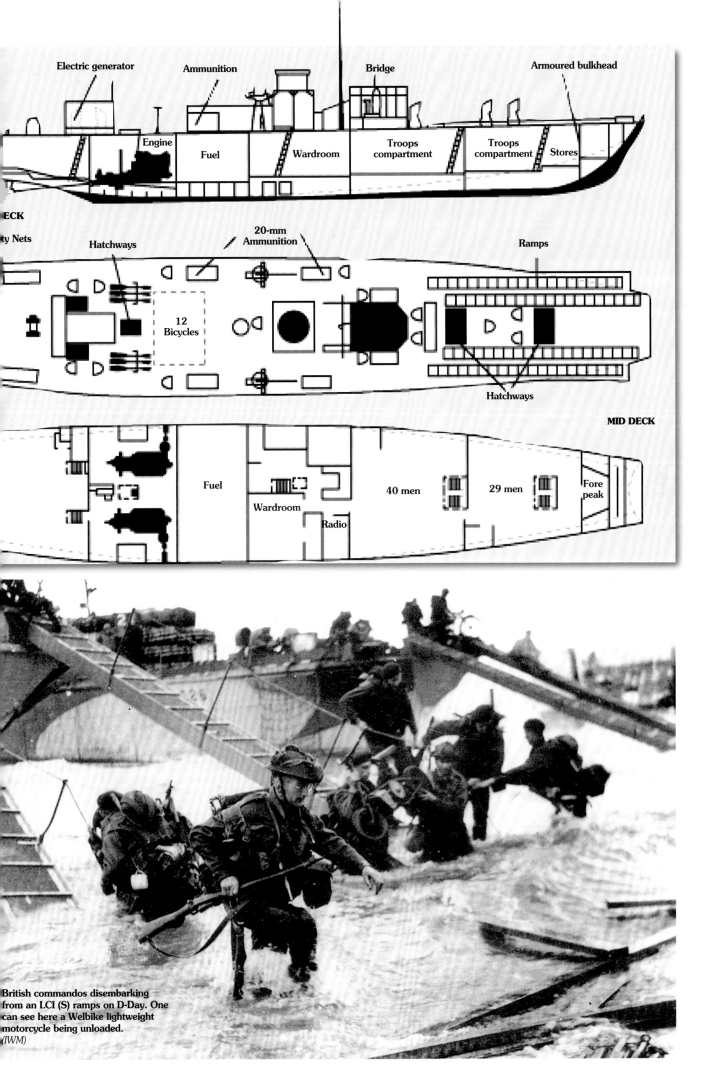

Electric generator　　Ammunition　　Bridge　　Armoured bulkhead

Engine　　Fuel　　Wardroom　　Troops compartment　　Troops compartment　　Stores

ECK

ty Nets　　Hatchways　　20-mm Ammunition　　Ramps

12 Bicycles

Hatchways

MID DECK

Fuel　　Wardroom　　Radio　　40 men　　29 men　　Fore peak

British commandos disembarking from an LCI (S) ramps on D-Day. One can see here a Welbike lightweight motorcycle being unloaded. (IWM)

47

14. RIVA-BELLA. — Œuvre des Colonies scolaires

Top.
Pre-war view of the Riva-Bella casino at Ouistreham.

Abov
In September 1942, the Germans demolished the casino, retaining on
ground floor, that was turned into a bunke
This was the objective of the 1er Bataillon de Fusiliers Marins Command
on the morning of 6 June and was taken by elements of Troop 1 supporte
by a Sherman III Duplex Drive of the 13/18 Hussar

Left.
Although it was named Riva-Bella, the school children holiday area was in
fact situated in the town of Colleville-sur-Mer.

Righ
The battalion's Normandy campaign drawn by Maurice Chauve
At number 7, the capture of Bavent on 17 August marke
the beginning of Operation 'Paddle
At number 11 is the correct Unit serial number '56' (vehicle tactic
marking) for No 4 Commande

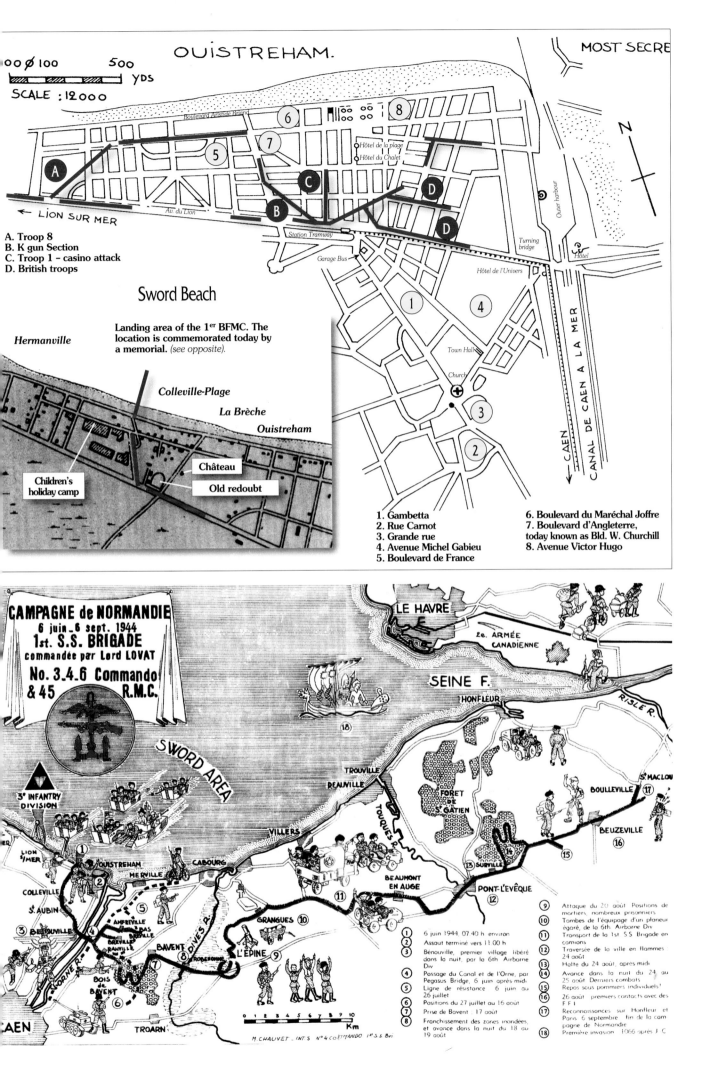

Below.
No 4 Commando landed in front of these ruins. Packs were left here before the attack on Ouistreham and were taken back in the afternoon for the advance towards Colleville, Saint-Aubin d'Arquenay, the bridges over the Orne canal and Amfreville in the 6th Airborne Division sector.
(IWM)

Operations in Holland and the end of the war

After the a period of leave and rest from 9 to 16 Septemb Kieffer's commando was reorganized into two Troops:
- Troop 5: Enseigne de vaisseau A. Lofi,
- Troop 6: Enseigne de vaisseau G. Vourch.

The K. Gun section was disbanded and its men reassigne Approximately 100 OF/OR remained. The unit was tra ferred to Belgium in October, still attached to No 4 Comman commanded by Lieutenant-Colonel Dawson, himself attach to the 4th Special Service Brigade (with 41, 47 and 48 Ro

Marine Commandos) placed under the command of Brigadier Leicester.

(continued page 54)

Right.
Metal sign of No 4 Commando. Number 4 in Roman numerals and S letters for Special Air Service.
(Musée de l'ordre de la Libération, Paris)

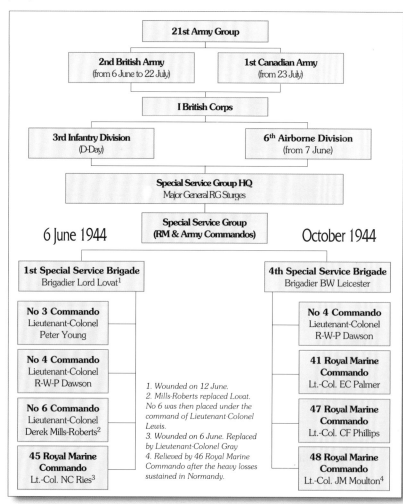

21st Army Group		

2nd British Army (from 6 June to 22 July)	**1st Canadian Army** (from 23 July)

I British Corps

3rd Infantry Division (D-Day)	**6th Airborne Division** (from 7 June)

Special Service Group HQ
Major General RG Sturges

6 June 1944

Special Service Group (RM & Army Commandos)

October 1944

1st Special Service Brigade Brigadier Lord Lovat[1]	**4th Special Service Brigade** Brigadier BW Leicester

No 3 Commando Lieutenant-Colonel Peter Young	**No 4 Commando** Lieutenant-Colonel R-W-P Dawson

No 4 Commando Lieutenant-Colonel R-W-P Dawson	**41 Royal Marine Commando** Lt.-Col. EC Palmer

No 6 Commando Lieutenant-Colonel Derek Mills-Roberts[2]	**47 Royal Marine Commando** Lt.-Col. CF Phillips

45 Royal Marine Commando Lt.-Col. NC Ries[3]	**48 Royal Marine Commando** Lt.-Col. JM Moulton[4]

1. Wounded on 12 June.
2. Mills-Roberts replaced Lovat. No 6 was then placed under the command of Lieutenant-Colonel Lewis.
3. Wounded on 6 June. Replaced by Lieutenant-Colonel Gray
4. Relieved by 46 Royal Marine Commando after the heavy losses sustained in Normandy.

VEHICLES OF THE BATAILLON DE FUSILIERS-MARINS COMMANDO
(ACI, 8 September 1943)

Bicycles (Airborne Folding)	35
Motorcycles, solo	9
Car, 4 Seater 4x2 GS	1
Cars, 5-cwt, 4x4 (Jeep)	18
Trucks, 15-cwt, 4x2, GS	8
Trailer 15-cwt Water Carrier	1
Lorries, 3-Ton, 4x2 GS	3

6 June 1944. Commandos head inland laden with their equipment. Shovels and picks were issued one to three men *(IWM)*.

No 4 Commando Jeep

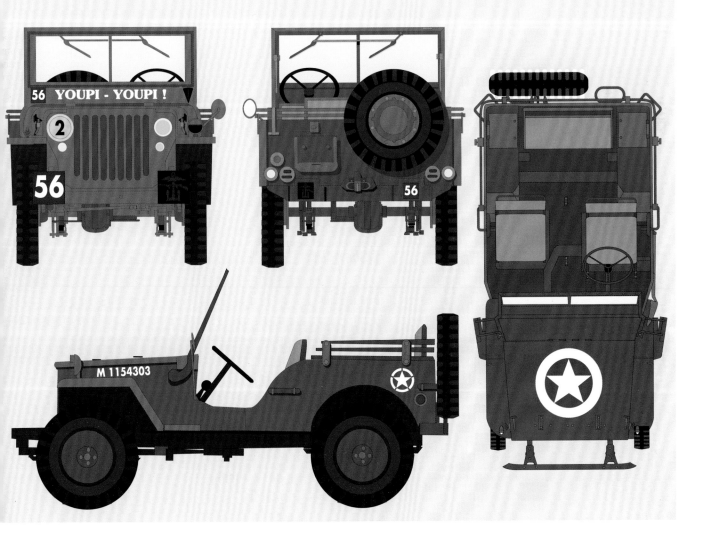

56 YOUPI - YOUPI !

2

56

56

M 1154303

Organisation of a French Commando Troop

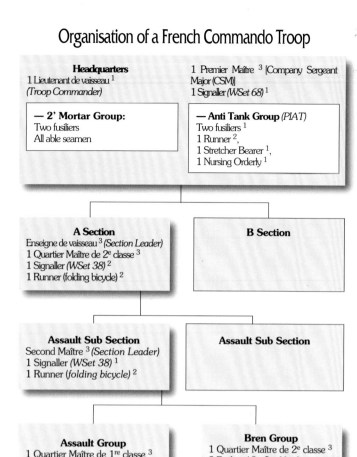

Headquarters
1 Lieutenant de vaisseau [1]
(Troop Commander)

1 Premier Maître [3] [Company Sergeant Major (CSM)]
1 Signaller *(WSet 68)* [1]

— 2' Mortar Group:
Two fusiliers
All able seamen

— Anti Tank Group *(PIAT)*
Two fusiliers [1]
1 Runner [2],
1 Stretcher Bearer [1],
1 Nursing Orderly [1]

A Section
Enseigne de vaisseau [3] *(Section Leader)*
1 Quartier Maître de 2e classe [3]
1 Signaller *(WSet 38)* [2]
1 Runner *(folding bicycle)* [2]

B Section

Assault Sub Section
Second Maître [3] *(Section Leader)*
1 Signaller *(WSet 38)* [1]
1 Runner *(folding bicycle)* [2]

Assault Sub Section

Assault Group
1 Quartier Maître de 1re classe [3]
6 Fusiliers [2]

Bren Group
1 Quartier Maître de 2e classe [3]
3 Fusiliers (2 rifles No 4,
1 Bren Light Machine Gun)

Notes: personal armament
1. Pistol, Automatic Cal .45 Colt
*2. Rifle, SMLE, No 4 Mk I * (sniper: Rifle No 1 Mk III)*

3. Thompson Machine Carbine Cal. 45.
Fairbairn Sykes knife issued to all personnel + 1 'Ack Pack' Flame Thrower per Troop

6 June 1944, the 1er Bataillon de Fusiliers-Marins Commandos land
on Colleville beach. The ruins of the children's holiday camp can be se
on the left of the illustration. As a headquarters runne
Maurice Chauvet has portrayed himself on the ram
pushing his Airborne, Folding Bicyc
(Maurice Chauvet Archiv

Previous page.
Operation 'Paddle'. Operational orders written up on 16 August 1944 by Lieutenant-Colonel Dawson, commanding No 4 Commando. The operation was due to start on 17 June 1944.

Below.
The French commandos in the Bavent woods. Period sketch made by Maurice Chauvet, of Troop 8. Everybody was hidden away in 'dugouts' under the trees. The details of the positions are very well rendered. On the far right-hand side is a German entrenching tool! One can also see the Compo Rations boxes that were issued from 7 June onwards at Amfreville.
(For details on rations, see 'The British soldier' volume 1 pages 122 and 123).

Above.
In the afternoon of 19 August at the exit of Briqueville-en-Ange, Brigadier Mills- Roberts, standing up in a Jeep, inspects the columns of commandos a short time before the decisive infiltration.
On this date, Mills-Roberts had replaced Lord Lovat, wounded on the 12th, as commander of the 1st Special Service Brigade. The illustrator has made a mistake, albeit understandable given the circumstances, by reversing the unit serial number on the jeep. It should be 56 and not 65.
Even though we have shown some of them, the 6 June photographs taken by the Army Film and Photography Units are very well known. The reader can find them in the books mentioned in this chapter's bibliography. We have chosen to show, with the kind permission of the author, a series of sketches made at the time, or from memory, by Quartier-Maître Maurice Chauvet. Full of accurate details, these sketches will delight enthusiasts of symbols, equipment and uniforms. An authentic Free French soldier, Maurice Chauvet landed on Colleville on 6 June 1944 with the 1er BFMC.
(Maurice Chauvet Archives).

(continued from page 50)

At this time, the Allied command mounted an important operation (code name 'Infatuate') designed to capture the island of Walcheren that covered the access to the port of Antwerp, the use of which was vital to the supply lines of the British and American armies.

No 4 Commando landed at Vlissingen on 1 November and advanced through the flooded areas before reaching Domburg in the North of the island. Fighting was over by the 8th and the enemy garrison surrendered.

During the winter of 1944-45, the Commando guarded the island of North-Beverland. A raid was undertaken against Schouven island on 14-15 February and this was occupied after a short period of fighting. Following the German capitulation on 8 May, the commando guarded POWs then paraded in Paris on 25 May (2 French troops and 1 British troop). In July, the French left No 4 Commando and were sent back to Great Britain and the FNFL depot at Portsmouth in order to carry out demobilization formalities, then the return to civilian life and for some, a career within the armed forces.

A sketch of Fusiliers-Commandos by Maurice Chauvet showing the evolution of head dress and insignia. The rubber soles screwed onto the regulation ankle boots are characteristic of the patterns used by commandos on operations (raiding boots).

THE COMMANDOS AT WALCHEREN

6 June 1944

1943

1942

FRENCH FUSILIERS MARINS RANK INSIGNIA

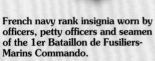

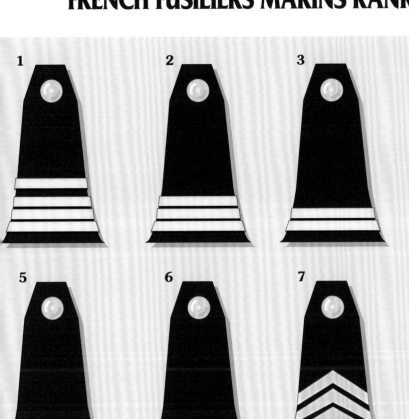

French navy rank insignia worn by officers, petty officers and seamen of the 1er Bataillon de Fusiliers-Marins Commando.

Officiers

Petty officers

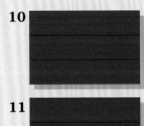

Seamen

Ranks stripes, worn on the front of the jacket, horizontally between the 2nd and 3rd button.

OFFICERS
1. Capitaine de corvette
2. Lieutenant de vaisseau
3. Enseigne de vaisseau de 1re classe
4. Enseigne de vaisseau de 2e classe

PETTY OFFICERS
5. Maître principal
6. Premier maître
7. Maître
8. Second maître (second service year)
9. Second maître

SEAMEN
10. Quartier Maître de 1re classe
11. Quartier Maître de 2e classe
12. Matelot breveté

RANK EQUIVALENTS

French Navy	Royal Navy
OFFICERS	
Capitaine de corvette	Lieutenant Commander
Lieutenant de vaisseau	Lieutenant
Enseigne de vaisseau de 1re classe	Sub-Lieutenant
Enseigne de vaisseau de 2e classe	Ensign
PETTY OFFICERS	
Maître principal	
Premier maître	Chief Petty Officer
Maître	
Second maître (2 years' service)	Petty Officer
Second maître	
SEAMEN	
Quartier Maître de 1re classe	Leading Seaman
Quartier Maître de 2e classe	
Matelot breveté	Seaman

Above.
Cap badge of the 1ᵉʳ Bataillon de Fusiliers-Marins Commando.
The 'Bllon' abbreviation is something that was added by the artist and does not correspond to any French or British designation. This rough sketch drawn by professional illustrator Maurice Chauvet at the end of 1943 was submitted to Contre-Amiral Thierry d'Argenlieu[1] in April 1944. The admiral replaced the star on the scroll with a second anchor. The cap badges were issued to Kieffer's men during a ceremony on 10 May 1944. 400 badges were made and numbered 1 to 400; with No 1 going t Lieutenant de Vaisseau Kieffer.

Left.
The **1re Compagnie de Fusiliers-Marins Commando** in 1942: seaman's ca with 'FNFL' tally, 'Commando' shoulder title (white letters on black), FNFL sign on left sleeve, red stripes on the blouse front for a quartier-maître de 1re classe. In a memo dated 7 December 1942, Capitaine de Vaisseau P. Kieffer requested the quartermaster to supply 100 sailor's caps and 100 red tufts for these, 100 'FNFL' tallies and 100 chinstraps.
(ECPAD France)

Belo
The cap badge of radio-operator Quartier-Maître radio Jean Couturi (died July 2006.) He was wounded on 6 June 1944 at Ouistreham an evacuated to a British hospital. The badge is of the second issue an numbered 215, given to him upon his return to the unit. The first badg 155, was lost during his transfer to hospita
(Private collection. Photos Pierre Courna

1. *Commander of Free French naval forces in Great Britain.*

Authorized in 1942 for the Royal Marine and Army Commandos, the beret adopted the distinctive green of the Light Infantry. After having successfully passed out of the commando school training course at Achnacarry (Scotland) the volunteers of the 1er Bataillon de Fusiliers-Marins Commando were authorized to wear the beret starting on 14 March 1943 (March 1944 for the K-Gun section).
This was Quartier-Maître Jean Couturier's beret and badge. The beret was worn sloped to the right with the badge placed vertically over the left eye.
(Private collection, photo Pierre Cournac)

THE GREEN BERET

Below.
1943. The 1er Bataillon de Fusiliers-Marins Commando after the issue of the green beret in March 1943. The woven FNFL badge is worn on the new head dress. It is replaced on the sleeves by the Combined Operations badge. At this time, the titles were those of No 10 Commando.
In the foreground, on the left, a Second Maître (rank on shoulder strap slip-ons), and at right, a Quartier-Maître de 2e classe (red stripes between the 2nd and 3rd buttons of his Battledress blouse).

Canvas K-Gun magazine pouches.

Above. **6 June 1944. Men of the K-Gun section of the 1ᵉʳ Bataill[on] de Fusiliers-Marins Commando. The Mk II helmet is worn here and not th[e] green beret. The K-Gunner was armed with a Colt 1911A1 pistol, an[d] the two ammunition carriers with the Rifle No 4 Mk** [...]

Opposit[e]
The K-Gun was an Aviation light machine-gun made by Vicke[rs] Armstrong Ltd. .303 (7.7 mm) calibre. It weighed 8.9 kg, i[ts] length was 1.016 m. The gun had an effective range of 1,50[0] metres and a practical range of 500 metres. It was gas operate[d] with its gas cylinder located below the barrel. Its rate of fire was 95[0] rounds per minute. It was fed by a drum magazine containing 96 rounds. Th[is] replaced the .303 Vickers MG in light units such as the Heavy Troops Roy[al] Marines and Army Commando[s]

(Reconstruction, from Militaria Magazine 113, Laurent Jégo article)

French commando Bren gunner during the Walcheren operation, November 1944. The Denison Smocks were issued during the battalion's stay in Belgium in October.

A Fusilier-Marin Commando's kit
(example, from the Royal Marines Museum archives*)

● **On the man**
— Mk II helmet
+ camouflage netting
— Battledress
— Field Dressing
— Handkerchief
— Raiding boots
— Anklets, ID disks
— Shirt
— Vest
— Underwear
— Socks
— Paybook
— Belt
— Straps
— Two pouches
— Water bottle
— Entrenching tool
— Climbing rope
— Pocket knife

● **Armament**
— No 4 Mk I* rifle
— Mk II bayonet

— Fairbairn-Sykes fighting knife
— Ten five-round rifle clips
— 10 clips bandoleer
— Two Bren magazines
— Two No 36. grenades

● **In the rucksack**
— Shirt
— Vest
— Underwear
— Socks
— Sweater (if not already worn)
— Leather Jerkin
— Denim trousers
— Ankle boots or plimsolls (depending on orders)
— Gas cape

— Respirator
— Beret with cap badge
— Mess tin
— Spoon, Fork
— Mug
— Housewife
— Toiletry kit
— Laces
— Toilet paper
— Four 24-hour rations packs
— One Emergency ration
— Tommy Cooker
— Solid fuel
— Water purifying tablets
— One tin self-heating soup
— Shovel or pick (one to three men)

* With thanks to Mrs Anna Lebbel, assistant curator

The K-Gun and its magazine.

...ergen rucksack marked with the name and battle honours of Quartier-Maître Jean
...uturier.
...rivate collection, photo Pierre Cournac).

FRENCH
COMMANDO INSIGNIA

1. Nationality shoulder title worn upon the creation of the unit along with fig. 2.

3. Title worn when unit became part of No 10 (Inter-Allied) Commando (printed type here) in 1942.

4. Title adopted upon transfer to No 4 Commando in March 1944.

5. Badge of the 'Forces Françaises Libres' designed in London in July 194 and issued in September. Given the amount of 'lost' badges, it was later issued to officers and NCOs only. Each badge is numbered according to th date of issue to the bearer. With the creation in 1941 of a second model, the first badge was reserved for personnel of the Forces Navales Française Libres. (FNFL)

6. Cloth FNFL badge that replaced fig. 5 for Navy personnel. It was first worn on the right breast of the French navy seamen's jumpers, then on th right sleeve of the Battledress blouse. With the issue of the green beret, this insignia became the cap badge for all of the battalion's personnel. It was replaced by the metal cap badge in May 1944. See page 56.

7. Combined Operations sign created at the beginning of 1942 and representing the three services: the anchor of the Royal Navy, the eagle o the RAF and a Thompson sub machine-gun for the Army. The eagle and Tommy gun point to the right on the left sleeve (left sleeve seen here).

8. Second pattern Combined Operations sign created in December 1944 and replacing fig. 7.

Left.
This sketch by M. Chauvet, that could be an early version of our own 'Allie in Battledress', shows a selection of soldiers and badges seen at the end o 1943 in Great Britain.
The physical appearance of the man in the middle is symbolic of the various ethnic origins of the Free French volunteers. If we are to believe th stylised badge pinned to his chest, this captain is a member of the FNFL.
At the top, a Polish soldier has attached the national eagle badge (Onzel Bialy) to the front of his Field Service Cap.
To the left can be seen the accurate portrayal of the right sleeve badges of a Belgian sergeant major. At the bottom are a few examples of shoulde titles worn by the Allies with, on the right, a set of shoulder straps. In the foreground, a French sergeants stripe on a dark blue loop. The shoulder strap with a longitudinal piping is that of a Polish officer cadet.
(Maurice Chauvet Archives)

Right.
Stamp issued in 1973 in memory of Colonel Pierre Bourgoin and Lieutenant de vaisseau Philippe Kieffer, both Compagnons de la Libération.

Left.
Quartier-Maître Maurice Chauvet (died 21 May 2010), seen here in England at the end of 1944.
(Author's collection)

Insignia on Battledress for the
Fusilier-Marins-Commandos (left)
and Chasseurs parachutistes (right)

THE 2ᵉ AND 3ᵉ REGIMENTS D

In September 1940, General de Gaulle followed the example of the British army and ordered the creation of a parachutist unit. 15 September saw the official creation of the '1re Compagnie d'Infanterie de l'Air (CIA) placed under the command of Capitaine Georges Bergé [1]. The unit

Three 2ᵉ RCP parachutists and two Resistance volunteers. On the le
Henri Corta, like many other junior officers, has retained his French air fo
cap despite regulations making it compulsory to wear the black be
(Royal Armoured Corps pattern). Rank stripes here are simply slipped ov
the shoulder straps of the Denison smoc

(Musée de la Résistance Bretonne de Saint-Mar

The 'Croix de l'ordre de la Libération' medal

● 2ᵉ RCP

Following the decree of 25 October 1944, the Regiment was officially awarded this decoration during a ceremony at the Arc de Triomphe in Paris on 11 November 1944. A parade then took place on the Champs-Elysées. Fifteen officers were bestowed the title of Compagnon de la Libération for the 1944-45 campaign:

— Lieutenant Michel Legrand
— Lieutenant F. Martin
— Commandant Pierre Bourgoin (DSO)
— Sous-Lieutenant Roger de la Grandière †
— Sous-Lieutenant Fauquet †
— Lieutenant Harent †
— Sergent-chef Ithuria †
— Lieutenant Lesecq
— Lieutenant Marienne †
— Commandant Puech-Samson (DSO)
— Lieutenant de Camaret
— Capitaine Betbeze
— Sous-Lieutenant Taylor † (MC)
— Lieutenant Varnier
— Lieutenant Louis Mairet

● 3ᵉ RCP (officers)

— Commandant Pierre Château-Jobert ('Conan')
— Aspirant Pierre Rosset-Cournand †
— Capitaine Paris de Bollardière
— Commandant Jean-Salomon Simon †
— Lieutenant Edgard Tupet-Thome (MC)

† *KIA or executed by the enemy.*
DSO: Distinguished Service Order. MC: Military Cross

comprised of thirty or so volunteers that gained their jump wings after u dergoing a training course at RAF Ringway, near Manchester (Lancashi in December 1940.

In 1941 the first sabotage and intelligence gathering missions were c ried out in occupied France and in July, General de Gaulle decided to se the 1re CIA to North Africa to fight alongside the British. Capitaine Ber met Major David Stirling at this time, the latter having just created the Sp cial Air Service (SAS), a unit comprising of small groups whose role w to carry out sabotage missions behind enemy lines. The 1re CIA was th attached to Stirling's unit.

From **June to August 1942**, many successful raids were carried o either by parachuting or by infiltrating by vehicle or boat. In December, t 1re CIA formed a second company for operations in Tunisia.

In March 1943, the 1re CIA returned to Great Britain followed by t survivors of the 2ᵉ CIA. The arrival of volunteers in May led to the creati of the 4ᵉ Bataillon d'Infanterie de l'Air (4ᵉ BIA) placed under the comma of Commandant Pierre Bourgoin. At the same time, the 3ᵉ Bataillon (BIA) was formed under Capitaine Pierre Château-Jobert (wartime ali 'Conan'). In November, the British command decided to create a Spec Air Service brigade that would operate in Europe in the spring of 194 The brigade fielded two British regiments, two French, and one Belgi squadron.

In March 1944, the 3ᵉ BIA became the 3ᵉ Régiment de chasseurs pa chutistes (RCP) and the 4ᵉ BIA the 2ᵉ RCP. These were known in the S/ Brigade as the 3rd and 4th SAS as of December 1943. Following a st in a secret camp for the preparation of missions and the continuation training, the 2ᵉ RCP sticks were the first of the Allied airborne forces to dropped during the night of 5 to 6 June as part of Operation 'Overlor Their mission was one of lines of communications sabotage, harassin

---

1. *The first French paratroopers had actually been created within the Air force 17 April 1937 and comprised of 3 officers (including one medical officer), 3 NCOs a 50 privates.*

HASSEURS PARACHUTISTES

German convoys and advising the Resistance groups.

Early fighting took place in Brittany near Saint-Marcel (Morbihan), fol-
ved by operations in central France, south of the Loire. Parachuted in
ly, the 3e RCP operated in the Poitou-Charentes, Rhône-Alpes and
urgogne then, in September, the Doubs. At the end of September, both
giments were rested for reorganisation and the induction of new person-
l. In December, during the German offensive in the Ardennes, the SAS
ught again the US sector, carrying out reconnaissance patrols and raids

(Continued on page 66)

1943 at Camberley, Surrey. Old Dean camp was the transit camp for all
of the FFL. Men of the 4ᵉ Bataillon d'Infanterie de l'Air are seen here with
Lieutenant de Mauduit wearing a French air force cap. The other men
wear the black beret of the Royal Armoured Corps with the pentagonal
grey-blue badge with an embroidered or metallic parachute. When this
photograph was taken the FAFL (Free French AF) jump wings had not yet
been issued. They are replaced here by the generic FAFL badge worn on
the right breast. The presence of the Polish jump wings indicates that the
bearers have successfully completed jump school under Polish supervision,
before the 8 graduation jumps at RAF Ringway.

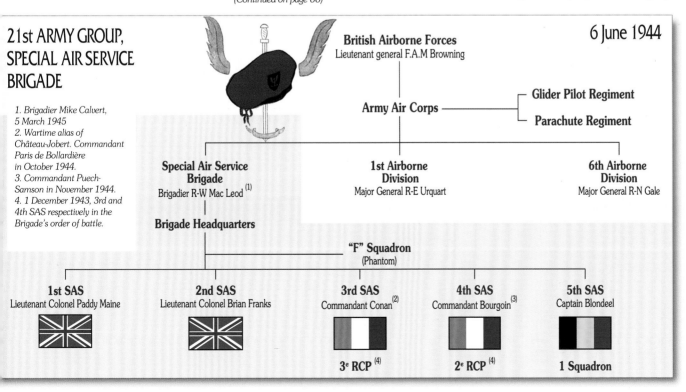

21st ARMY GROUP, SPECIAL AIR SERVICE BRIGADE

6 June 1944

1. Brigadier Mike Calvert, 5 March 1945
2. Wartime alias of Château-Jobert. Commandant Paris de Bollardière in October 1944.
3. Commandant Puech-Samson in November 1944.
4. 1 December 1943, 3rd and 4th SAS respectively in the Brigade's order of battle.

British Airborne Forces
Lieutenant general F.A.M Browning

Army Air Corps
— **Glider Pilot Regiment**
— **Parachute Regiment**

Special Air Service Brigade
Brigadier R-W Mac Leod [1]

Brigade Headquarters

1st Airborne Division
Major General R-E Urquart

6th Airborne Division
Major General R-N Gale

"F" Squadron
(Phantom)

1st SAS
Lieutenant Colonel Paddy Maine

2nd SAS
Lieutenant Colonel Brian Franks

3rd SAS
Commandant Conan [2]

3ᵉ RCP [4]

4th SAS
Commandant Bourgoin [3]

2ᵉ RCP [4]

5th SAS
Captain Blondeel

1 Squadron

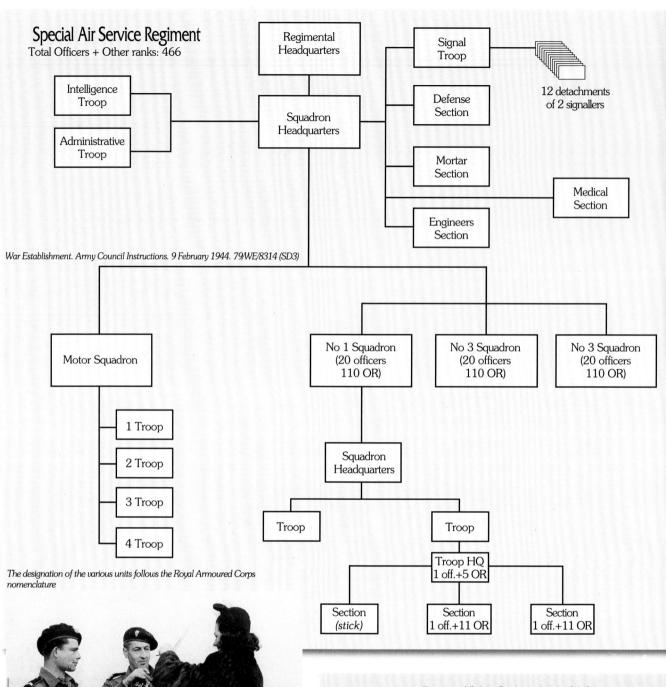

Special Air Service Regiment
Total Officers + Other ranks: 466

- Regimental Headquarters
- Intelligence Troop
- Administrative Troop
- Squadron Headquarters
- Signal Troop
- Defense Section
- Mortar Section
- Medical Section
- Engineers Section

12 detachments of 2 signallers

War Establishment. Army Council Instructions. 9 February 1944. 79/WE/8314 (SD3)

- Motor Squadron
  - 1 Troop
  - 2 Troop
  - 3 Troop
  - 4 Troop

The designation of the various units follows the Royal Armoured Corps nomenclature

- No 1 Squadron (20 officers 110 OR)
- No 3 Squadron (20 officers 110 OR)
- No 3 Squadron (20 officers 110 OR)
- Squadron Headquarters
  - Troop
  - Troop
    - Troop HQ 1 off.+5 OR
    - Section (stick)
    - Section 1 off.+11 OR
    - Section 1 off.+11 OR

Right.
October 1944, Camberley, Surrey. Capitaine Larralde receives the HQ company pennant from actress Betty Stockfield. The soldier with the rifle is Sergeant Remy.

France 1944, 3rd and 4th SAS operations

Code name	Unit	Region	Period
Dingson	4th SAS	Brittany	5 June – 25 August
Samwest	4th SAS	Brittany	5 June – 25 August [1]
Cooney	4th SAS	Brittany	5 June – 25 August [1]
Lost	4th SAS	Brittany	5 June – 25 August [1]
Dickens	3rd SAS	Vendée	17 July-7 October
Moses	3rd SAS	Vienne-Indre-Vendée	2 August-4 October
Derry	3rd SAS	Brittany	5 August-18 August
Samson	3rd SAS	Haute-Vienne-Vendée	10 August-28 Sept.
Marshall	3rd SAS	Corrèze-Indre	11 August-12 October
Snelgrove	3rd SAS	Creuse-Indre	13 August-12 October
Harrod	3rd SAS	Saône & Loire	13 August-4 Sept.
Barker	3rd SAS	Saône & Loire	13 August-4 Sept.
Jockworth	3rd SAS	Loire-Rhône	15 August-8 Sept.
Newton	3rd SAS	Loire-Rhône [2]	18 August
Spencer	4th SAS	Loire valley	26 August-15 Sept.
Abel	3rd SAS	Doubs	17 August-25 Sept.

1. Reinforcements for Dingson. 2. Reinforcement operation.

AS OPERATIONS IN FRANCE AND HOLLAND

Weekly strength report, 7 April 1944

	Officers	Aspirants	Adj. chefs	Adjudants	Sgt. chefs	Sergents	Cap. chef	Caporaux	1re cl.	2e cl.	Total
aff command and IA mmand section [1]	4					2	3	3	6		18
3e Bataillon d'Infanterie de l'Air											
Q		3		1		1		1	3		9
mmand section [2]	12	5	1	5	4	10	5	13	84	20	159
st Squadron	6	3		1	2	10	8	9	63	3	105
nd Squadron	3	4			2	11	5	15	59	8	107
rd Squadron	5	1			1	12	3	12	76		113
	29	13	1	7	9	44	21	50	285	34	511
4e Bataillon d'Infanterie de l'Air											
Q											
mmand section [2]	12	4	3	7	5	24	3	19	88		165
st Squadron	6	4		2	3	12	10	21	48		106
nd Squadron	8	1			4	14	16	12	49		104
rd Squadron	5	3		1	5	16	6	12	58		106
tal	31	12	3	10	17	66	35	64	243		481
rand total	64	25	4	17	26	112	59	117	534	34	992

or the French 'Demi-brigade de chasseurs parachutistes' associating both battalions. Lieutenant-Colonel N. Durand, Capitaine H. de Mauduit, Lieutenant H. Déplante, Lieutenant Clevenot + 14 NCOs. British Liaison: Major Cary-Elwes, Squadron Leader Smith, Captain Fay. 2. Including Medical Officer.

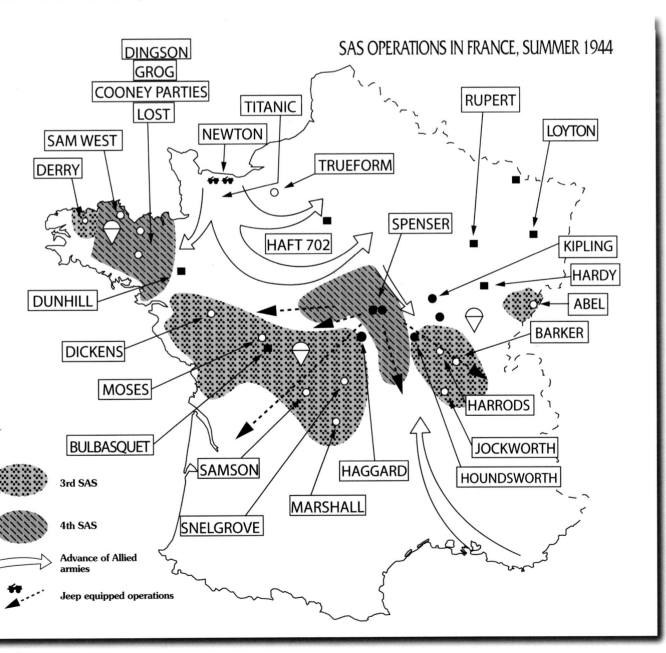

SAS OPERATIONS IN FRANCE, SUMMER 1944

3rd SAS

4th SAS

Advance of Allied armies

Jeep equipped operations

3rd SAS (3e régiment de chasseurs parachutistes) 22 March 1944

Battalion Commander	Capitaine 'Cona'n (Château-Jobert
Second in Command	Capitaine Simor
Adjutant	Lieutenant Poissor
British Liaison	Lieutenant Landsmanr

Headquarters Squadron

Squadron Commander	Lieutenant Lazor
Administrative Officer	Lieutenant Combaud de Roquebrune
Signal Officer	Sous-lieutenant Dreyfus
Quartermaster	Sous-lieutenant Florentin
Intelligence officer	Lieutenant Vallières
Engineer officer	Aspirant A Ka
Medical officer	Lieutenant Poro

No 1 Squadron

Squadron Commander	Capitaine Paumier
Troop 1, Troop Leader	Lieutenant Rouar
Troop 2, Troop Leader	Lieutenant Colcombe

No 2 Squadron

Squadron Commander	Capitaine Sicauc
Troop 3, Troop Leader	Lieutenant Tupet-Thome
Troop 4, Troop Leader	Sous-lieutenant Queler

No 3 Squadron

Squadron commander	Capitaine Fournier
Troop 5, Troop Leader	Lieutenant Leblond
Troop 6, Troop Leader	Sous-lieutenant Chate.

Note: several modifications were made to the unit establishment before operations began. Consequently, ranks indicated are post-6 June 1944. Many promotions were made during the campaign.
1. Killed in action.

Capitaine Pierre Château-Jobert (1912-2005) Wartime alias: 'Conan'

An artillery Sous-Lieutenant in 1935, he joined the air observers school at Dinard in 1940. Wounded on 13 June, he escaped from the hospital in Vannes and on the 21st, reached England by boat to join the Free French forces where he enlisted under the name of 'Conan.' Following the Erythrean, Syrian and Libyan campaigns (he was wounded in the latter in February 1942), he returned to Great Britain where he took over the 3e Bataillon d'Infanterie de l'Air, which became the 3e RCP (3rd SAS). His unit was parachuted into France in July 1944 and operated mainly between the Vendee and Doubs regions.

He was promoted to the rank of Chef de Bataillon in December 1944 and handed over command of the 3e RCP to Lieutenant-Colonel Paris de Bollandière.

Above.
Capitaine Château-Jobert looks at a pennant commemorating a period spent in Scotland. The Infanterie de l'air wings are placed over a piece of tartan. The officer wears the maroon beret in the British fashion, sloped to the right. The Airborne Forces badge on the Denison smock is unusual.

● **2e RCP decorations** [2]
— Croix de la Légion d'honneur following 6 air force level citations
— Fourragère in the colours of the Légion d'honneur with Croix de Guer 1939-45 olive and Légion d'honneur.
— Croix de compagnon de la Libération
— Croix de Guerre 1939-45 with one silver and one bronze palm
— Belgian Croix de Guerre 1940-45 with palm
— Dutch Bronzen Loeeuw

● **3e RCP decorations**
— Croix de Guerre 1939-45 with two palms following two air force lev citations
— Fourragère in the colours of the Croix de Guerre.
— Dutch Bronzen Loeeuw
Note. 1996 saw the creation of a fourragère in the ribbon colours of the Cro de Guerre for units that had received this decoration.

The flag of the Demi-Brigade de parachutistes SAS

to create confusion behind enemy lines. The two regiments returned to Great Britain in February 1945 and trained again with new volunteers from the Resistance that had arrived to make up the losses. At the beginning of April, the Allied command decided to undertake an airborne operation in Holland in order to assist the advance of the 1st Canadian Army by capturing bridges (operation 'Amherst').

The two French SAS regiments were committed during the night of 7-8 April and fighting continued during almost two weeks. After 8 May 1945, the 2e and 3e RCP first went back to Great Britain before being gathered in Nantes for demobilization of the oldest soldiers. The remainder went to Tarbes in September where the 2e and 3e RCP were amalgamated to form the new 2e RCP.

On 1 August, the parachutists left the French air force and came und army command.

Strength

The term 'Régiment' used to designate the 2e and 3e RCP fro April 1944 onwards, did not correspond to any tactical organisation use

(Continued on page 7

2. Along with the Normandie-Niemen fighter squadron, the 2e RCP is the most decorated French army unit of the Second World War.

	Theoretical strength, 3e and 4e BIA						Strength on 7 April 1944				
	One Rgt.	Total for 2 Rgts	1st ref.	Total 2 Ref.	½ Brig.	Total	½ Brig.	3e BIA	4e BIA	CH R	Total
Officers	47	94	11	22	5	**121**	4	29	31	2	
Officer cadets								13	12	3	**89 + 5**
WOs	6	12			2	**14**		8	13		**21**
NCOs	44	88	3	6	4	**98**	2	53	83	3	**138 + 3**
Corporals	38	76	11	22	2	**100**	6	71	99	2	**178**
Other ranks	369	738	71	142	17	**897**	6	319	243	12	**578 + 12**
TOTAL	**504**	**1008**	**96**	**192**	**30**	1230	**18**	**493**	**481**	**22**	992 + 22

Note: From 7 April, men were transferred due to physical or mental reasons, thus decreasing these numbers. The lack of officers led to senior NCOs being promoted to subaltern rank; these men were selected for their command aptitudes.

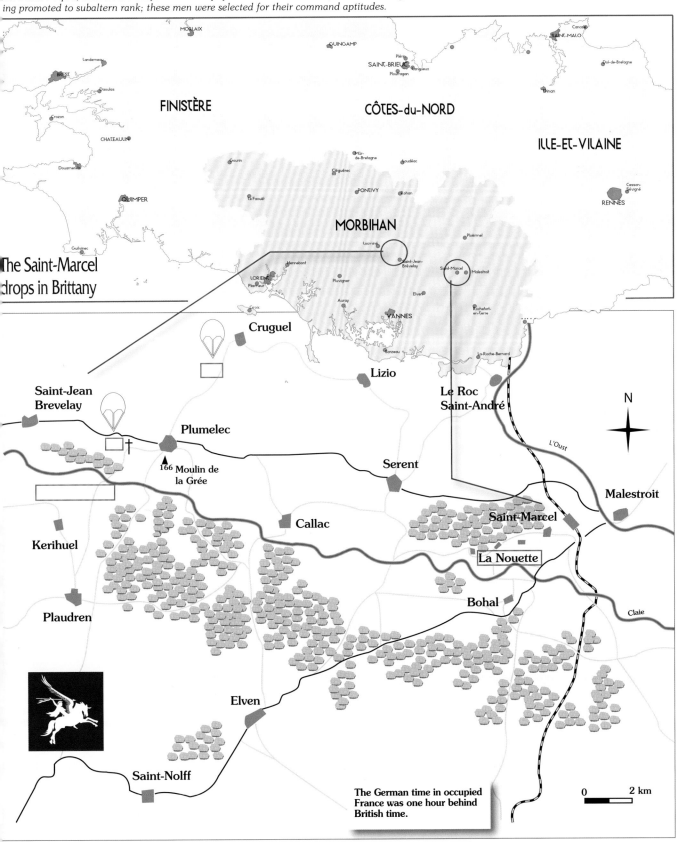

Saint Marcel

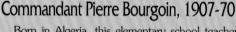

Commandant Pierre Bourgoin, 1907-70

Born in Algeria, this elementary school teacher
and reserve officer joined the Free French as early as
June 1940. In June 1941 he took part in the Syrian campaign with Bataillon de marche n° 2. Twice
wounded in North Africa, he joined the British secret services after having gone through jump school.
He took part in the fighting in Tunisia in February 1943. Seriously wounded there, he lost his
right arm. Having returned to Great Britain in November 1943, he took over command of the 4e Bataillon d'infanterie
de l'air, which became the 2e Régiment de Chasseurs Parachutistes
(4th SAS in the British order of battle). Dropped into Brittany during
the night of 9 to 10 June 1944, he led his unit in the liberation of the
province and several French departments.

He handed over command in November 1944 to Commandant Puech-Samson and was promoted to inspector general of airborne troops
with the permanent rank of Lieutenant-Colonel.

Below.
**Seen here with his staff officers, Lieutenant Déplante
and Capitaine Puech-Samson, Commandant Bourgoin (left) wears
here the rank insignia of a lieutenant-colonel in order to be on equal
footing with his British counterparts, according to a memo
from Brigadier McLeod dated 30 May 1944.**
(Musée de la Résistance Bretonne de Saint-Marcel, 56)

FRENCH SAS LOSSES

● France, 1944
2e RCP. 77 killed, of which 23 were executed by the Germans or
French Milice, 197 wounded.
3e RCP. 37 killed, 72 wounded, 4 missing.

● Holland, 1945 'Operation Amherst [1]'
2e RCP. 17 killed, 15 wounded, 56 missing.
3e RCP. 16 killed, 25 wounded, 40 missing
(Total: 33 killed, 40 wounded, 96 missing [2])

---
1. Out of 650 enlisted men.
2. Of which 67 later rejoined their unit.

4th SAS (2e Régiment de Chasseurs Parachutistes), 22 March 1944

Battalion Commander	Commandant Bourgoin [1]
Second in Command	Capitaine Lambert
Adjutant	Lieutenant Tissier
British Liaison	Sous-lieutenant Skinner
Headquarters Squadron	
Squadron Commander	Lieutenant Bodolec
Administrative Officer	Adjudant chef Marie-Victor
Signal Officer	Adjudant chef Hoffmann
Quartermaster	Sous-lieutenant Galiaudan
Intelligence officer	Sous-lieutenant de Camaret
Medical officer	Lieutenant Sassoon [2]
No 1 Squadron	
Squadron Commander	Capitaine Laralde
Troop, Troop Leader	Lieutenant Tisné
Troop, Troop Leader	Lieutenant Mairet
No 2 Squadron	
Squadron Commander	Capitaine Leblond
Troop, Troop Leader	Lieutenant Viaud
Troop, Troop Leader	Lieutenant Martin
No 3 Squadron	
Squadron commander	Capitaine Puech-Samson
Troop, Troop Leader	Lieutenant Botella
Troop, Troop Leader	Lieutenant Marienne [2]

---
1. Promoted Lieutenant-Colonel on 15 November 1944
2. Killed in action.

Operation AMHERST April 1945

North Sea

THE NETHERLANDS

Leeuwarden
Groningen
Winschoten
Emden
Papenburg
Wilhemshaven

3ᵉ SAS 4ᵉ SAS
Assen
Appelsga
Eɪ·p
Beilen Westerbock
Diever
Spier
Hoogeven
Coevorden

ZUIDERSEE
Zwolle
Ommen
Nordhorn
Almelo
Rheine
Holen
GERMANY
Münster

Utrecht

Rhine
Arnhem
Waal
Nimègue
Emmerich
Rhine

0   50 Km

▸ 1st Canadian Army offensive
--- 2ᵉ and 3ᵉ RCP sectors

N

2e RCP Citation for the Croix de la Libération

"The Croix de la Libération is awarded to the 2ᵉ Régiment de Chasseurs Parachutistes of the Armée de l'Air.

General de Gaulle, president of the provisional government of the French Republic, cites in the name of the nation with the following citation of the Croix de la Libération:

The 2ᵉ RCP, commanded by Lieutenant-Colonel Bourgoin, an elite unit that had the honour of being the first French unit to fight again on the soil of the motherland. Parachuted over Brittany in the month of June, it rallied more than ten thousand resistance fighters. With this help and at the price of heavy losses, it went on to successfully attack enemy units, and destroyed several telephone networks, ammunition dumps and lines of communications that were of the utmost importance to the enemy. It also played an important role in the Allied offensive from the Normandy bridgehead and laid the foundations to the liberation of Brittany."

Paris, 25 October 1944.
Signed: Charles de Gaulle

The Special Air Service wings

Designed in Egypt in 1941 by British Lieutenant Jack Lewes, it was based on the 'Ba' bird that is often seen in ancient Egyptian imagery. It is seen as being one of the five elements of personality.

1. 'Ba' bird amulet.
(Musée du Louvre, Paris, département des antiquités égyptiennes)

2. Special Air Service wings (made official in March 1946). They could only be worn after having taken part in actual combat.

The SAS wings, worn by French SAS Lieutenant Hoffmann in 1945.
(P. Lengrand collection)

FRENCH SAS INSIGNIA

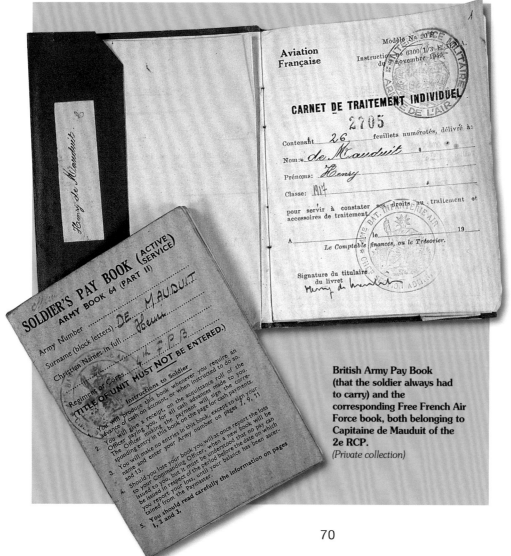

British Army Pay Book (that the soldier always had to carry) and the corresponding Free French Air Force book, both belonging to Capitaine de Mauduit of the 2e RCP.
(Private collection)

Right
Caporal Emile Bouetard of the 2e RC with the Polish jump wings received afte passing out of Ringway. He wears on th sleeve a variant of the first pattern Frenc parachute badge. Born on 4 September 1915 at Pleudihe (Côtes du Nord [1]), he was part of a nin man group led by Lieutenant Pierr Marienne. Parachuted on 5 June 194 at 23:30, he was spotted by a Germa observation post. Seriously wounded afte a short fight, he was finished off at 01.3 by Osttruppen soldiers. Caporal Bouetar was the first soldier to lose his life durin Operation 'Overlord'. A commemorativ plaque bearing his name can be found i the hamlet of Hallinger near Plumelec (Morbihan)

1. Today known as 'Côtes d'Armor' in Brittan

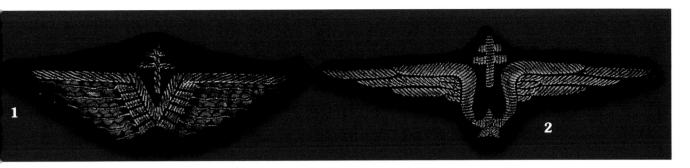

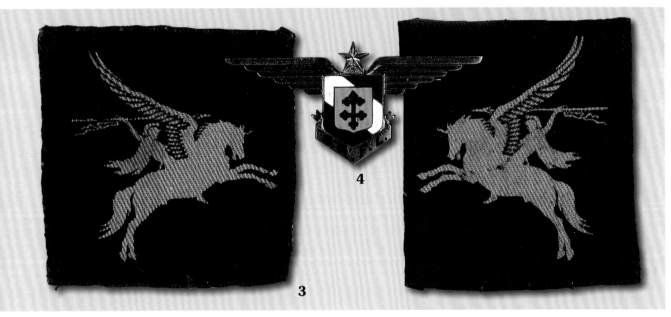

Upholding the traditions of the French air force infantry, the RCP retained some of the air force badges.

1. Cap badge of the Forces Aériennes Françaises Libres (FAFL).

2. Aircrew FAFL wings, worn over the right pocket of the dark blue tunic. Officers and NCOs.
(Collection Patrick Lengrand.)

3. British Airborne Forces formation signs. Embroidered or printed, they were only worn on the Battledress blouse from January 1944, after the 2e and 3e RCP became part of the British SAS Brigade.

4. Breast badge of the Forces Aériennes Françaises Libres (FAFL) made by the British manufacturer Gaunt. The badge was designed in October 1940 in Great Britain by soldat Drabier, a former art school student. The number on the reverse in theory relates to the chronological order of the bearer's enlistment (here No 13237). No 1 was presented to General de Gaulle. After August 1943, the FAFL initials were replaced by FAFC (Forces Aériennes Françaises Combattantes).
(From G. Le Marec, 'Les Français Libres and leurs emblèmes').

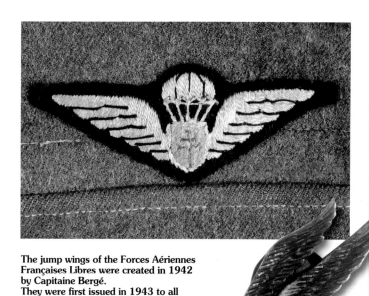

The jump wings of the Forces Aériennes
Françaises Libres were created in 1942
by Capitaine Bergé.
They were first issued in 1943 to all
personnel who had completed jump shool at
Ringway. A French made version was issued
at the end of 1944 and in 1945. The model
seen here is of British manufacture.

Polish jump wings.
It was decided, at the end of
1942, to send some officers
and NCOs for two weeks to the
Polish jump school based in Largo,
Scotland. This commando type training ended with a jump made from a
25 metre high steel tower. The French detachment, joined by its Polish
instructors and brothers in arms, then went to Ringway where, after the
eight regulation jumps, they were allowed to wear the Polish and French
jump wings.
276 French military personnel underwent the Largo training course, 56 in
1942 and 220 in 1943.

by the French infantry. However, it derived from the 1er Régiment
Chasseurs Parachutistes formed in Algeria in 1943. It is a traditional te:
used in the British army corresponding here to a Parachute Regiment b
talion, although considerably lightened in the cas of Special Air Serv
units: 466 OF/OR instead of 616 (regular unit). The strength cited cou
therefore in theory form two French units on the basis of the War Depa
ment decision of 9 February 1944. It is however stipulated in the do
ment accompanying the 7 April establishment that numbers were la
lowered for physical or morale reasons. During the course of the ca
paign, volunteers from the Resistance joined the two RCP, thus allowi

(Continued on page 7

Beret badges

1. The first headdress badge worn in 1943 on the Royal
Armoured Corps black beret. The design was based on the collar
tabs worn by Polish parachutist officers on their service dress
tunic: grey-blue background with a metallic or bullion embroidered
parachute. It was also worn on the left sleeve before the adoption of
the Airborne Forces sign in January 1944.

2. British Parachute Regiment badge worn on the black beret at the
end of 1943. The British imperial crown and lion have been removed
to show the French identity of the bearer.

3. Special Air Service badge, designed in Egypt by Corporal Tait in
1941. Worn on the sand coloured beret until 1945 and beyond. The
sword is Excalibur, the weapon of King Arthur who fought for freedom
(period badge from the beret worn by Sergent Clément. Author's
collection)

Left, top to bottom.
1. French air force type nationality shoulder title.
2. General issue shoulder title.
3. Special Air Service title. In some circumstances, in 1945 notably, the
'France' titles were not worn, or replaced by these Special Air Service title:
4. Non-regulation 3rd SAS title.

The black beret of the Royal Armoured Corps was adopted in 1943. It replaced the French air force dark blue sidecap or the British army Field Service Cap. The beret was worn sloped over the left ear contrary to British fashion. The badge was placed by the two ventilation eyelets. *(Patrick Lengrand collection)*

THE BERETS

The SAS were authorized to wear the Army Air Corps maroon beret in November 1944, although some had been issued beforehand depending on availability. The beret was worn sloped to the left, unlike the British who wore it sloped to the right with the badge positioned vertically over the left eye [1]. Wearing it sloped to the left meant that badge had to be sewn over the ventilation eyelets.

The beret seen here was worn by Sergent Paul Clément (aka. 'Freval') who joined the FAFL in June 1943. Assigned to the 3e RCP, he dropped into France on 15 August 1944 (Operation 'Jockworth') and fought with the Regiment until December 1944.

1. Except for some Irish regiments.

(Author's collection)

Right and below.
The beret netting cover. This rare item was made from the camouflage netting used on British vehicles. This was not made on an individual basis, but in small quantities at unit level, and fits perfectly the shape of the beret. It has a khaki cloth braid around the inside edge. The beret netting is worn here during an exercise in May 1944 by Sergent Marty of the 2e RCP (left). Taken prisoner on 12 July 1944, he was shot the same day.
(Collection P. Lengrand)

FRENCH SAS RANK INSIGNIA

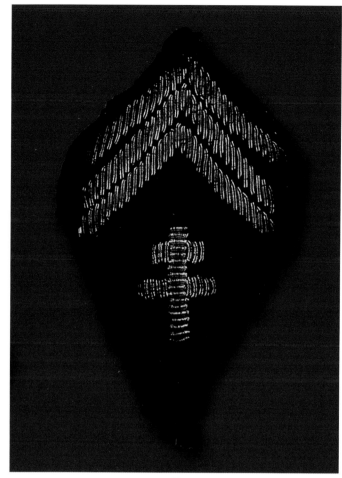

Abov
**Regulation rank insignia for a French Air Force Captain, with air fore
button and flying eagl**
(Photo Militaria Magazir

Opposite, left.
**FAFL service chevrons worn on the dark blue tunic, left sleeve. One
chevron indicates a year of service, the two lower chevrons six months
each.** *(Photo Militaria Magazine)*

FRENCH SAS RANK INSIGNIA
worn on the Battledress blouse and Denison smock

	FRENCH ARMY	BRITISH ARMY
1	Colonel	Colonel
2	Lieutenant-colonel	Lieutenant-Colonel
3	Commandant	Commandant Major
4	Capitaine	Captain
5	Lieutenant	1st Lieutenant
6	Sous-lieutenant	2nd Lieutenant
7	Aspirant	Cadet
8	Adjudant-chef	Company Sergeant Major *(CSM)*
9	Adjudant	Company Quarter Master Sergeant *(CQMS)*
10	Sergent-chef	Staff-Sergeant
11	Sergent	
	after two years of service	
12	Sergent	Sergeant
13	Caporal-chef	Lance Sergeant
14	Caporal	Corporal
15	Soldat de 1re classe	Lance-Corporal

12, 14 and 15 show examples of rank badges placed on a black
cloth loop that is most commonly seen worn on officer's Denison
smocks.

Left.
**Sergent rank insignia placed on a black cloth shoulder strap affixed to tha
of the Battledress blouse. The flying albatros is that of the RAF often used
by tailors due to the lack of French sparrow hawks. The British parachute
qualification badge shows that the owner successfully passed out of the
Ringway parachute school. The Airborne Forces 'Pegasus' sign, issued
at the end of 1943 – beginning 1944, indicates that at this time only the
FAFL parachute badge should be worn.**
(Photo Militaria Magazine)

to partially make up the personnel deficit. Some of the latter went throug
parachute school in Great Britain.

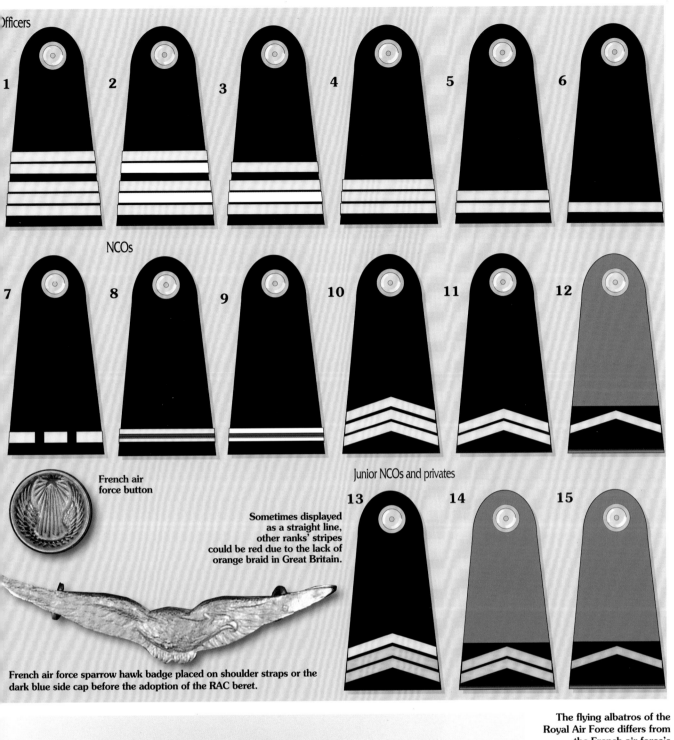

Officers

1 2 3 4 5 6

NCOs

7 8 9 10 11 12

French air
force button

Junior NCOs and privates

13 14 15

Sometimes displayed
as a straight line,
other ranks' stripes
could be red due to the lack of
orange braid in Great Britain.

French air force sparrow hawk badge placed on shoulder straps or the
dark blue side cap before the adoption of the RAC beret.

The flying albatros of the
Royal Air Force differs from
the French air force's
sparrow-hawk.

75

UNIFORMS AND EQUIPMENT

Free French Air Forces command in Great Britain, Instruction No 2942/CAL/FAFL

"London, 15 April 1944

The orders mentioned in this instruction will be brought to the attention of all personnel and strictly adhered to from Thursday 20/4/44 onwards.

Memorandum concerning uniforms of the FAFL in Great Britain.
[Paragraphs I and II concern aircrew and ground crew on air bases.]

III. Special measures for air infantry.

Uniform of Infanterie de l'Air personnel is thus defined:

Walking out uniform (reminder of memo 2035 dated 21/3/1942)

Below.
1943. The walking out uniform[1] for officers, as defined by instruction 2035 of 21 March 1942, is worn here by Lieutenant de Mauduit. The Armée de l'air cap bears the generic FAFL badge. On the right-hand side of the tunic re the FAFL aircrew wings to which the parachutists were assimilated. On the left, in the regulation position, is the Polish parachutist badge awarded after the training courses at Largo and Ringway. Lieutenant de Mauduit's badge, numbered 2192, corresponds to course No 51 that took place from 27 December 1942 to 7 January 1943. The left sleeve bears a sewn on variant of the of the first type of the French air force parachute badge.

1. All officer's uniforms, whatever their purpose, were privately purchased.

CLOTHING ISSUE, FRENCH PARATROOPERS
(officer cadets, NCOs and ORs)

Item	Quantity	Item	Quantity
- Battledress (trousers[1])	2	- PT vest	1
- Battledress (blouse)	2	- Rain coat	1
- Hair brush	1	- Comb	1
- Toothbrush	1	- Mug	1
- Shaving brush	1	- Razor	1
- Trouser braces (pair)	1	- French towel	1
- Shoes (pairs)	2	- British towel	1
- Greatcoat	1	- Kit bag	1
- Tie	1	- Housewife	1
- Jack knife	1	- Vest	2
- Muffler	1	- Denim trousers	1
- Socks (pairs)	3	- Denim jacket	1
- Longjohns	2	- Field dressing	1
- Underwear	2	- British respirator	1
- PT shorts	1	- Gas mask bag cover	1
- Sweater	1	- Gas mask eyepieces	1
- Wool shirts	3	- Anti-gas ointment	1
- Spoon	1	- Gas detection armlet	1
- 'France' shoulder titles	6	- Anti-dimming	1
- Toilet roll	1	- Anti-gas cape	1
- Anti-gas wallet	1	- Wind jacket (Smock, Denison)	1
- Plimsolls (pair)	1	- Wind jacket (Oversmock)	1
- Anklets (pair)	1	- Parachute wings	6
- Mess tin	1	- Breast insignia	2
- Woolen gloves (pair)	1	- Leather edged black beret	2
- Fork	1	- Paratroop helmet	1
- Leather laces	1	- British webbing equipment[2]	1

1. The 'Trousers, Parachutists' were issued in the last week of May 1944.
2. The 1937 Pattern 'Large pack' was replaced by a Bergen rucksack.

French paratrooper officer's badges on a 1937/40 Pattern Battledress blouse. This belonged to Capitaine de Mauduit of the 2e RCP.
(J.B. Favier collection)

Capitaine Henri, Comte de Mauduit (1897-1977) was mobilized in 1917 and served with a dragoon regiment where he was awarded the Croix de Guerre. A colonial administrator, he joined the Free French in Great Britain in 1941. After undergoing parachutist training, he was sent to the 2e RCP and dropped into Brittany during the night of 7 to 8 June. After the fighting in Brittany and south of the Loire, he took part in the liberation of Paris on 25 August 1944.

For officers
uniform comprises of:
Cap, greatcoat (in winter) or navy blue raincoat, trousers and tunic, rk blue fine cloth (air force type), dark blue or black socks, black oes, white shirt (RAF type blue shirt is authorized), black tie and tan loured leather gloves.

Officer cadets, NCOs and privates
uniform comprises of:
Walking out: leather-bound British Armoured Corps type beret, own greatcoat, brown Battledress, shirt, and tie, black socks, French ound forces in Great Britain type gaiters.
For officer cadets and warrant officers, the wearing of the air force e fine cloth cap, raincoat and white shirt is authorized for walking t, but this is not the case for other NCOs and men.

Field uniform
The field uniform for all ranks comprises of: The black beret (RAC e), brown Battledress [1], shirt and tie, ankle boots and canvas an-ts, web belt, special 'Paratroop' helmet.

Rank insignia
Rank insignia are worn in the following way: the Battledress blouse oulder straps are totally covered by a black cloth upon which are ced the rank insignia."
Signed: General de Brigade Aérienne Valin, commander of the FL

(From the Archives du Service Historique de la Défense, départe-nt de l'Armée de l'Air)

Right.
Sergent of the 2e Régiment de Chasseurs Parachutistes (4th SAS).
Under the British Airborne Forces sign is the French air force parachute badge as stipulated for parachute instructors in 1936 and then issued to all qualified parachutists the following year. Normally, in 1943, it was replaced by the Forces Aériennes Françaises Libres wings worn n the right breast. The metal Croix de Lorraine is worn in regulation fashion on the right (memo No 484 du 25/2/1944).
(Reconstruction, Christophe Deschodt collection)

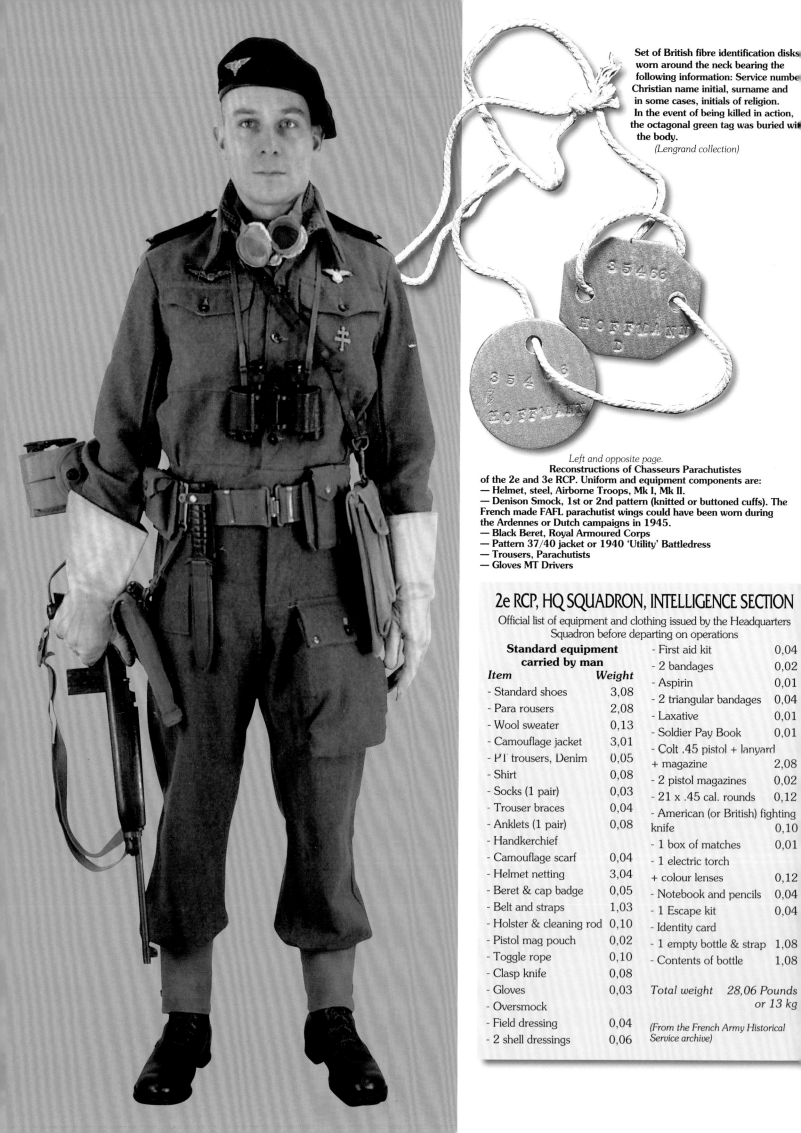

35466

HOFFMANN
D

354 6
HOFFMANN

Left and opposite page.
Reconstructions of Chasseurs Parachutistes of the 2e and 3e RCP. Uniform and equipment components are:
— Helmet, steel, Airborne Troops, Mk I, Mk II.
— Denison Smock, 1st or 2nd pattern (knitted or buttoned cuffs). The French made FAFL parachutist wings could have been worn during the Ardennes or Dutch campaigns in 1945.
— Black Beret, Royal Armoured Corps
— Pattern 37/40 jacket or 1940 'Utility' Battledress
— Trousers, Parachutists
— Gloves MT Drivers

2e RCP, HQ SQUADRON, INTELLIGENCE SECTION

Official list of equipment and clothing issued by the Headquarters Squadron before departing on operations

Standard equipment carried by man		
Item		*Weight*
- Standard shoes		3,08
- Para rousers		2,08
- Wool sweater		0,13
- Camouflage jacket		3,01
- PT trousers, Denim		0,05
- Shirt		0,08
- Socks (1 pair)		0,03
- Trouser braces		0,04
- Anklets (1 pair)		0,08
- Handkerchief		
- Camouflage scarf		0,04
- Helmet netting		3,04
- Beret & cap badge		0,05
- Belt and straps		1,03
- Holster & cleaning rod		0,10
- Pistol mag pouch		0,02
- Toggle rope		0,10
- Clasp knife		0,08
- Gloves		0,03
- Oversmock		
- Field dressing		0,04
- 2 shell dressings		0,06
- First aid kit		0,04
- 2 bandages		0,02
- Aspirin		0,01
- 2 triangular bandages		0,04
- Laxative		0,01
- Soldier Pay Book		0,01
- Colt .45 pistol + lanyard + magazine		2,08
- 2 pistol magazines		0,02
- 21 x .45 cal. rounds		0,12
- American (or British) fighting knife		0,10
- 1 box of matches		0,01
- 1 electric torch + colour lenses		0,12
- Notebook and pencils		0,04
- 1 Escape kit		0,04
- Identity card		
- 1 empty bottle & strap		1,08
- Contents of bottle		1,08

Total weight   28,06 Pounds or 13 kg

(From the French Army Historical Service archive)

EQUIPMENT CARRIED IN THE BERGEN RUCKSACK

Designation	Weight
Rucksack	5,10

Clothing

3 pairs of socks	0,09
PT shorts	0,05
2 handkerchiefs	
1 shirt	0,08
1 Battledress blouse	2,06
1 pair overshoes	0,03
1 pair PT shoes	1,03
Small pack and straps	1,05
Shoe laces	0,01
Towel	0,10
mess tins (both)	1,03
Spoon	0,01
Housewife	0,02
Toilet paper	0,01
Toilet roll	0,06
Soap (3 cakes)	0,06
String Vest	0,12
Sleeping bag	3
Anti-gas cape	1,08

Ammunition and various items

2 No 36 grenades	3? 04
20 x .45 cal. rounds	0,12
Kit bag	
Spare bulb	

- Batteries	0,08
- Lifebelt	
- Solid fuel	0,04

Rations

- 2 x 24hr-ration cartons	4,04
- 1 packet coffee	1
- 1 packet sugar	1
- 3 matchboxes	0,03
- 1 x 1b margerine	1
- 2 oz. salt	0,02
- 1 oz. pepper	0,01
- 1 lb tobacco	
- 1.5 lb. chocolate	0,08

*Total weight
34,01 pounds
or 15,15 kg*

In order to respect the load capacities of transport aircraft, the weight of equipment carried was of paramount importance. The carrying of unlisted items could only be done once something on the list, of equal weight, was removed.

(From the French Army Historical Service archive)

Also note the issue of the folding stock US Army M1A1 carbine, together with the American M3 fighting knife. The British parachutists' kit bag hung from the parachute harness during the last phase of the descent.

...t mentioned in the official list, along ...th a few other items, were these crepe ...led patrol boots issued before departing for Brittany. ...ey were not taken by all men.
...usée de l'Armée, Paris)

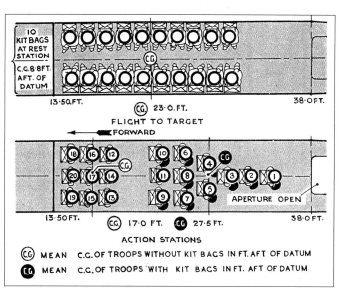

Emplacement of parachutists transported by the Stirling bomber. The men jumped via a hatch in the plane's floor.

The Motorcycle Lightweight, Welbike.
Total all-up weight: 38 kg. Engine: 2 stroke, single cylinder temps, 97 cm³. Fuel tank: 7 litres. Range: 145 km. Particular characteristics: removable handlebars to enable it to be parachuted.
This motorbike was issued to airborne troops, commandos and X units depending on the type of operations.

TRANSPORT AIRCRAFT

Armstrong Whitworth Albemarle Mk V

Power plant: 2 X Bristol Hercules radial engine 1,186 hp
Maximum speed: 265 mph, 426 km/h
Cruise speed: 170 mph, 274 km/h
Ceiling: 18,000 ft (5,486 m)
Range: 1,300 mi (2,092 km)
Wingspan: 77 ft (23.47 m)
Length: 59 ft 11 in (18.26 m)
Height: 15 ft 7 in (4.75 m)
Wing area: 804 ft² (74.6 m²)

Loaded weight: 36,500 lb (16,556 kg)
Armament: 4 x Vickers .303 MG in dorsal turret
Capacity: 10 parachutists
Squadrons No 295, 296, 297 and 570 of 38 Group were equipped with the Albemarle. Several parachute operations used the twin-engine Albemarles of 38 Group as well Dakotas Mk III of 46 Group, Squadron 233.

Short Stirling Mk IV

Power plant: 4 X Bristol Hercules radial engine 1,186 hp
Maximum speed: 255 mph
Cruise speed: 200 mph
Ceiling: 16,500 ft (5,030 m)
Range: 2,330 mi (3,750 km)
Wingspan: 99 ft 1 in (30.2 m)
Length: 87 ft 3 in (26.6 m)
Height: 22 ft 9 in (6.9 m)
Wing area: 1,460 ft²

(135.6 m²)
Loaded weight: 59,400 lb (26,944 kg)
Armament: 2 x MG in tail turre
Capacity: 22 parachutists
Two Stirlings dropped the pathfinders of the 2e RCP on 5 June at 23.30 (36 OF/OR), during operations 'Dingson' and 'Samwest.'

Handley Page Halifax Mk V

Power plant: 4 X Bristol Hercules XVI radial engine 1,615 hp
Maximum speed: 282 mph (454 km/h)
Cruise speed: 346 kph
Ceiling: 24,000 ft (7,315 m)
Range: 1,860 mi (3,000 km)
Wingspan: 104 ft 2 in (31.75 m)
Length: 71 ft 7 in (21.82 m)
Height: 20 ft 9 in (6.32 m)
Wing area: 1,190 ft² (110.6 m²)

Loaded weight: 54,400 lb (24,675 kg
Armament: 5 x .303 Vickers MG (4 in tail and 1 front)
Capacity: 10 parachutists + containers. The plane illustrated (s/n LL 326) was flown by Squadron Leader Norman and towed one of the Waco gliders transporting the jeeps of Lieutenant Bodolec of the 2e RCP.

DOUGLAS DAKOTA MK III

Power plant: 2 x Pratt and Whitney R-1830-92, 895 hp each
Maximum speed: 230 mph (370kph)
Cruise speed: 298 kph
Ceiling: 23,200 ft (7,100 m)
Range: 3,420 km
Wingspan: 95 ft 2 in (29.0 m)

Length: 64 ft 8 in (19.7 m)
Height: 16 ft 11 in (5.16 m)
Wing area: 987 sq ft (91.7 m2)
Loaded weight: 14.061 kg
Capacity: 25 parachutists. No 48, 233, 271, 512 and 575 Squadrons of RAF 46 Group were equipped with this aircraft.

Standard contents of a stick's additional armament container*

Equipment	Weight
— 1 Bren Gun (with sling)	22
— 2 spare barrels	12
— 2 rifles (with sling)	20
— 1 sniper's telescope	3
— Felt pads	10
— 30 boxes (48 x .303 rounds each)	80
— 10 fifty round. 303 bandoleers	
— 24 empty Bren magazines	27
— 10 No 36 grenades	15
— 10 x No 77 grenades	10
Total weight	*200 pounds or 90 kg*

Demolition supplies
— Plastic explosives
— 24 boxes of 5 detonators
— 48 x safety fuse
— 200 x Cordtex
— 8 pull switches (1 oz each)
— 8 pressure switches (1 oz each)
— 10 fog signals
— 50 friction fuses
— 10 strikers
— 12 tyre-burster
— 5 black time pencils
— 25 red time pencils
— 5 white time pencils

— 5 yellow time pencils
— black PTI (10 mn) and six red PTI (30 mn).
— 60 Primers
— 10 Lewes bombs (unfused)
— 10 boxes of matches
— 5 rolls adhesive tape
— 1 roll trip wire
— 10 lighters
— 10 'balloons' (waterproofing system of the explosive charge fuse).
— 1 adjustable spanner
Total weight   91 Pounds or 40 kg

(*) Sometimes dropped with the stick

IMENTS DE CHASSEURS-PARACHUTISTES

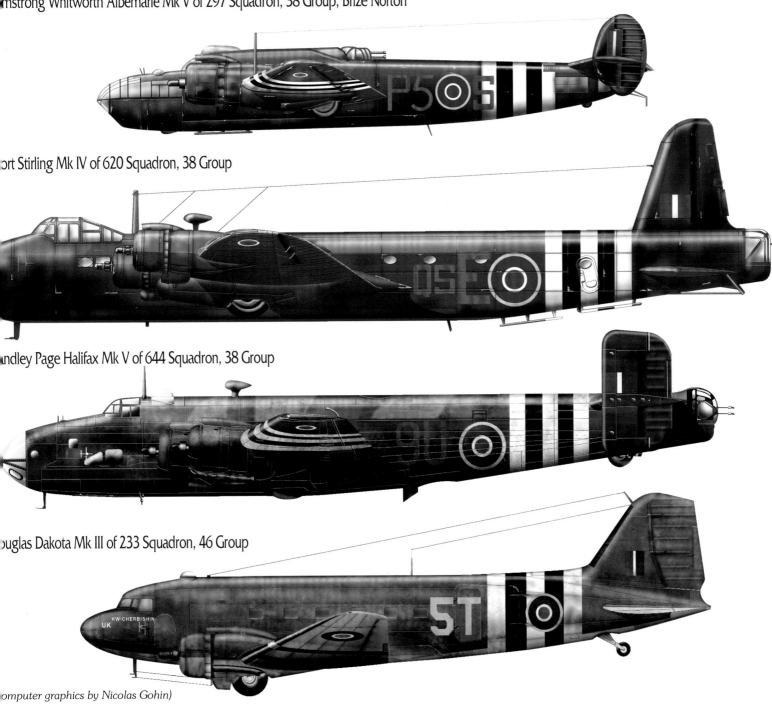

mstrong Whitworth Albemarle Mk V of 297 Squadron, 38 Group, Brize Norton

ort Stirling Mk IV of 620 Squadron, 38 Group

ndley Page Halifax Mk V of 644 Squadron, 38 Group

ouglas Dakota Mk III of 233 Squadron, 46 Group

omputer graphics by Nicolas Gohin)

SAS VEHICLES AND ARMAMENT

TRANSPORT

Vehicles	Numbers
Bicycles, folding, Airborne	25
Motorcycles, solo, lghtweight, Welbike	23
Cars, 4-Seater, 4x2[1]	1
5-cwt, 4x4 (Jeep)	20
Trucks, 15-cwt, 4x2 GS [1]	7
Trucks, 15-cwt, 4x2 Water[1]	4
Lorries, 3-Ton, 4x2 GS [1]	10

ARMAMENT [2]

- Automatic Pistol (Colt) M1911A1
- Automatic Pistol,

- 9 mm Browning, Inglis Canada
- Sten Mk V, Airborne
- Carbine, USM1, M1 A1[2],
- Patchett Machine Carbine, cal. 9 mm. 14 were issued, outside the regulation scales, to the 4th SAS in June 1944
- USM3 Fighting knife
- Fairbairn-Sykes Fighting knife
- Pistol, Signal, RAF
- Bren, .303, Light Machine Gun
- 2-in Mortar, Airborne
- Projector, Infantry, Anti-Tank (PIAT)
- No 36, 69, 70, 82 grenades

- Mines, Hawkins 75, GS Mk II, GS Mk V

RADIO EQUIPMENT

- MCR1 and PCR radios,
- WSet 38, WSet 68, SCR-536 (USA)
- B Mk II

SAS PERSONNEL PARACHUTE

- British Type X Mk II

1. Brought in during the course of the campaign by sea and land.
2. Issued depending on the mission as substitute for the standard issue Rifle No 4 Mark I".

JEEPS PARACHUTED IN BRITTANY

A 2e RCP Jeep in a Paris
street on 26 August 1944. On the evening
of the previous day, men of the 2ᵉ RCP entered
into Paris with General Leclerc's 2ᵉ DB and assisted
in mopping up snipers. On the morning of the 26th
a small group of men led by Capitaine de Mauduit laid a
wreath on the tomb of the Unknown Soldier
at the Arc de Triomphe before the official ceremonies.

(Musée de la Résistance Bretonne de Saint-Marcel, Morbihan)

SAS JEEP MARKINGS EXAMPLES

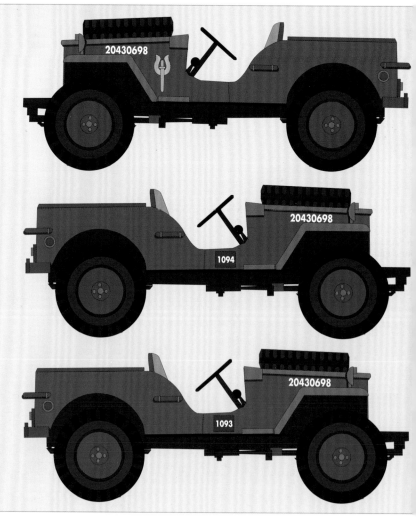

Letters and numbers are 8.9 cm in height and 5.1 cm in width.
Unit Serial Numbers:
1093: 3rd SAS (3ᵉ RCP)
1094: 4th SAS (2ᵉ RCP)

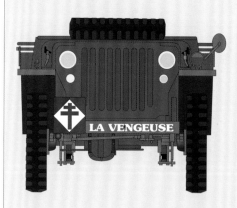

LA VENGEUSE

A few nicknames…
*Denise, Mickey, Maryvonne,
La Madelon, Mort aux doryphores,
Un peu juste!, Le Forban, Colette,
Varsovie, Le Moustique,
La Vengeuse, Le Flibustier,
Le Corsaire, Le Pirate,
Oradour-sur-Glane.*

Jeeps as they would have appeared in the Battle of the Bulge at the end of 1944 and during the Dutch campaign in April 1945. Armour plating has been added to the radiator and the windscreen. Semi-circular unshatterable glass shields protect the heads of the driver and gunner.
(Musée de la Résistance Bretonne de Saint-Marcel, Morbihan)

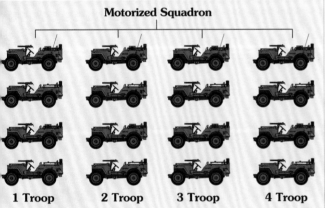

Motorized Squadron

1 Troop 2 Troop 3 Troop 4 Troop

Right.
The Jeep positioned on its air-drop cradle. They were dropped with four parachutes in order to ensure a soft landing.

Below.
An SAS Jeep is loaded into the bomb bay of a specially equipped Halifax four-engine bomber.
(IWM)

Operations carried out by jeep			
Date	**Mission**	**Unit**	**Number of Jeeps**
June 1944	Dingson	4th SAS	4 Jeeps parachuted in
August	Dingson	4th SAS	6 Jeeps parachuted in
5 August	Dingson	4th SAS	10 Jeeps landed by Waco glider
August	Newton, Dickens, Moses, Harrods	3rd SAS	19 Jeeps from 'Newton' infiltrated through enemy lines
August	Spencer	4th SASS	54 Jeeps infiltrated
December	Franklin	4th SAS	40 Jeeps infiltrated
April 1945	Amherst	3rd SAS	

(Patrick Nonzerville Collection)

Car 5-cwt, 4 x 4 'Jeep'

Main modifications for air-dropped SAS jeeps:

Addition of two extra fuel tanks: one over the right rear wheel, another under the passenger seat. Removal of lifting handles, jerrycan support, spare wheel, rear bumpers, tool racks, windscreen and running boards. Ends of bumpers cut off square at spar ends. Parts of the radiator grill were not systematically removed. Some vehicles with the classic 'Airborne' jeep alterations and brought in by glider did not undergo the SAS set of modifications.

See also 'D-Day Paratroopers, the British, Canadan and French', page 129.

JEEPS FLOWN IN BY WACO GLIDERS

At the beginning of August 1944, HQ Special Service Brigade agreed to despatch jeep reinforcements to the 2e RCP, that had been fighting in Brittany as part of Operation 'Dingson' since 6 June. Drawn from the Motorized Squadron, this eleven vehicle detachment was placed under the command of Lt. Bodolec with three men of the 2e RCP. The glider flight was planned for the night of 5-6 August with the landing zone situated in the Sainte Hélène and Locoal-Mendon sector, 12 km east of Lorient. The jeeps were loaded on American Waco 'Hadrian' gliders (chosen for their superior handling compared to the British Horsa) and flown by Glider Pilot Regiment crews. The glider tows were four-engine Halifax bombers from 298 and 644 Squadrons, 38 Group Royal Air Force. At 20.05 hrs 5 August, the first planes took off from Tarrant Rushton (Dorset) led by Squadron Leader Norman. One Halifax had to abort due to a technical fault but the other ten gliders reached the LZ that had been lit up by red lights positioned by the SAS and resistance fighters. All the landings went

ahead smoothly, apart from the glider flown by Staff Sergeant Ross-Da and Sergeant Newton that crashed into trees. The two injured pilots we taken to hospital in Auray that was under resistance control. Along wi the other Glider Pilot Regiment pilots, they later reached the spearhea of the 4th US Armoured Division when it entered Brittany.

On 6 August, Lt. Bodolec's jeeps began operations in the Auray ar Vannes sector with the latter being liberated on 7 August by Commanda Bourgoin on board the jeep 'Vengeuse' that had been flown in on the 5th.

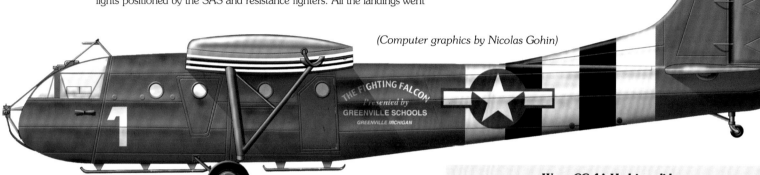

(Computer graphics by Nicolas Gohin)

Waco CG-4A Hadrian glider

Wingspan: 26,82 m.
Length: 20,42 m.
Empty weight: 3 900 kg.
Loaded weight: 7 020 kg.

Maximum tow speed: 150 mph (241 km/h).
Landing speed: 74 mph (120 km/h).

Below.
The liberation of Vannes (Brittany) on 7 August by elements of the 2e RCP. The Jeeps were flown in on Waco gliders during the night of 5-6 August. The vehicles did not feature all of the specific SAS modifications: radiator grills not cut out for example. The aerial identification stars had been cut out from the wings and fuselage of the gliders.
(Musée de la Résistance Bretonne de Saint-Marcel, Morbihan)

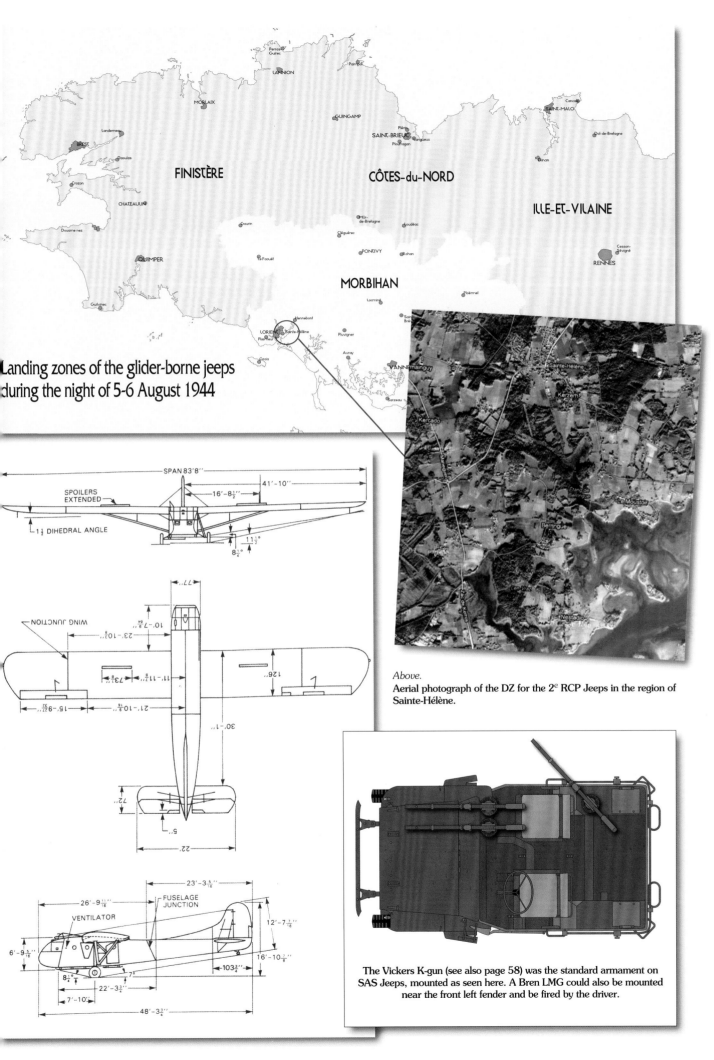

Landing zones of the glider-borne jeeps during the night of 5-6 August 1944

Above.
Aerial photograph of the DZ for the 2e RCP Jeeps in the region of Sainte-Hélène.

The Vickers K-gun (see also page 58) was the standard armament on SAS Jeeps, mounted as seen here. A Bren LMG could also be mounted near the front left fender and be fired by the driver.

OTHER FRENCH UNITS

Having become head of the provisional government of the French Republic, General de Gaulle set about, from September 1944 onwards, to ensure that French soldiers were present wherever battle was being waged. Apart from the large units formed in 1943 in North Africa and already committed alongside the Allies, it was now imperative to mobilize the Forces Françaises de l'Intérieur (FFI) who had fought with the Resistance and integrate them into the regular armed forces.

As it was not possible to call upon the Unites States to equip these combatants, negotiations carried out with Great Britain since March 1944 led to several agreements that would allow the formation of numerous units, of which some would be placed under British command. The documents shown below shed some light on the decisions taken by the French provisional government that led to the creation of such units.

General pattern insignia of the Forces Françaises de l'Intérieur attributed with a certificate of authenticity bearing the same number. These were made by Arthus Bertrand beginning in September 1944 (the badge here bears No 66608).

The decrees

Decree dated 19 September 1944 concerning the organisation of French interior forces

"**Art. 1** – The FFI are an integral part of the army and therefore subject to military regulations and discipline. They come under the sole authority of the ministry for war.

Formations still on operations form groups that are placed, for these operations, under the orders of a commander designated by the president of the government and head of the armed forces. The other formations are placed, in each military district, under the regional commander.

Art. 2 – FFI units will be forthwith formed into reserve infantry battalions, or, whenever possible, into equivalent units of the other arms and services. The number, composition and operational sectors of these units will be determined by the minister for war.

Current FFI officers and NCOs will be used to form these units.

Art. 3 – As training and the supply of armaments progress, units thus formed will be: either attached, keeping their composition, to existing formations, or merged into new formations.

Art. 4, 5…"

Signed C. de Gaulle
For the provisional government of the French Republic:
the minister of war A. Diethelm

Decree dated 20 September concerning the status of the FFI

"**Art. 1** – The FFI are defined as all personnel having voluntarily fought against the enemy, during the course of the fighting for the liberation, acts of war in combatant units and services defined in the first decree of 9 June 1944.

Art. 2 – FFI personnel are endorsed by the military authorities designated by the minister of war under the stipulations of the ministerial decree. Service certificates will bear the date of enlistment into the FFI as well as the actions in which the recruit has taken part.

Art. 3 – There will be no recruitment into the FFI in any part of France that has already been liberated."

Memo from Gen. de Gaulle to André Diethelm, minister for war.

"Paris, 16 October 1944.

Please find included here the summary of the meeting that has taken place between General Juin and General Marshall.

Whatever may follow these new negotiations, the time has come for France to direct by itself its military effort. The total control maintained up to now by the Americans on French rearmament, that has been restrictive, is no longer acceptable. At this stage of the war, our country must, by its own means, proceed with the formation of a certain number of divisions and army corps structured in a way of our own choosing, that is to say removed from the organisational tables of US type formations.

In other words, French units must be formed with what we already have and with what we can manufacture ourselves, with Allied supplies being seen as a supplement to complete our own equipment. Such is the case of heavy materiel that our own industry will not be able to supply before a long time. This means that what we ask of our allies (from the Americans but also the British who have just opened talks with us), should no longer concern the number of divisions, but materiel (tanks, guns, vehicles, engineer vehicles and equipment and so on), with how all of this is to be used being decided by ourselves.

Concerning this problem, I will wait and see what the next National Defence Committee has to say in order to immediately proceed with the formation of a certain number of new formations according to available manpower resources and the projected industrial output to equip them. Naturally, we will not alter the structure of our eight first divisions, or the equipment programs for our security and pioneer battalions that are in the process of being formed. Also, it would be better to maintain the armaments along the lines of US and British units for divisions due to leave for the Pacific."

Note. Apart from the fire support provided by Allied artillery units, a French group of two batteries using captured German 155 GPF guns was also in action 1st battery in December 1944, 2nd battery in March 1945.

Locally made title for units in action around 'Festung Dunkerque'. This was supplied, among others to the 'Groupe Français Marine Dunkerque'.
(Jean-Yves Nasse collection. Militaria Magazine 120)

FRENCH INFANTRY REGIMENTS
IN ACTION AT THE DUNKIRK POCKET

Four infantry regiments were formed and took the numbers of the first d second 1939 military districts: 1st district (Nord and Pas-de-Calais dé- rtemens), 2nd region (Somme, Oise, Aisne and Ardennes).

Strength

With an approximate strength of 6,000 men, these units mostly com- ised of volunteers from the resistance movements who had enlisted for e duration of the siege of Dunkirk and the pursuit of the war against ermany. Also present were men from the class of 1943 (decree of '1/1945). Losses by 9 May totalled 117 killed, 240 wounded and 26 ssing.

Armament

British or captured German weapons.

Equipment

British clothing, either new or previously worn and repaired. Canadian iforms purchased by the provisional French government were also is- ed as replacement clothing. Other clothing came from French stocks covered from German army depots in the Toul region (very poor quality iforms and boots according to a period report). 1944 Pattern French ittledress may have also been issued.

(Continued on page 90)

ove.

aining with the 2-inch mortar. The officers wear rank insignia the shoulder straps in the fashion of the liberation army that was formed North Africa in 1943. The wearing of breeches, as seen by the officer on e left, was forbidden with the Battledress blouse.

Right.

Mk II helmets and British Battledress, civilian boots, no anklets. As was often the case, clothing supplied by the Royal Army Ordnance Corps was incomplete and some items had be found from other sources.

Winter 1944-45 at the Dunkirk Pocket. French infantry are seen here with a captured MG 42. This must have been an exception, given the circumstances, as generally speaking, the Allied command demanded that captured weapons must be handed over, with most usually being destroyed.

INFANTRY UNITS

33ᵉ régiment d'infanterie (33ᵉ RI)
Type: independent unit
CO: colonel Gros
Origin: FFI Nord and Pas-de-Calais
Strength in May 1945: 79 officers, 1,601 other ranks.
Role: Ensuring security in Calais, Lille, Arras and Boulogne. Engaged in Dunkirk sector beginning on 4 April 1945.

51ᵉ régiment d'infanterie (51ᵉ RI)
Type: independent unit
CO: lieutenant-colonel Lehagre (1/2/45)
Origin: FFI Oise and No rd.
Strength in May 1945: 72 officers, 1,640 other ranks.
Role: Ier, IIe, IVe bataillons took part in the fighting around Dunkirk as of 1 February 1945. The IIIe battalion was placed in reserve (COM Z) of the 12th US Army Group.

67ᵉ régiment d'infanterie (67ᵉ RI)
Type: independent unit
CO: lieutenant-Colonel Bern
Origin: FTP from Oise and Somme, FFI from Somme and Aisne.
Strength in May 1945: 104 officers, 2,350 other ranks.
Role: in action at the Dunkirk Pocket beginning on 10 February 1945.

110ᵉ régiment d'infanterie (110ᵉ RI)
Home regiment of Dunkirk town.
CO: Chef d'escadron, then Lieutenant-Colonel Lehagre until February 1945.
Origin: Organisation Civile and Militaire (OCM), Organisation de la Résistance de l'Armée (ORA) of the Pas-de-Calais. FFI and FTP Nord.
Role: took part in Dunkirk operations beginning in October 1944. Retired from operations in February 1945 to form the 51ᵉ and 67ᵉ regiments.

Above.
Badges of the French infantry units in action at the Dunkirk Pocket:
1. 51ᵉ RI.
2. 67ᵉ RI.
3. 110ᵉ RI. The badge features Dunkirk's coat of arms (post 1945 manufacture).

patrol sets off along the flooded areas around 'Festung Dünkirchen'. They e equipped with French 1926 Pattern helmets (often from civil defence ocks), British or Canadian greatcoats and captured German Kar. 98K les and ammunition carriers. This photo illustrates well the dearth of uipment within newly formed French units.

Officers and NCOs of the 4ᵉ Bataillon de marche de Normandie photographed at Evreux in November 1944. From left to right, Jacques Bayet, Jacques Chasles, Capitaine Thirault and Gérald Balcan. They had previously served with the Mouvement de Résistance Libération-Nord. They wear 37/40 or 'Utility' 1940 Pattern Battledress. The rank insignia is placed on shoulder straps and cap as stipulated in the 1943 regulations. *(Courtesy of Editions Alan Sutton)*

Vehicles

Various previously used British and Canadian vehicles were issued after reconditioning in the workshops of the Royal Electrical and Mechanical Engineers.

Assignments

These units took part in siege of the 'Festung Dunkerque' under the command of the 1st Czech Independent Armoured Brigade Group (see chapter concerning this unit).

Badge of the 2e Bataillon de marche de Normandie (Orn 600 were made by Arthus Bertrand.
(Private collection)

The Bataillons de marche de Normandie

Eight units were formed as early as September 19⁴ and placed at the disposal of the 21st Army Group lin of communication.

Personnel was made up of resistance volunteers wł had signed up for the duration of hostilities against German Armament was of British origin that had either been previous dropped to the Maquis, or captured German weapons.

Clothing was entirely British.

They were organised along the lines of a security battalion and were n supplied with heavy weapons.

Their role was mainly one of guarding lines of communications, pip lines and POW camps. They were, however, given various other missio such as looking for German stragglers.

At the beginning of 1945, these battalions were disbanded and the men sent to the 1st French army fighting in the Vosges.

The Groupe France Marine Dunkerque

This Navy unit of Marines was made up with volunteers from the Bo logne-sur-Mer harbour firemen.

They were commanded by Capitaine de Corvette Acloque and ha a strength of 37 petty officers and seamen. A battalion was formed March 1945 and placed under the command of Enseigne de Vaisseau o 2e Classe Denielou. At this point there were 397 men in the followir units:

– Battalion staff (30 men) 4 officers, 3 petty officers, 23 other ranks.
– HQ company (99 men) 2 officers, 7 petty officers, 90 other ranks.
– 1st fusilier company (134 men) 4 officers, 13 petty officers and 11 other ranks.
– 2nd fusilier company (134 men) 4 officers, 13 petty officers and 11 other ranks.

Officers and petty officers were armed with the Pistol, Revolver No Mk I*, other ranks the No 4 Mark I Rifle, captured German Kar-98 rifl and the Sten Machine Carbine. Heavier weaponry consisted of the Bre Light Machine Gun and the 2-Inch Mortar.

The Fusilier-Marins were issued with a Jeep for liaison duties, five moto cycles, eight Bedford QL 3-Ton lorries, eleven 3/4-Ton GS Bedford Q trucks, six Universal Carriers and six bicycles.

They were not issued with signals or tentage. Dixie tins and tools wei issued, the uniforms were British, as were the blankets.

The Groupe Franc was placed under the command of the 110e RI, the the 51e RI from February 1945 onwards where it served on the Dunkir Pocket.

(Documents kindly supplied by Jean-Yves Nasse, see also Militaria Mag. 120)

On the left, Quartier-maître Fostier, Médaille Militaire, Croix de Guerre. O the right, Maître Duboc (June 1945).
(Jean-Yves Nasse collection)

THE BATAILLONS DE MARCHE DE NORMANDIE

Battalion	Département	Origin	CO	Strength	Formed	Disbanded
1er	Eure	OCM and FTP	Cdt. Leblanc	800	September 1944	March 1945[1]
2e	Orne		Cdt. Mazeline	500	November 1944	March 1945[1]
3e	Eure	OCM and FTP	Cdt. Fromager	?	November 1944	March 1945[1]
4e	Eure	Libé-Nord	Cdt. Stouls	685	September 1944	March 1945
5e	Seine Maritime	ORA/OCM/FTP and Libé-Nord	Cdt. Multrier	809	September 1944	March 1945
6e	Seine Maritime	FTP	Cdt. Caron	?	September 1944	February 1945
7e	Seine Maritime	?	Capitaine Filoque	616	September 1944	February 1945
8e	Calvados – Eure	?	Cdt. Chaulieu	50	October 1944	February 1945

1. Formed in March 1945 into the 129e Régiment d'Infanterie. The other battalions joined the French 1st army where they were sent as reinforcements to the badly mauled regiments from Africa, especially those of the 4e Division Marocaine de Montagne.

OCM: *Organisation Civile and Militaire.* **FTP:** *Francs Tireurs Partisans.* **ORA:** *Organisation de la Résistance de l'Armée.*

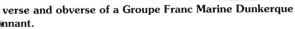

verse and obverse of a Groupe Franc Marine Dunkerque
nnant.

an-Yves Nasse Collection)

e Pioneer battalions

Decree DM No 379/Etat Major General Guerre dated 6 October 1944
to the creation of pioneer units to be used by the British 21st Army
oup. Groupements 3 and 4 were thus formed by 1re Région Militaire
and 4e Bataillons de Pionniers Nord-Africains, BPNA).

Unit strength was 28 officers, 79 NCOs and 1,070 men. A great major-
were of North African origin and had previously worked under German
pervision on the Atlantic Wall and V-rockets launching sites. Equipment,
nament and uniforms were supplied by the British (small arms only).
is was also the case for light, but no heavy machinery was forthcoming.
The role of these Groupements mainly consisted of repairing and main-
ning lines of communications as a source of extra help to the Pioneer

Corps near supply centres and dumps. These units were disbanded in
March 1945.

FFI transport groups

At the end of August 1944, five motor regiments were formed with
former FFI personnel and placed under the command of Chef d'Escadron
Dunat. Numbered 1 to 5, these supply units were tasked with transport-

**Evreux, 10 October 1944. The 4e Bataillon de marche de Normandie
parades in front of General de Gaulle. Armament comprises of the No 4
Mark 1 rifle for the other ranks and the Enfield Revolver No 2 Mark 1
(in a Pattern 1942 holster) for the unit commander.
All of the men wear Battledress but they have
not been issued with anklets.**
(Photo Editions Herissey, Evreux)

First vehicle in a convoy bound for Paris, this Canadian Dodge, 3 Ton, 4x2 General Service, is driven by a man wearing a civilian beret. His Battledress blouse bears a 'France' shoulder title.
(US National Archives)

A 4x4 Ford FT semi-trailer 6-Ton (Canada) tractor. The trailer is permanently attached to the tractor. It bears an automobile regiment insignia on the door. The officer wears a British 1940 Pattern.
(Period postcard, 1944-45)

INFANTRY RANK BADGES

Infantry rank badges in use within former FFI units organised into infantry battalions or regiments. Motorized supply units adopted the ranks and nomenclature of the French transportation service: silver stripes, 'Brigadier' and 'Brigadier-chef,' 'Maréchal des logis' and 'Maréchal des logis-chef' for corporals and sergeants.

On the cuffs:
1. Général de division
2. Général de brigade
On the shoulder straps:
3. Colonel
4. Lieutenant-Colonel
5. Commandant
6. Capitaine

7. Lieutenant
8. Sous-Lieutenant
9. Aspirant
10. Adjudant-chef
11. Adjudant left sleeve,
Between shoulder and elbow:
12. Sergent-chef
13. Sergent

14. Caporal-chef
15. Caporal
16. Soldat de 1re classe.
17. The wearing of rank insignia was defined by a ministerial instruction dated 22 May 1945. Previously, the type of insignia was determined

according to empirical criteria seen in the army of 1940 and in the army of liberation in 1943. It is this criteria that is shown here.

1. 'France' shoulder title (French made)
2. 2e Régiment automobile (made by Arthus Bertrand)
3. 5e Groupement d'Infanterie formed with Normandy volunteers. The badge has the Normandy leopard and the formation sign of the British Lines of Communication Troops.
4. Title of the Groupes Automobiles Français (FTG).
5. Embroidered badge worn on the arm or chest by the Paris 5e Regt Automobile. The winged cog wheel bears the Allied flags, including that of the USSR with the hammer and sickle. This unit was formed in November 1944 with staff from the Paris Métro underground, operating in Normandy and Belgium.

FRANCE

NORMANDIE

2

5e G.I.

3

4

5e REGIMENT AUTOMOBILE

5

Above.
Identification armband issued by the French home office (and created by the Vichy government for lines of communications guards) and worn by volunteers of the Rouen group tasked with guarding convoys in liberated areas. The shield bears a cogged wheel in its centre.
(Private collection)

supplies to large liberated towns. They used American, Canadian and British vehicles.

The 2e Regiment 'Normandie' was created in Bayeux on 28 August. The other regiments were called 'Brittany' (1er, Anjou (3e), Maine (4e) and Paris (5e).

Packet of cigarettes for the *Amis des Volontaires Français* (AVF), founded by the Free French HQ in London to raise funds for military personnel in hospital or rest centres. The AVF also commissioned various patriotic wares that were sold in canteens.

A.V.F.
AMIS DES VOLONTAIRES FRANÇAIS
A V F
Tabac Blond

NORWEGIANS IN BATTLEDRESS

Invaded by the German army in April 1940, Norway was forced to capitulate on 10 June despite being reinforced by a French, British and Polish contingent.

King Haakon VII and his son Prince Olav left for Great Britain on the 7th, accompanied by members of parliament in order to form a government in exile. An armed Norwegian force was formed using naval and air force personnel and placed under British command. The Norwegian

Above.
Norway, May 1945. Prince Olav, wearing battledress, greets Major-General RE Urquart. The man in the centre is one of the underground leaders. After the cessation of hostilities on 8 May 1945, an Allied contingent landed in Norway and was placed under the command of Major-General RE Urquart, with elements of the 1st British Airborne Division reformed after the disaster of Arnhem, various other British and American units, the Norwegian Brigade and the 99th Norwegian Infantry Battalion, a unit formed in the United States in 1942. Attached to the 1st US Army in 1944, the Battalion took part in the French campaign and the Battle of the Bulge in 1944-45.

The Norwegian Mountain Infantry Brigade 1944-45

— **Headquarters**
— **Signals, Medical sections, Supply**
— **School Training Group**
— **1st Mountain Infantry Battalion**
1st, 2nd, 3rd Companies (260 OF/OR each)
— **Artillery battery**
8 x 25-Pounder Howitzers (a second battery was formed at the end of 1944)
— **Parachute Company**
— **Reconnaissance Squadron**
(Armoured cars, Jeeps, Universal carriers)
Strength:
1, 400 officers NCOs and men in 1941.
3, 900 officers, NCOs and men in 1944.

1. Insignia worn on the MK II helmet, the General Service cap and battledress blouse.

2. Cap badge with King Haakon VII's cipher, worn by other ranks.

3. Nationality shoulder title worn on the left arm. The same applied to the Norwegian flag placed on the right sleeve.

3. Norwegian War Cross fourragère bearing the Norway shield with a rampant crowned lion brandishing an axe.

Regulation British Army arm of service strips:

4. Infantry. The numbers of strips identify the 1st, 2nd or 3rd Infantry Mountain Company.

5. Artillery. **6.** Reconnaissance.

7. Formation Badge of the Norwegian Mountain Infantry Brigade, worn on left sleeve. *(Military Heraldry Society collection)*

The Norwegian flag. Previously attached to Denmark, then Sweden in 1821, Norway adopted this flag upon its independence in 1905. The white Scandinavian cross of the previously used Danish flag is superimposed with the blue cross. The three colours derive from the French tricolour, the symbol of freedom.

Right.
7 June 1945, after five years in exile, King Haakon VII returns to his kingdom. He is welcomed by his son, Prince Olav, Commander-in-Chief of the Norwegian armed forces. In the background can be seen Prince Olav's wife Princess Martha, and her three children, Prince Harald and Princesses Ragnhild and Astrid, who took refuge in the United States for the duration of the war.
(The National Geographic Magazine)

...ountain Infantry Brigade was created in 1941 ...d commanded by Major-General Major Fleis-...er. Operating independently from the 21st ...rmy Group, the brigade was placed under the ...ntrol of the Scottish Command. It carried out ...ids in the Spitzbergen and the northern tip of ...orway in November 1944. After 8 May 1945, ...took part in the disarming of the 340,000 ...rong German garrison.

...Norwegian volunteers joined No 10 Comman-...o (Inter-Allied), as the 5th (Norwegian) Troop. ...hey carried out many raids to harass the enemy ...n the Norwegian coast and took part in the ...hting at Walcheren in November 1944.

...In liaison with the SOE and the Norwegian re-...stance, they destroyed a heavy water plant that ...uld have been used by the Germans to develop ...a atomic bomb.

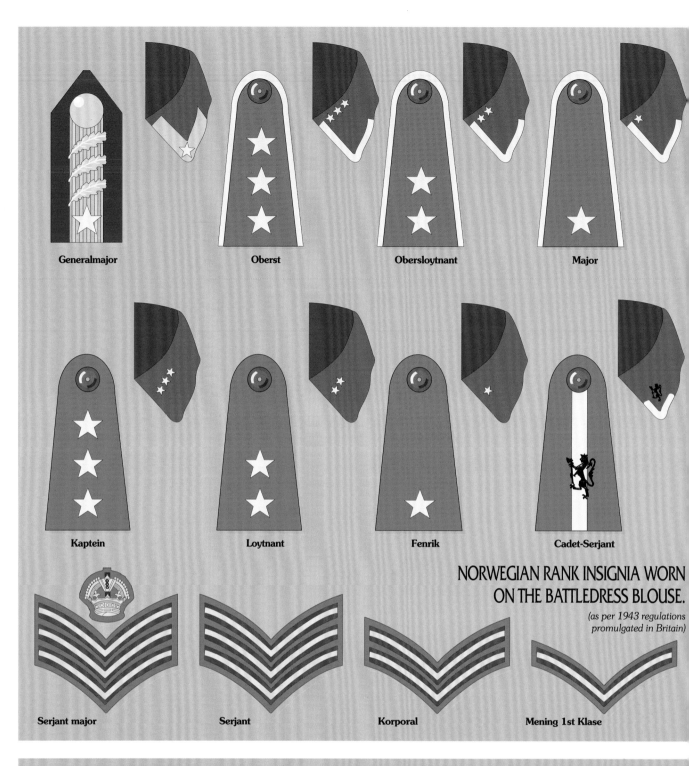

Generalmajor

Oberst

Oberstloytnant

Major

Kaptein

Loytnant

Fenrik

Cadet-Serjant

NORWEGIAN RANK INSIGNIA WORN ON THE BATTLEDRESS BLOUSE.

(as per 1943 regulations promulgated in Britain)

Serjant major

Serjant

Korporal

Mening 1st Klase

MAIN NORWEGIAN DECORATIONS

1. Order of St. Olav (*St Olavs-Orden*, 1847), in three classes.

2. St. Olav medal (*St Olavs medaljen*, 1939). Silver oak leaf device for awards to military personnel. Ribbon identical to number 1.

3. War Cross (*Krigsmedaljen*, 1941). One or more swords on the ribbon for citations *(Krigs Korset)*.

4. Liberty Cross (*HaakonVII's Frihetskors*, 1945). For actions contributing to the liberation of Norway

5. 1940-45 Campaign Medal (*Delta Kermedljen 1940-45*, Sept. 1945). The rose indicates overseas service.

6. War Medal (1941). Awarded to personnel who did not rate the War Cross.

(Compiled by Patrick Beaufigeau)

HE DANISH

Denmark was invaded by the armed forces of the 3rd Reich on 9 April [19]40. Its small army defeated within a day, the country was occupied. [Ber]lin had stated that any resistance would lead to the destruction of all [ma]jor towns and the ultimatum was thus accepted. King Christian X and [the] government remained in place.

However, as early as April 1940, the Danish ambassador to the United [Sta]tes of America, Henrik Kauffman, founded the 'Free Denmark' move[me]nt, joined in April 1942 by Christian Moeller, an escaped member of [par]liament in Great Britain.

Under their leadership, resistance at home became more organised. In [Au]gust 1943, the increase in hostile actions towards the occupying forces, [in t]he shape of strikes and acts of sabotage, led the Germans to remove all [exe]cutive power from the Danes.

Due to a lack of manpower, the Free Denmark movement did not cre[ate] military ground force units, but several hundred volunteers were as-

The Danish flag (*Dannelbrog)* is one of the oldest in the world. According to legend, it fell from the sky in 1219 during a battle when the Christian Danes defeated the pagan Estonians. It became the emblem of King Valdemar IV Alterdag in the 14th century. At the beginning, the white cross was symmetrical, but later took the shape of other Scandinavian flags (Finland, Sweden, Norway and Iceland).

Danish rank insignia and decorations

Kaptajn Captain

Premierlojtnant Lieutenant

Lojtnant 2d Lieutenant

Oversergent Staff Sergeant (CQMS)

Sergent Sergeant

Korporal Corporal

Konstabel Lance Corporal

King Christian X Medals

Commemorative medal 1940-45 (1946)

Army good conduct (1945)

National title for personnel with the 21st Army Group

signed to the Royal West Kent Regiment (The Buffs) of which King Christian X was Colonel-in-Chief. A thousand other volunteers were part of No 10 Commando or joined the Royal Air Force. Sixty parachutists joined the SOE and operated in Denmark in liaison with the resistance networks. As soon as the Germans occupied the country, all Danish merchant shipping placed itself at the disposal of the Allies under their own flag.

On 15 November 1943, A Danish Brigade ('Danforce') was formed in Sweden with escaped volunteers. Placed under the command of K. Knudtzon, it comprised of a headquarters, the 1st and 4th Light Infantry Battalions, the 5th Medium Machine-Gun Battalion and various support units. Armed and equipped by Sweden, it took part in, from 5 May 1945, the disarming of 280,000 German soldiers stationed in Norway, together with the underground and advanced elements of the 21st Army Group.

Norwegian soldiers in Great Britain

The Norwegian flag is painted on the helmet.

In Sweden (on battledress copies made from grey Swedish cloth.)

In Great Britain

Danish forces in Great Britain and Sweden

8 August 1944, a Ford WOT 2H-15-cwt 4x2 landing at Courseulles beach. The unit serial number 114 on a blue-red background indicates that the vehicle belongs to the Field Artillery Battery. *(IWM)*

THE ROYAL NETHERLAND

After May 1940, the Princess Irene brigade [1] was formed in Great Britain with members of the Dutch armed forces that had managed to escape from Holland, but also Dutch nationals recruited in the UK, USA, Canada and South Africa. Attempts to form a full brigade with its own artillery and tank regiment failed due to a lack of recruits, however. Officially created on 11 June at Congleton (Cheshire), the brigade finally comprised of a HQ, three companies strengthened with machine-guns, mortars and anti-tank and aircraft guns. It also had an armoured reconnaissance unit, an artillery troop and support and supply units. A reinforcement company was also formed with naval troops trained in the United States. In July 1943, the brigade, commanded by Luitenant-Kolonel AC de Ruyter van Steveninck, was attached to Montgomery's 21st Army Group.

It trained, therefore, with British units and was tasked with guarding the coastline in the Harwich sector. On 6 August 1944, the brigade was sent by sea to Normandy where it landed on 7-8 August, assembling around Douvres la Délivrande and Plumetot. It then fell under the command of the 6th Airborne Division east of the Orne. It went into the front lines on 12 August 1944 and from the 17-31 August, took part in the advance towards the Seine river (operation 'Paddle'). It fought in the outskirts of Pont-Audemer on the 25th. After crossing the Seine, the brigade was initially attached to the 1st Canadian Army before being placed under the command of the British 2nd Army on 5 September. Following a rapid advance via Brussels, the Albert canal was soon reached near Beerlingen

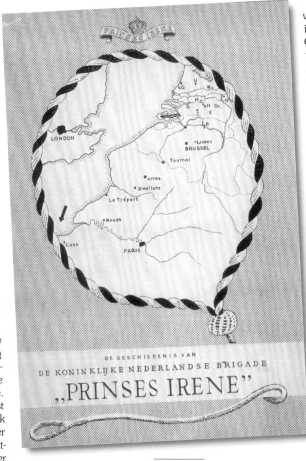

DE GESCHIEDENIS VAN
DE KONINKLIJKE NEDERLANDSE BRIGADE
,,PRINSES IRENE"

where the brigade played an active r
in the fighting. During operation 'Mark
Garden' that began on 17 Septemb
the brigade was transferred to Grave
20-21 September where it was task
with guarding and reconnaissance un
17 October. On this date it was sent
the Wilhelmine canal south of Oirso
and attached to the 51st (Highland) Di
sion. It took part in operations design
to push the Germans out of the cen
and western part of Northern Braba
On 25 and 26 October, Tilburg w
captured it despite fierce opposition
front of Broekhoven. When this tov
had been taken, the brigade found its
successively around Weelde, Rijd
and Raamsdonk.

Then, from 5 to 11 Novemb
it guarded the Maas in the region
Waalwijk. On 9 November, its co
mander was promoted to Colon
After the brigade had been sent ba
to Wuustwezel in Belgium on 11 N
vember, it was transferred to Zeelan
where it was tasked with guarding th
area all winter, in particular the nor
of Beveland and Walcheren.

During this period it served w
the 52nd (Lowland) Division ur
the end of November, then the 4
Commando brigade until 23 Mar
1945. It then came under the co
trol of the 'Netherlands District'.

1. Princess Irene was the second granddaughter of Queen Wilhelmina, born on
5 August 1939. Her Christian name means 'peace' in Greek. This name was
given to the brigade on 27 August 1941 during a ceremony in which the brigad
(in fact a regiment) received its colours from the Queen. The choice of name
shows that the Queen and her people aspired to peace!

Right.
With the river Risle [flo]wing through it, Pont-Audemer in the north the Eure department, was reached by the Royal Netherlands brigade on 24 August 1944. The town was [to]tally liberated on the [26]th by elements of the [Bel]gian Reconnaissance [S]quadron and the 6th British Airborne.

[B]RIGADE

('PRINCESS IRENE' BRIGADE)

PRINCE BERNHARD

THE ROYAL NETHERLANDS BRIGADE

STRENGTH

	OF	OR
Brigade headquarters	16	104
including Defence platoon, Medical, Ordnance, Provost Sections, Chaplains, British Liaison, Postal Unit		
Reconnaissance Unit	2	121
Signals Section	1	40
Transport/Supply	1	42
Field Artillery Troop [1]	4	88
Independent Coy [2]	11	238
Independent Coy [2]	11	238
Independent Coy [2]	11	238
Total:	**58**	**1124**

LOSSES

14 August to 5 July 1945: 345 killed and 180 wounded

COMMAND

- **Brigade commander**
Luitenant-Kolonel A.C. de Ruyter van Steveninck [4]
- **Second in command**
Majoor C.F. Pahud de Mortanges
- **Chief of Staff**
Majoor Jhr. MHL van der Wijck

---

1. *From January 1945: 8 OF, 196 OR.*
2. *From March 1945: 12 OF, 269 OR.*
3. *From 8 May 1945 to 5 July, killed by mines and accidents.*
4. *Kolonel 9 November 1944.*
5. *Formed in Normandy, August 1944.*

- **Signals Troop**
1st Liutenant H.V. Oosterom
- **Artillery Battery**
Kapitein J.A. Risseauw
- **Reconnaissance Coy**
Kapitein MCG Imminck

- **Medical Section**
Dirigeerend Off. van Gezondheid 3rd Klass J.W. Boerma
- **Ordnance**
Kapitein-Intendant M. Hertzdalh
- **Workshop-LAD**
Kapitein J. Bredt
- **Transp./Supply**
Kapitein H.J.J. Westernberg

- **Chaplain, Catholic**
Veldpediker, Major CD Buenk
- **Chaplain, Protestant**
Aalmoezenier, Major, Pater LJA Laureyssen
- **Chaplain, Jewish**
Rabbijn, Majoor S. Rodrigues Pereira

- **1st Independent Infantry Coy**
Majoor A.A. Paessens
- **2nd Independent Infantry Coy**
Majoor F. Molenaar
- **3rd Independent Infantry Coy**
Majoor J.J.L. Huber, 16 March 1945: Majoor PC V. Scherpenberg
- **Replacement Coy** [5]
Majoor F. Looringh V. Beek

Prince Bernhard was the commander-in-chief of all Dutch forces, including those of the underground. On this 1945 dated photograph, he wears the rank badges of a Luitenant-General on the collar of his jacket. The sleeve bears the bullion embroidered badge of the Dutch forces general staff. Worn from September 1944 onwards, it was made official by Army Order No 9 of 1945. A cotton woven version existed for other ranks.
The Prince also wears, on the right hand side of his chest, RAF pilot wings and on the left, Dutch pilot wings. German born, Prince Bernhard von Lippe-Biesterfeld married Princess Juliana in January 1937, the daughter of the reigning sovereign, Queen Wilhelmina. Prior to the marriage, he had asked Chancellor Adolf Hitler for the authorization to relinquish his German nationality.
(Private collection)

Opposite.
On the British General Service Cap, the cap badge was worn over the left eye. Routine orders of 9 February 1944 stipulated the deletion of the Field Service Cap and its replacement by the GS Cap for all arms and services with the exception of the cavalry that had adopted the black beret of the Roy Armoured Corps.

ROYAL NETHERLANDS BRIGAI
RANK INSIGN
**1 to 9. On jacket coll.
10 to 15. On sleeves, identical
British Army. Six-point star placed
a piece of khaki cloth or sewn direc
onto the coll.
Silver or gold for high ranking office
orange for other office**
*(Taken from the Dutch magazi
Armamentaria, published 194*

Orange is the predominant colour in Dutch heraldry, going back to 16th century. At this time in history, the upper band of the Dutch flag was orange (it became red in 1630), the colour of William the First of Orange (1533-1584) who freed Holland from Spanish rule and founded the house of Orange-Nassau, the future holders of the Dutch crown. The orange band was joined by 'Nassau blue' (royal blue).

1

2

3

5

4

6

Abo
**Cap badge placed on piece of oran
cloth (except for the cavalry). T
rampant, crowned lion brandishi
a sword and lightning rod is t
emblem of Flanders and Limbu
(this cap badge was common to .
arms and servic**

Opposite.
**Head dress and sleeve insignia.
1. Cap badge with orange backing
2. Shoulder title [1]
3. Formation Sign [2]
4. Arm-of-service strip (Infantry)
5. Volunteer badge [2]
6. Parachute qualification badge**

1. Worn on both sleeves of the BD blouse and greatcoat.
2. Worn on left sleeve of blouse.

Queen Wilhelmine visited the brigade at Walcheren. The naval troop contingent was attached elsewhere and left the brigade on 31 March. This led to reorganisation and the disbanding of the reconnaissance unit. From 10 to 14 April 1945, with the Allied advance in Eastern Holland and Germany in full swing, the brigade was relieved by a battalion of the Belgian brigade and transferred to the area of Meuse Heusden-Hedel.

The brigade then came under the command of the British 116th Royal Marine Brigade and captured a bridgehead at Hedel during the advance in the Bommerlerwaard on 23 April. It remained in this bridgehead despite strong German counter attacks. However, the advance became bogge down and the brigade received the order to withdraw.

On 4 May, the 116th brigade was relieved by the 308th (Br.) Infant brigade. On 5 May, after the German capitulation, the unit was sent Wageningen and on the 6th, was the first Allied unit to enter The Hague

The brigade was disbanded at the end of 1945 and reformed as th Princess Irene Regiment on 16 April 1946 (later the Guards Regimen thus upholding its traditions.

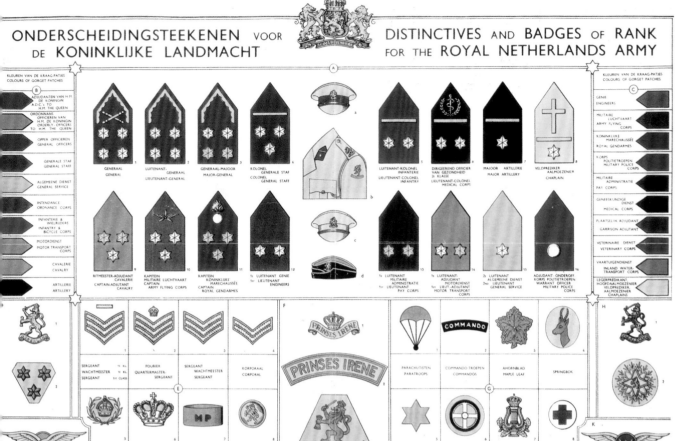

ONDERSCHEIDINGSTEEKENEN VOOR DE KONINKLIJKE LANDMACHT

DISTINCTIVES AND BADGES OF RANK FOR THE ROYAL NETHERLANDS ARMY

KLEUREN VAN DE KRAAG-PATIES / COLOURS OF GORGET PATCHES

ADJUDANTEN VAN H.M. DE KONINGIN / A.D.C.'S TO H.M. THE QUEEN
ORDONNANS OFFICIEREN VAN H.M. DE KONINGIN / ORDERLY OFFICERS TO H.M. THE QUEEN
OPPER OFFICIEREN / GENERAL OFFICERS
GENERALE STAF / GENERAL STAFF
ALGEMEENE DIENST / GENERAL SERVICE
INTENDANCE / ORDNANCE CORPS
INFANTERIE & WIELRIJDERS / INFANTRY & BICYCLE CORPS
MOTORDIENST / MOTOR TRANSPORT CORPS
CAVALERIE / CAVALRY
ARTILLERIE / ARTILLERY

GENERAAL / GENERAL
LUITENANT-GENERAAL / LIEUTENANT-GENERAL
GENERAAL-MAJOOR / MAJOR-GENERAL
KOLONEL GENERALE STAF / COLONEL GENERAL STAFF
LUITENANT-KOLONEL INFANTERIE / LIEUTENANT-COLONEL INFANTRY
DIRIGEEREND OFFICIER VAN GEZONDHEID 2e KLASSE / LIEUTENANT-COLONEL MEDICAL CORPS
MAJOOR ARTILLERIE / MAJOR ARTILLERY
VELDPREDIKER / CHAPLAIN

RITMEESTER-ADJUDANT CAVALERIE / CAPTAIN-ADJUTANT CAVALRY
KAPITEIN MILITAIRE LUCHTVAART / CAPTAIN ARMY FLYING CORPS
KAPITEIN KONINKLIJKE MARECHAUSSÉE / CAPTAIN ROYAL GENDARMES
1e LUITENANT GENIE / 1st LIEUTENANT ENGINEERS
1e LUITENANT MILITAIRE ADMINISTRATIE / 1st LIEUTENANT PAY CORPS
1e LUITENANT-ADJUDANT MOTORDIENST / 1st LIEUT.-ADJUTANT MOTOR TRANSPORT CORPS
2e LUITENANT ALGEMEENE DIENST / 2nd LIEUTENANT GENERAL SERVICE
ADJUDANT-ONDEROFF. KORPS POLITIETROEPEN / WARRANT OFFICER MILITARY POLICE CORPS

KLEUREN VAN DE KRAAG-PATIES / COLOURS OF GORGET PATCHES

GENIE / ENGINEERS
MILITAIRE LUCHTVAART / ARMY FLYING CORPS
KONINKLIJKE MARECHAUSSÉE / ROYAL GENDARMES
KORPS POLITIETROEPEN / MILITARY POLICE CORPS
MILITAIRE ADMINISTRATIE / PAY CORPS
GENEESKUNDIGE DIENST / MEDICAL CORPS
PLAATSELIJK ADJUDANT / GARRISON ADJUTANT
VETERINAIRE DIENST / VETERINARY CORPS
VAARTUIGENDIENST / INLAND WATER TRANSPORT CORPS
LEGERPREDIKANT, HOOFDAALMOEZENIER VELDPREDIKER, VELDPREDIKER, AALMOEZENIER / CHAPLAINS

SERGEANT 1e KL. WACHTMEESTER 1e KL. / SERGEANT 1st CLASS
FOURIER / QUARTERMASTER-SERGEANT
SERGEANT WACHTMEESTER / SERGEANT
KORPORAAL / CORPORAL

PRINSES IRENE
PRINSES IRENE
PRINSES IRENE NEDERLAND

PARACHUTISTEN / PARATROOPS
COMMANDO TROEPEN / COMMANDOS
AHORNBLAD / MAPLE LEAF
SPRINGBOK

SERGEANT-MAJOOR OPPERWACHTMEESTER SERGEANT-MAJOR
VELD- EN DAGELIJKSCHE TENUE / BATTLE DRESS
GEKLEEDE TENUE / SERVICE DRESS
ARMBAND POLITIEDIENSTEN / POLICE DUTY ARMLET
UNIFORM-KNOOP / UNIFORM BUTTON

VRIJWILLIGERS / VOLUNTEERS
CHAUFFEURS EN MOTOR-ORDONNANSEN DRIVERS AND DESPATCH-RIDERS
MUZIKANTEN / BANDSMEN
GENEESKUNDIG PERSONEEL / MEDICAL PERSONNEL

VLIEGER / PILOT
WAARNEMER / OBSERVER

Right.
Soldaat 1 Klass wearing a Mk II helmet with a transfer representing the orange lion of Flanders and Limburg on a Nassau blue disk. Above the sleeve chevron is sewn the maple leaf of volunteers that had come from Canada.
(Reconstruction, courtesy of Mike van Dobbelsteen)

Below. A humorous postcard printed after the end of the war. The battledress and insignia are accurately portrayed.
(Mike van Dobbelsteen Collection)

DE BRIGADE „ON DUTY"

GALLANTRY AND COMMEMORATIVE MEDAL RIBBONS

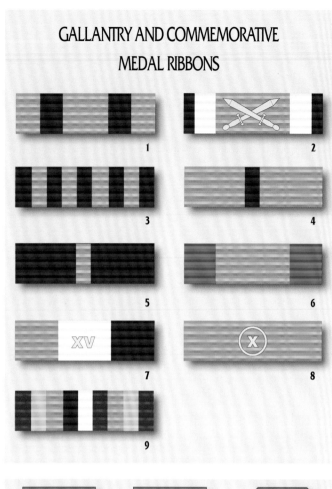

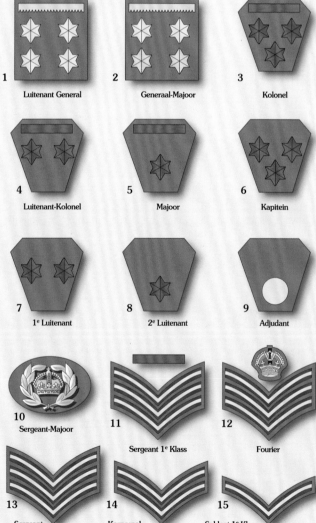

1. *Militaire Willemsorde.* Military William order (est. 1815), existed in four classes

2. *Orde van Orange-Nassau.* Medal of honour of the Order of Orange-Nassau (1815), existed in three classes.

3. *Bronzen Leeuw.* Bronze lion, for gallantry or command in the presence of the enemy (1944).

4. *Bronzen Kruis.* Bronze cross, acts of bravery in combat. (1941).

5. *Mobilisatie Oorlogskruis.* War commemorative cross 1940-45 (1946).

6. *Oorlogs Herinnerings Kruis.* War Cross awarded all military personnel for more than 6 months active service, or directly if involved in a distinctive action (March 1944).

7. *Onderscheidingsteken Voor Langdurige Dienst als Officer.* Long service cross for officers (1844).

8. *Langdurige Dienst als Onderofficer.* Long service cross for NCOs (1825).

9. *Huweliijksmedaille 1937.* Medal for the wedding of Princess Juliana and Prince Bernhard (1937).

1. **Medal of honour of the Orange-Nassau Order.**
2. **Bronze cross. 3. War cross (also awarded to the French SAS involved in operation 'Amherst' in April 1945).**
(Patrick Nonzerville collection)

Rank equivalents

	Dutch	British
1	Luitenant General	Lieutenant General
2	Generaal-Majoor	Major General
3	Kolonel	Colonel
4	Luitenant-Kolonel	Lieutenant Colonel
5	Majoor	Major
6	Kapitein	Captain
7	Eerste Luitenant	1st Lieutenant
8	Tweede Luitenant	2nd Lieutenant
9	Adjudant	Staff Sergeant Major
10	Sergeant-Majoor	Warrant Officer Class I
11	Sergeant Eerste Klass	Warrant Officer Class II
12	Fourier	Quarter Master Sergeant
13	Sergeant	Sergeant
14	Korporaal	Corporal
15	Soldaat 1st Klass	Lance Corporal

rly August 1944, liaison officers from the 'Prinses Irene' Brigade pose
r the photo on the beach at Courseulles. Standing on with a British
telligence Corps captain are, on the left, 1e Luitenant R. Fack wearing
e scarlet infantry strip and parachute qualification badge, on the right, 1e
uitenant B. Dubois. *(IWM)*.

Above.

Normandy 23 August 1944. Visiting the front line, Prince Bernhard listens
to an operations report from Luitenant-Kolonel de Ruyter van Steveninck,
commanding the Royal Netherlands brigade.
(IWM).

Luitenant-Kolonel Albert Cornelis de Ruyter van Steveninck, 1895-1949

Following high school studies at Leewarder, de Ruyter van Steveninck joined the army in August 1915 and went to the military academy at Breda where he underwent artillery officer training. Specialised in ground to air liaison, he was commissioned as a second lieutenant in 1918 then promoted to lieutenant in August 1922. Promoted to Kapitein in January 1936, he was attached to the HQ of the Belgian army during the German invasion of May 1940, then to the military attaché in Paris. At the end of June 1940, Kapitein de Ruyter van Steveninck decided to join the Dutch government in exile in Great Britain. After travelling via North Africa, he arrived in London in February 1941. Promoted to Major, he took command of the 1st Infantry Battalion, the core of the future 'Prinses Irene' brigade (Royal Netherlands brigade) which he organised and trained with the rank of Luitenant-Kolonel (February 1943). After the brigade had been attached to the 21st Army Group and landed at Courseulles on 8 August 1944, Luitenant-Kolonel de Ruyter van Steveninck led his formation in Normandy (operation 'Paddle'), during operation 'Market-Garden' in September 1944, as well as through fighting in the Zeeland province in south-west Holland. At the end of the war and with the disbanding of the brigade on 13 July 1945, de Ruyter van Steveninck was given various commands within the Dutch army. He was promoted to Kolonel in May 1946 then Generaal-Majoor in March 1949.

Main decorations
Holland: Order of Orange-Nassau with swords. Bronze Lion 1944. Commemorative war cross 1944, Long Service Decoration (15 years of service).
Great Britain: Distinguished Service Order, Member of the British Empire.
France: Croix de Guerre 1939-45 with 2 palms.
Belgium: Ordre de Léopold, Chevalier du Mérite militaire, Croix de Guerre 1940 with palms.

(Sidebar authored by Arjen Bosman)

Embroidered badge worn by Dutch HQ personnel in Great Britain.

Dutch Infantry Korporaal

PRINSES IRENE.

PRINSES IRENE.

Right.
A sergeant and pathfinder Korporaal of the III Independent Company examine the route of advance.
(Reconstruction, courtesy Mike van Dobbelsteen)

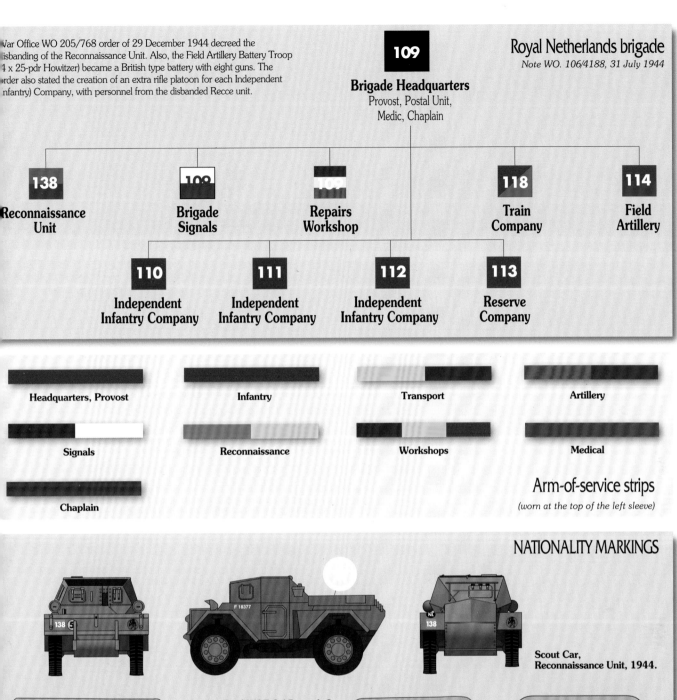

War Office WO 205/768 order of 29 December 1944 decreed the disbanding of the Reconnaissance Unit. Also, the Field Artillery Battery Troop (4 x 25-pdr Howitzer) became a British type battery with eight guns. The order also stated the creation of an extra rifle platoon for each Independent (Infantry) Company, with personnel from the disbanded Recce unit.

109
Brigade Headquarters
Provost, Postal Unit,
Medic, Chaplain

Royal Netherlands brigade
Note WO. 106/4188, 31 July 1944

138 Reconnaissance Unit

108 Brigade Signals

109 Repairs Workshop

118 Train Company

114 Field Artillery

110 Independent Infantry Company

111 Independent Infantry Company

112 Independent Infantry Company

113 Reserve Company

Headquarters, Provost

Infantry

Transport

Artillery

Signals

Reconnaissance

Workshops

Medical

Chaplain

Arm-of-service strips
(worn at the top of the left sleeve)

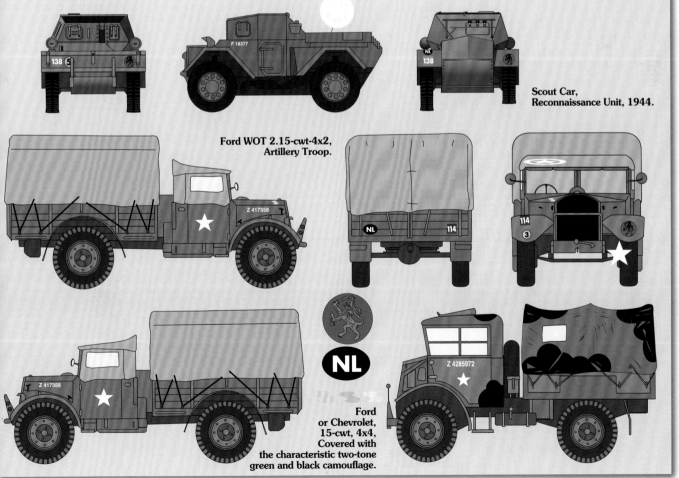

NATIONALITY MARKINGS

F 18377

138

NL 138

Scout Car,
Reconnaissance Unit, 1944.

Ford WOT 2.15-cwt-4x2,
Artillery Troop.

Z 417358

NL 114

114 3

Z 417358

NL

Z 4285972

Ford
or Chevrolet,
15-cwt, 4x4,
Covered with
the characteristic two-tone
green and black camouflage.

VEHICLES AND ARMAMENT OF THE ROYAL NETHERLANDS BRIGADE, 1944
(except infantry component, see table below)

- **Headquarters Company**
  13 x M' Cycles
  9 x 10-cwt light trucks
  8 x 15-cwt trucks
  4 x 3 ton trucks
  3 x ambulance
  3 x trailers, 1 x Water trailer
  3 x 20 mm AA guns
- **Signals Company**
  5 x M' Cycles
  5 x Armoured Cars
  1 x 10-cwt truck
  4 x 15-cwt truck
  2 x 3-ton truck
- **Repair Company**
  1 x M' Cycle
  2 x 10-cwt
  1 x 15-cwt
  1 x Recovery
  1 x Workshop trailer
  1 x 3-ton truck (Machinery)

- **Transport Company**
  3 x M' Cycles
  1 x 10-cwt
  1 x 15-cwt
  12 x 3-ton
  1 x Recovery
  1 x Water trailer

RECCE SQUADRON [1]

- **Squadron HQ**
  1 x M' Cycle, 1 x light car
  1 x 15-cwt truck
  6 x 3-ton truck
  2 x Universal Carriers
  1 x Light Scout Car
  1 x Water trailer
- **2 Recce troops** (each:)
  5 x M' Cycles
  5 x Armoured Cars, Daimler

- **2 Carrier troops** (each:)

6 x Universal Carriers
1 x 15-cwt truck
- **1 Anti-Tank troop:**
  4 x Loyd Carriers
  2 x 6-pdr Anti-tank guns
  1 x 15-cwt truck

FIELD ARTILLERY BATTERY [2]

- **Battery HQ**
  5 x M' Cycles
  1 x Jeep, 6 x 15-cwt, 5 x 3-ton
  2 x Artillery Limbers
- **2 Gun troops** (each:)
  1 x Loyd Carrier
  2 x 25-Pdr Field Guns
  2 x Artillery Limbers
  3 x Artillery Tractors

_____

1. Disbanded in January 1945. Personnel reassigned to the infantry.
2. From 8 September 1944, equipped with eight 25-Pounder guns instead of four.

VEHICLES IN THE INFANTRY COMPANY (*WO instruction No 106/4 188*)

- **Company Headquarters**
Bicycle
Motorcycle (x 2)
Kapitein (Second in Command)
Majoor (Company Commander)
Jeep - Liaison
15-cwt – Office
Carrier, Universal
SUPPORT GROUP
- **Group HQ** *Kapitein*
- **MMG Platoon**
Motorcycle
Luitenant (Platoon Commander)

Universal carrier - Rangetaker
Universal carrier - Gun numbers (x 2)
Universal carrier - MMG 303 in (x 4)
15-cwt - Ammunition
- **3-inch Mortar Section**
Motorcycle
15-cwt - Sergeant
Universal carrier - Rangetaker
Universal carrier - 3-in. Mortar (x 2)
- **Antitank Section**
Motorcycle - Subaltern

Motorcycle - Orderly
15-cwt - Sergeant
Loyd carrier (x 2)
Loyd carrier - 6-pdr AT gun (x 2)
- **Anti-Aircraft section**
Motorcycle - Sergeant
15-cwt- 20-mm AA gun (x 2)
- **Administrative Section**
Bicycle - Sergeant
Truck, 15-cwt, GS
15-cwt - Medical Sergeant Ambulance
Lorry, 3-Ton, GS - Stores (x 2),

Lorry, 3-Ton, GS - Petrol
Lorry, 3-Ton, GS - Baggage (x 2)
Lorry, 3-Ton, GS - Ammunition
Lorry, 3-Ton, GS - Kitchen
Lorry, 3-Ton, GS - Officers' mess
- **Troop carrying section**
Motorcycle - Sergeant
Lorry, 3-Ton - Troop carrying (x 4)
- **Rifle platoons** (No 1, 2, 3), **each**:
15-cwt - General Service
15-cwt - Tools
15-cwt - 2-in. Mortar

Company Headquarters

Kapitein Second in command   Major Coy. Cdr   Jeep Liaison   15-cwt Office   Carrier, Universal

SUPPORT GROUP

Group Headquarters

Kapitein

Medium Machine Gun Platoon

Luitenant (Platoon Cdr)   Range taker   Gun Numbers n° 1   Gun Numbers n° 2   15-cwt Ammunition

Carrier MG .303 in.   Carrier MG .303 in.   Carrier MG .303 in.   Carrier MG .303 in.

VEHICLES IN THE INFANTRY COMPANY (continued)

3 inch Mortar Section

Subaltern

Sergeant

Universal Carrier, Range Taker

Universal Carrier, 3 inch Mortar

Antitank Section

Subaltern   Orderly

Sergeant

Loyd Carrier   Loyd Carrier + 6-pdr antitank gun

Loyd Carrier   Loyd Carrier + 6-pdr antitank gun

Anti Aircraft Section

Sergeant

Truck 15-cwt, 20 mm AA gun

Truck 15-cwt, 20 mm AA gun

Administrative Section

Sergeant

Truck 15-cwt

Medical Sergeant Ambulance

Bicycle

Lorry 3-ton. Stores

Lorry 3-ton. Stores

Lorry 3-ton. Petrol

Lorry 3-ton. Baggage

Lorry 3-ton. Baggage

Lorry 3-ton. Ammunition

Lorry 3-ton. Kitchen

Lorry 3-ton. Officers' Mess

Troop Carrying Section

3-ton. Troop carrying

3-ton. Troop carrying

3-ton. Troop carrying

3-ton. Troop carrying

Rifle platoons x 3 (Nos 1, 2, 3)

Truck 15-cwt, tools

Truck 15-cw, tools

Truck 15-cw, 2-in. mortar

107

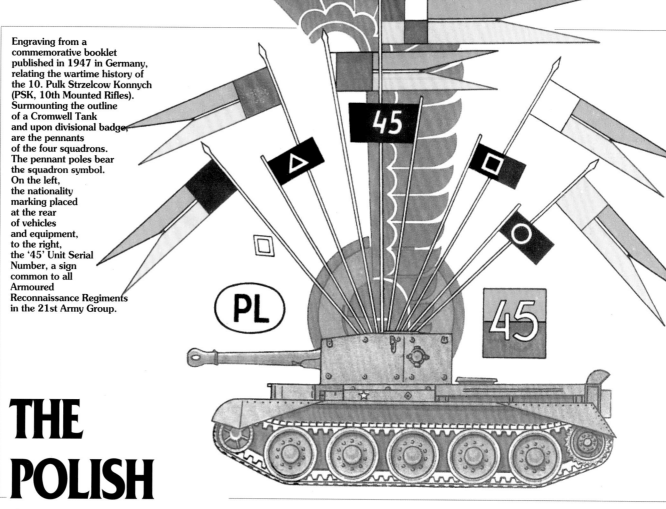

THE POLISH

The German army invaded Poland on 1 September 1939, thus setting the Second World War in motion. Attacked in the rear by the Soviet army on the 17th, the Polish army laid down its arms on 5 October. With Eastern Poland occupied by the Russians, the main part of the country became a province governed by the 3rd Reich (conscription in the Wehrmacht was decreed).

Many Polish military personnel managed to escape captivity, however, and rallied in France via Romania and Hungary. Reorganised, they took part in the fighting in May-June 1940 [1]. After the armistice of 22 Ju between France and Germany, the remaining men reached Great Brita where they were gathered in Scotland.

On 26 February 1942, the British government and General Sikorski the commander of Polish armed forces exiled in London, agreed to t formation of the 1st Polish Armoured Division. It was placed under t command of General Brygady Stanislaw Maczek, a veteran of the Poli and French campaigns.

THE 1st POLISH ARMOURED DIVISION

As well as men that had survived the Battle of France, the Division comprised of volunteers that arrived from all over the world and later, by large contingents that had travelled via the Middle East and Soviet prisoner camps following agreements signed by both governments.

After 18 months of training and outfitting, the Division, whose training was carried out along British lines, was deemed as ready for operations.

Loaded onto ships in the south of England on 28 July 1944, the Division landed on the coast of Normandy at Juno Beach, Arromanches and Courseulles.

The Division was concentrated between 29 July and 4 August between Bayeux and Caen near Magny-en-Bessin, Crépon and Tierceville; it was then attached to II Canadian Corps/1st Canadian Army.

Following the campaigns of France, Belgium, Holland and Germany and the capitulation of German armed forces on 8 May 1945, the 1st Polish Armoured Division was tasked with occupying part of the British sector. The spring of 1947 saw it depart for Great Britain where it was disbanded.

Organisation and structure

There was a notable difference between the Polish division's establishment and that of an equivalent British formation as stipulated by the War Establishment Tables of November 1943, eventually modified in the first three months of 1944.

It should be noted that in March 1944 the Motor Battalion (10th Dragoons) was equipped with US half-tracks (M5, M9) as a replacement for the previously used trucks. During the course of the campaign other equipment was issued. This will be covered in this chapter.

However, the main modifications affected the armoured regiments. No longer needed due to the lack of enemy air activity, the anti-aircraft troops

were disbanded and their men transferred as reinforcements to the armour regiments that had seen the most fighting (October 1944). Also disband were the reconnaissance troops, due to their lack of tactical use and also, part, to make up for the chronic lack of infantry. Their M5 light tanks h their turrets removed and they were fitted out to carry five riflemen (Nove ber 1944).

Command structure (August 1944-May 1945)

HQ/Divisional Commander
eneral Brygady Stanislas Maczek
Chief of Staff
odpulkownik Ludwik Stankiewicz
0th ARMD CAVALRY BRIGADE
ulkownik Tadeuz Majewski
ulkownik Franciszek Skibinski
6.01.1945)
1st Armoured Regiment
odpulkownik Aleksander Stefanowicz
2nd Armoured Regiment
odpulkownik Stanislas Koszutski
Iajor Michal Gutowski (29.04.1945)
24th Uhlans
odpulkownik J. Witold Kanski
8.08.1944)
odpulkownik Romuald Dowbor
9.081944)
10th Dragoons (Motor)
Iajor Wladislaw Zgorzelski
otmistrz Waclaw Kownas (09.09.1944)
Iajor Bohdan Mincer (19.11.1944)
Iajor Andrzej Szajowski (04.12.1944)
odpulkownik Wladislaw Zgorzelski
?.01.1945)

3rd RIFLE BRIGADE
ulkownik Marian Wieronski
ulkownik Franciszek Skibinski
?4.08.1944)
ulkownik Wladyslaw Dec (13.01.1945)
1st Podhale Rifle Battalion
odpulkownik Karol Complak
8th Rifle Battalion
odpulkownik Alexander Nowaczynski
9th Rifle Battalion
odpulkownik Zdzislaw Szydlowski
Iajor Konrad Stepien (15.01.1945)

DIVISIONAL ARTILLERY
Pulkownik Bronislaw Noël
– 1st Motorized Artillery Regt (SP)
Pulkownik Joseph Krautwald
– 2nd Mot. Artillery Regt (Towed)
Podpulkownik Karol Maresch
– 1st Anti-tank Artillery Regt
Major Romual Dowdor
Major Otton Z Eysymont (25.08.1944)
– 1st Light Anti Aircraft Art. Regt
Podpulkownik Olgierd Eminowicz
Major Witold Berendt (08.08.1944)

DIVISIONAL TROOPS
– 10th Mounted Rifle Regt (PSK)
Major Jan Maciejowski (KIA 20 Aug.
1944), *Major* Jerzy Wasilewski
– 1st Independent MMG squadron
Major Marian Kochanowski
– 1st Signal Battalion
Pulkownik Jan Gradjkowski
– Engineers units
Podpulkownik Jan Durantt
– Supply and Transport
Major Henryk Gwiazdowski
– Ordnance & Field Park
Major Teodor Lesser
– Divisional Workshops
Major Michal Wasowicz
– Medical Services
Podpulkownik Lekarz Marian
Pawlowicz
– Replacement Tank Squadron
Rotmistr Bronislaw Skuliez
– Replacement Infantry Brigade
Podpulkownik Jerzy Deskur
– Traffic Control Squadron
Rotmistr Anatol Pieregrodzki

Theoretical strength, June 1944
(War Establishment Tables, March 1944)

– Divisional Headquarters,
Provost, Postal unit, Employment
platoon, Field Security Section, etc.:
464 OF/OR
– Divisional Signals: 730
– Armoured Recce Regt: 692
– Independent MMG Coy: 211
– Armoured Rgt. (x3): 692
– Motor Battalion: 854
– Rifle Battalion (x3): 845
– Field Artillery Regt,
Self Propelled: 645
– Field Arty Regt, Towed: 673
– AT Battery, Self Prop. (x2): 176
– Anti-tank Bat., Towed (x2): 180
– Light AA Bty. (x3): 273
– Divisional Engineers: 680
– Transport and Supply: 1791
– Medical Services: 559
– Ordnance Field Park: 68
– Divisional Workshops: 677

Grand total: 14, 939 OF/OR

*The above list does not include Headquarters
and Brigade personnel: They are included in
the strength with the Divisional Headquarters.*

Losses from 1 August 1944 to 8 May 1945

— 99 officers killed, 353 wounded
— 1,191 ORs killed, 3,471
wounded, 22 missing.
Total: 1, 290 killed, 3824 wounded
22 missing.
*These losses were partially made
good during the course of the
campaign by prisoners or deserters
forcibly enrolled into the German
army.*

Detailed losses for combat units:
— 10th Mounted Rifle (PSK)
90 killed, 231 wounded
— 1st Armoured Regiment
56 killed, 147 wounded, 4 missing
— 2nd Armoured Regiment
65 killed, 253 wounded
— 24th Uhlans
69 killed, 147 wounded

— 10th Dragoons
194 killed, 502 wounded
— Podhale Rifle Battalion
173 killed, 477 wounded, 10 missing
— 8th Rifle Battalion
187 killed, 632 wounded, 6 missing
— 9th Rifle Battalion
219 killed, 726 wounded

Normandy, August 1944:

— 21 officers killed, 35 wounded

— 304 ORs killed, 967 wounded.

Total: **325 killed**[1], 1,002
wounded and 114 missing

---
*1.Including 44 killed on 8 August 1944
and 93 on 14 August by Allied bombers
that dropped short.*

e Division's armament

Cavalry Brigade
183 Sherman tanks: in three Armoured Regiments; **61 Crom-
ells**: Armoured Reconnaissance Regiment (PSK); **Challenger**: supplied
the PSK in October 1944; **44 Stuarts Mk V:** 11 in each Armoured
giment including the PSK. At the beginning of the Netherlands cam-
ign, the Stuarts had their turrets removed in order to carry a half-rifle
ction (5 men). In all, the division had 288 medium and light tanks.
Field Artillery
1 regiment of twenty-four **25-pdr Self-Propelled Sexton**
1 regiment of twenty-four **25-pdr Towed Anti-tank Artillery**
Anti-tank Artillery (1 regiment)
2 batteries with twenty-four **17-pdr Self-Propelled M10.**
2 batteries with twenty-four **17-pdr Towed.**

Light Anti-aircraft Artillery regiment:
thirty-six **40 mm Self Propelled, Towed**
Independent Medium Machine Gun Coy:
4 x **4.2 in Mortar**
22 heavy machine-gun **.303 Vickers MG**
Anti-Tank Platoons
24 x **6-pdr Anti-Tank Guns,** 6 per Rifle Battalion
During the NW Europe campaign, from August 1944 to May 1945,
the division lost: 172 Shermans, 35 M5 Stuarts, 51 Cromwells, 12 Sex-
tons, 15 artillery guns, 138 Universal and Loyd Carriers, 15 Half Tracks,
12 White Scout-cars. From this total 66 were destroyed and eighty damaged but repairable, during the Battle of Normandy. Heer and Waffen-SS
reports indicate the destruction of 173 Allied tanks for the sole dates of 8
to 9 August 1944.

Right.
**Rifle section of the 10th
Dragoons, Normandy,
August 1944.**

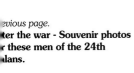

evious page.
**ter the war - Souvenir photos
r these men of the 24th
lans.**

---
*Also in Norway, notably at Narvik.
Killed in an accident on 4 July 1943
d replaced by General Sosnkowski.*

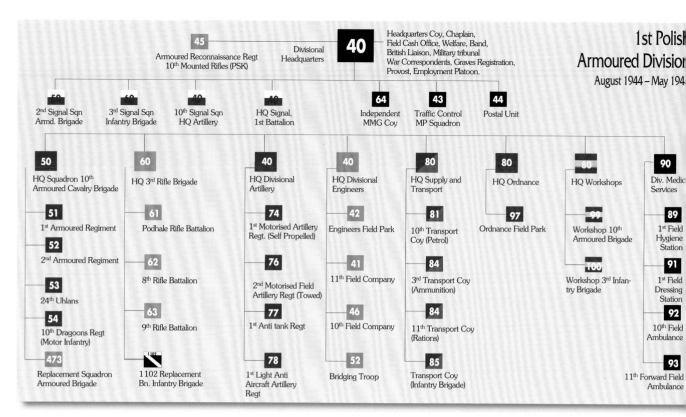

45 Armoured Reconnaissance Regt 10th Mounted Rifles (PSK)

Divisional Headquarters

40 Headquarters Coy, Chaplain, Field Cash Office, Welfare, Band, British Liaison, Military tribunal War Correspondents, Graves Registration, Provost, Employment Platoon.

- **50** 2nd Signal Sqn Armd. Brigade
- **60** 3rd Signal Sqn Infantry Brigade
- **40** 10th Signal Sqn HQ Artillery
- **40** HQ Signal, 1st Battalion
- **64** Independent MMG Coy
- **43** Traffic Control MP Squadron
- **44** Postal Unit

50 HQ Squadron 10th Armoured Cavalry Brigade	**60** HQ 3rd Rifle Brigade	**40** HQ Divisional Artillery	**40** HQ Divisional Engineers	**80** HQ Supply and Transport	**80** HQ Ordnance	**80** HQ Workshops	**90** Div. Medical Services
51 1st Armoured Regiment	**61** Podhale Rifle Battalion	**74** 1st Motorised Artillery Regt. (Self Propelled)	Engineers Field Park	**81** 10th Transport Coy (Petrol)	**97** Ordnance Field Park	**99** Workshop 10th Armoured Brigade	**89** 1st Field Hygiene Station
52 2nd Armoured Regiment	**62** 8th Rifle Battalion	**76** 2nd Motorised Field Artillery Regt (Towed)	**41** 11th Field Company	**84** 3rd Transport Coy (Ammunition)		**100** Workshop 3rd Infantry Brigade	**91** 1st Field Dressing Station
53 24th Uhlans	**63** 9th Rifle Battalion	**77** 1st Anti tank Regt	**46** 10th Field Company	**84** 11th Transport Coy (Rations)			**92** 10th Field Ambulance
473 Replacement Squadron Armoured Brigade	**1102** 1102 Replacement Bn. Infantry Brigade	**78** 1st Light Anti Aircraft Artillery Regt	**52** Bridging Troop	**85** Transport Coy (Infantry Brigade)			**93** 11th Forward Field Ambulance

Translation of unit designations

Sza Dywizja Pancerna: 1st Armoured Division
10. Brygada Kawalerii Pancernej: 10 Armoured Cav. Brigade
1. Pulk Pancerny: 1st Armoured Regiment
2. Pulk Pancerny: 2nd Armoured Regiment
24. Pulk Ulanow: 24th Lancers Regiment
10. Pulk Dragonow: 10th Dragoon Regiment
Brygada Strzelcow: 3rd Rifle Brigade
Battalion Strzelcow Podaalariskich: Podhale Rifle Battalion
8 Battalion Strzelcow: 8th Rifle Battalion
9 Battalion Strzelcow: 9th Rifle Battalion
DIVISIONAL UNITS
10. Pulku Strzelcow Konnych (PSK): 10th Mounted Rifles Regiment
1 Samodzielny Swadron: 1st Machine Gun Company
1, 2 Pulk Artylerii Motorowej: 1, 2 Field Artillery Regiments
1 Pulk Artylerii Przeciwlotniczej Lekkiej: 1st Light AA Regt.
1 Pulk Artylerii Przeciwpancernej: 1st Anti tank Regiment
1 Battalion Saperow: 1st Engineers Battalion
1 Battalion Lacznosci: 1st Signals Battalion
Oddzialy Zaopatrywania: Supply and Transport
1 Park Materialowy: 1st Ordnance Field Park
1 Oddzialy Warsztatowa-Naprawce: Divisionals Workshops

vious, far left.
ese men of the 24th Uhlans show their
nting spirit, something that is clearly
pressed on the written sign placed in front
the windscreen.

mous for its 12th century square keep,
 small town of Chambois in the Orne
partment, is now known for one of the final
ases of the fighting in lower Normandy. In
 evening of 19 August, the Falaise Pocket
s, in theory, closed, but fierce fighting
ntinued until the 21st. Contrary to what
ny battle of Normandy historians claim,
 fighting was not over. The 21st Army
oup, along with other units, crossed the
ine in force at Vernon on 25 August. The
ttle for Le Havre did not end until the
rrison capitulated on 12 September, thus
nging to the Battle of Normandy to a close.

Above.
24th Uhlans, Headquarters Squadron,
Reconnaissance Troop. During the advance
towards Belgium, the crew of a Stuart Light
Tank M5 pose for a photograph taken by
the Canadian Film and Photo Unit. An RAC
helmet bearing the unit code can be seen in
the foreground.

et, top.
ris, 25 February 1945. During an awards
remony by French army chief-of-staff
neral Juin, Major Michael Gutowski, CO
 the 10th Mounted Rifle (PSK) is awarded
 Croix de guerre with palm (he later took
mmand of the 2nd Armoured Regiment).
e Major wears Polish Battledress, modified
 the addition of a zip closure in place of the
ttons.

Right.
Challenger tanks were issued to the 10th
Mounted Rifles (PSK) in November 1944.

10th Mounted Rifles (PSK) tank crew. In the turret, right, is Major Jan Maciejowski, killed on 20 August 1944 at Hill 124 north of Chambois.

10th Mounted Rifles (PSK)

Regimental Commander
Major Jan Maciejowski (KIA 20.08. 44), Temporary commander: *Podpulkownik* Franciszek Skibinski then *Major* Jerzy Wasilewski
Headquarters Squadron
Major Otton Ejsymont
Regimental Headquarters
Podporucznik Pawel Borzemski
Reconnaissance Troop
Porucznik Marian Plichta
Anti-Aircraft Troop
Plutonowy Aleksander Szczechla
Communication Troop
Podporucznik Witold Szwedzicki
'A' Squadron
Rotmistrz J. Wasilewski
'B' Squadron
Rotmistrz M. Gutowski
'C' Squadron
Rotmistrz Hermann Cieseslinski
Regimental workshops
Podporucznik W. Zienkiewez

STRENGTH

— 37 Officers
— 8 Warrant Officers
— 46 Sergeants
— 63 Corporals
— 538 Privates
Total: 692

EQUIPMENT

— 55 Cruiser Tanks
— 6 Close Support Tanks
— 11 Light Tanks
— 6 Ant- Aircraft Tanks
— 3 Armoured Recovery Vehicle

ARMAMENT

— 357 Pistols (Enfield)
— 211 Sten SMG
— 124 Rifles No 4 Mk I*
— 40 Bren LMG

TRANSPORT

— 8 Motorcycles
— 11 Cars, Utility, Jeep
— 23 Trucks 15-cwt
— 54 Lorries 3-Ton
— 4 Carriers, Universal
— 9 Scout Cars, Humber
— 3 Half Tracks M5, M9

LOSSES
(8 August 1944 to 8 May 1945,
— 5 officers killed, 16 wounded
— 40 Other ranks killed, 75 wounde
— 16 Cromwell tanks destroyed 12 damaged
— 4 Stuart tanks destroyed, damaged

LOSSES SUMMARY
(from 8 August 1944 to 8 May 1945)

— 7 officers killed, 41 wounded
— 83 Other ranks killed, 192 wounde

General Brygady Stanislas Maczek, 1892-1994

Following a period commanding a dragoon unit, the first Polish mechanised troops, he was promoted to the rank of Pulkownik in 1938 and was given command of the 10th Cavalry Brigade that he led during the German invasion of his country in September 1939.

With the Polish armed forces having laid down its arms, Stanislas Maczek made his way to France, joining the units being formed in Champagne and Burgundy in May-June 1940. He then managed to reach Great Britain.

The reformed 10th Cavalry Brigade then led to the formation of the 1st Polish Armoured Division that was commanded by General Brygady Stanislas Maczek throughout the fighting in Europe from August 1944 to May 1945.

General Brygady Stanislas Maczek with his staff during the battle of Normandy.

Metal button bearing the crowned Polish eagle. These buttons could be worn by officers on their service dress jacket, but also, albeit contrary to regulations, on the 1940 Pattern Battledress blouse or the 1946 Pattern issued after the cessation of hostilities in Europe.

DIVISIONAL TRANSPORT

—Bicycles	86	—Scout Cars	81
—Motorcycles	87	—ACV	19,
—Cars [1]	387		
—Trucks [2]	754		
—Lorries [3]	1329		
—Tractors [4]	160		
—Ambulances	32		
—Carriers	274		

1. Sherman and Cromwell tanks.
2. Jeep (5-cwt), 4 Seater 4x4 Humber, car, 2 Seate 4x2 Hillman, etc.
3. Truck 15-cwt Half Track (regulation British de nomination), 2. Truck 15-cwt 4x2, 4x4.
4. Lorry 3-Ton 4x2, 4x4, 6x4. Of which 62 were a tached to the Field Artillery Regt and the AA Regt.

Registration numbers observed on period photos

Motorbike, solo, Ariel : 140C078
Lorry, Fordson WOT-8 3-Ton: L 1278902
Studebaker 2,5 Ton: L 1278700
Scammell, Breakdown: H 4782322
Humber, Light Reconnaissance car: M 1279282
Challenger, (1st Armoured Regt): T 272020
Cromwell, (2nd Armoured Regt): T 188015
Cromwell (1st Armoured Regt): T 121790
Humber Mk III Field Engineers: M 4709065
Carrier, Universal, (Motor Battalion): T 137521
Carrier, Universal, (Motor Battalion): T 248539
Half Track, International Harvester: Z 5620129

Half Track, International Harvester: L (?) 5580571
Cromwell 95 mm Howitzer, Close Support (1st Armoured Regt): T 120529
Challenger (PSK): T 272089
Jeep (Light anti-aircraft Regt): M 5538992
Sherman M4A4: T 232480
Sherman M4A4: T 228988
Sherman 'Firefly' M4A4 (1st Armd. Regt. C Sqn): T 228699
Sherman M4A4: T 232392
Cromwell (PSK C. Squadron): T 187914
Cromwell (PSK C. Squadron): T 120517
Cromwell (Divisional HQ): T 187921
Crusader Anti aircraft: T 126727
Carrier, Universal (10 Dragoons): T 218525

M4A4 (Sherman V) tanks were the mainstay of the Polish armoured regiments. *(IWM-B8830)*

Below.
PSK Cromwell tanks. (PSK).

The route taken by the 1st Polish Armoured Division from 7 August 1944 to 5 May 1945, from Normandy to the North Sea.

Inset, right. **Combat zone of the division from 7 to 22 August 1944. On 19 August, the 10th Dragoons (Motor) closed the 'Falaise Pocket' by linking up with elements of the 90th (US) Infantry Division advancing from the south.**

113

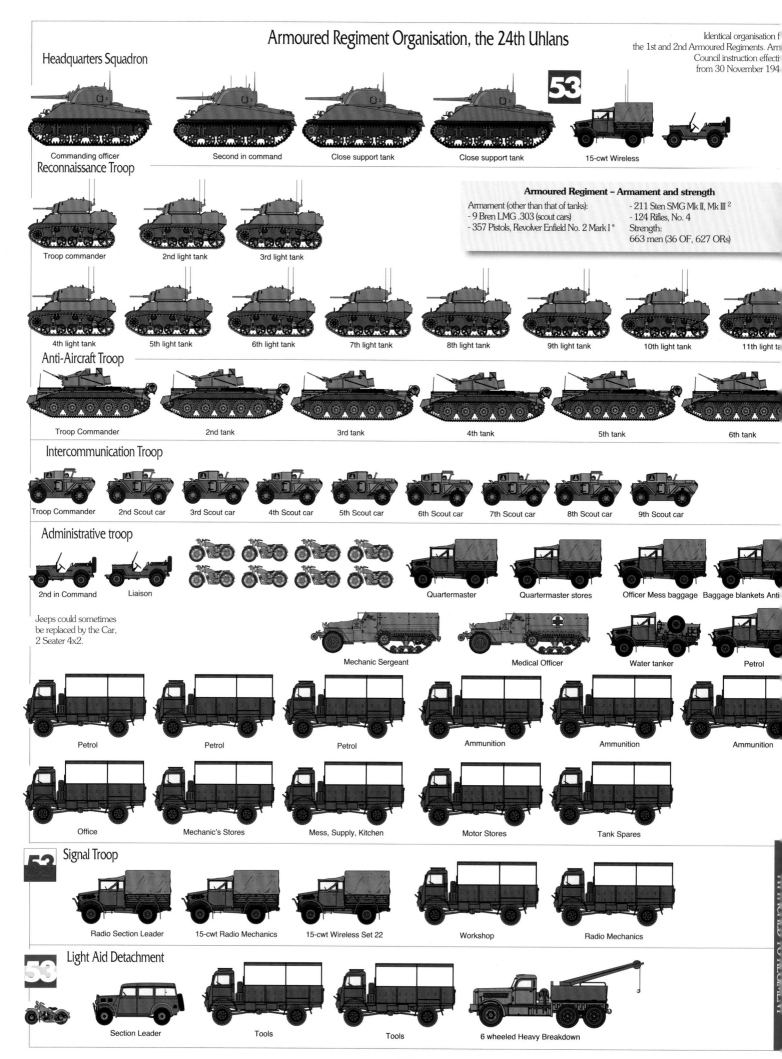

Armoured Regiment Organisation, the 24th Uhlans

Identical organisation f
the 1st and 2nd Armoured Regiments. Arm
Council instruction effecti
from 30 November 194

Headquarters Squadron

Commanding officer — Second in command — Close support tank — Close support tank — 15-cwt Wireless

53

Reconnaissance Troop

Troop commander — 2nd light tank — 3rd light tank

Armoured Regiment – Armament and strength

Armament (other than that of tanks):
- 9 Bren LMG .303 (scout cars)
- 357 Pistols, Revolver Enfield No. 2 Mark I *
- 211 Sten SMG Mk II, Mk III [2]
- 124 Rifles, No. 4
Strength:
663 men (36 OF, 627 ORs)

4th light tank — 5th light tank — 6th light tank — 7th light tank — 8th light tank — 9th light tank — 10th light tank — 11th light ta

Anti-Aircraft Troop

Troop Commander — 2nd tank — 3rd tank — 4th tank — 5th tank — 6th tank

Intercommunication Troop

Troop Commander — 2nd Scout car — 3rd Scout car — 4th Scout car — 5th Scout car — 6th Scout car — 7th Scout car — 8th Scout car — 9th Scout car

Administrative troop

2nd in Command — Liaison

Quartermaster — Quartermaster stores — Officer Mess baggage — Baggage blankets Anti

Jeeps could sometimes
be replaced by the Car,
2 Seater 4x2.

Mechanic Sergeant — Medical Officer — Water tanker — Petrol

Petrol — Petrol — Petrol — Ammunition — Ammunition — Ammunition

Office — Mechanic's Stores — Mess, Supply, Kitchen — Motor Stores — Tank Spares

53 Signal Troop

Radio Section Leader — 15-cwt Radio Mechanics — 15-cwt Wireless Set 22 — Workshop — Radio Mechanics

53 Light Aid Detachment

Section Leader — Tools — Tools — 6 wheeled Heavy Breakdown

24th Uhlans Armoured Squadron (x 3)

Identical organisation for 'B' and 'C' Squadrons

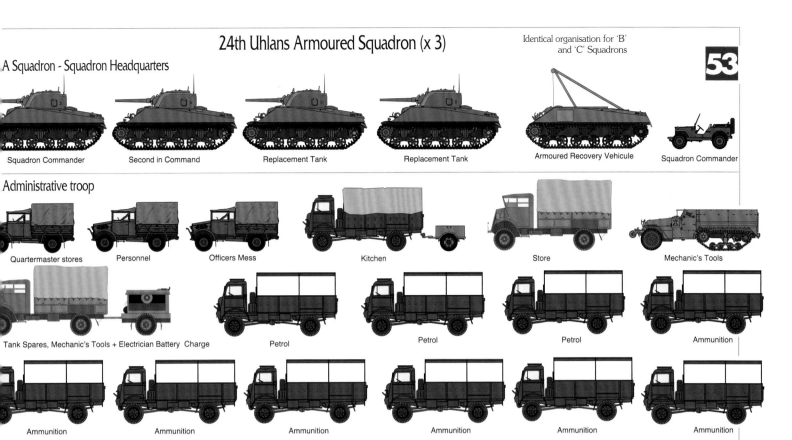

A Squadron - Squadron Headquarters

Squadron Commander — Second in Command — Replacement Tank — Replacement Tank — Armoured Recovery Vehicle — Squadron Commander

Administrative troop

Quartermaster stores — Personnel — Officers Mess — Kitchen — Store — Mechanic's Tools

Tank Spares, Mechanic's Tools + Electrician Battery Charge — Petrol — Petrol — Petrol — Ammunition

Ammunition — Ammunition — Ammunition — Ammunition — Ammunition — Ammunition

Note: The War Establishment prescribed the issue of 2 Close Support Tanks for the Regimental Headquarters (Sherman IB 105-mm Howitzer). As these had not been supplied by the USA by this date, they were replaced by the Sherman M4A4 75 mm. One 'Firefly' per troop was theoretical and were only supplied during the course of the campaign.

Sherman tank variants [1]

US/British designation	Gun/calibre	Engine
M4A1 (76)/Sherman II A [2]	76,2 mm	9 cyl. radial. Air cooled, gasoline
M4A4/Sherman V	75 mm	5 x 6-cylinder coupled engines, gasoline.
M4A4/Sherman VC Firefly	76,2 mm 17-Pounder	5 x 6 cylinder coupled engines, gasoline.
M4A2/Sherman III	75 mm	2 Diesel engines coupled engines. Gasoline.
M4/Sherman I	75 mm	9 cyl. Radial. Air cooled. Gasoline.

1. Most of the armoured regiments of the 10th Armoured Brigade were equipped with Sherman Vs and strengthened, depending on availability, with Sherman VC Fireflies.

2. The Sherman II A was supplied to the Division in Holland in October 1944.

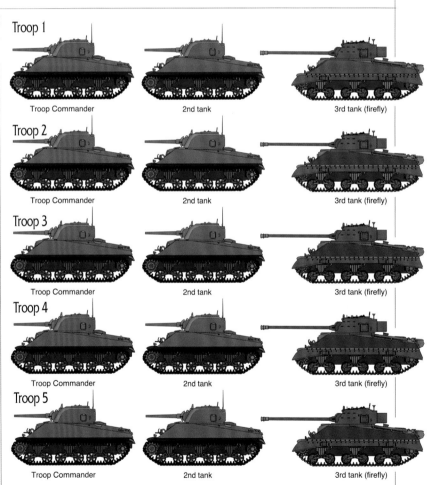

Troop 1 — Troop Commander — 2nd tank — 3rd tank (firefly)

Troop 2 — Troop Commander — 2nd tank — 3rd tank (firefly)

Troop 3 — Troop Commander — 2nd tank — 3rd tank (firefly)

Troop 4 — Troop Commander — 2nd tank — 3rd tank (firefly)

Troop 5 — Troop Commander — 2nd tank — 3rd tank (firefly)

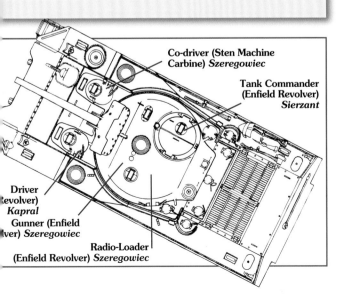

Co-driver (Sten Machine Carbine) *Szeregowiec*

Tank Commander (Enfield Revolver) *Sierzant*

Driver (Enfield Revolver) *Kapral*

Gunner (Enfield Revolver) *Szeregowiec*

Radio-Loader (Enfield Revolver) *Szeregowiec*

Crew locations in a M4A3 Sherman; in the Firefly, the co-driver's position was removed and replaced by shell racks.

COMMAND STRUCTURE OF AN ARMOURED REGIMENT

CO	Podpulkownik	Recce Troop	Porucznik	Troop Commander	Porucznik
Second in Command	Major	Intercom. Troop	Porucznik	Tank Commander	Sierzant
Squadron HQ	Major	Administrative Troop	Porucznik		
Anti-aircraft Troop	Porucznik	Squadron	Major		

1st POLISH INDEPENDENT PARACHUTE BRIGAD

General Brygady Stanislas Sosabowski, 1892-1967

Born in Stanislaswow in May 1892, Sosabowski studied law and science at Cracow university. During the First World War, he was mobilised as a NCO and fought against the Russians, then joined the new Polish army. Stanislas Sosabowski then occupied various positions within the general staff and at the military academy.

In September 1939, having reached the rank of Pulkowik, he commanded the 24th Warsawski Regiment ('children of Warsaw') during the German invasion. After the Polish defeat, he made his way to France and the 4th Polish infantry division with whom he fought in May-June 1940.

Having reached Great Britain, he formed the 1st Polish Independent Parachute Brigade. Promoted to General Brygady on 15 June 1944, he was dropped into Holland with his brigade during operation 'Market Garden'.

Having previously shown strong differences of opinion with General Browning, commander of the British airborne forces, he was relieved of his command by the latter in December 1944. General Brygady Stanislas Sosabowski ended the war within the general staff of the Polish army in Great Britain.

1st Polish Independent Parachute Brigade
September 1944

109

Brigade Headquarters
Reconnaissance Troop, Administrative Section,
Postal Unit, Provost Section, Chaplains, British Liaison, War Correspondent, Band.

109
Airborne Signals
Company

116
Airborne Engineers
Troop

118
Airborne Supply
and Transport
Company

115
Airborne Light
Artillery Battery

Troop   Troop
4x75 mm Howitzers
(US)

114
Airborne Anti-Tank
Battery

Troop   Troop
Troop
4x6 Pounder Anti-Tank Gun

117
Airborne Medical
Company

110
1st Parachute
Infantry Battalion
Headquarters Company

Mortar Platoon   Anti-Tank
4x3-in. Mortars   Platoon 10 x PIAT

1st Parachute   3rd Parachute
Infantry Company   Infantry Company

2nd Parachute
Infantry Company

Section   Section   Section

111
2nd Parachute
Infantry Battalion

Mortar Platoon   Anti-Tank
4x3-in. Mortar   Platoon 10 x PIAT

4th Parachute   6th Parachute
Infantry Company   Infantry Company

5th Parachute
Infantry Company

112
3rd Parachute
Infantry Battalion

Mortar Platoon   Anti-Tank
4x3-in. Mortar   Platoon 10 x PIAT

7th Parachute   9th Parachute
Infantry Company   Infantry Company

8th Parachute
Infantry Company

113
Reserve
Battalion

Structure is identical to a British para brigade.

First Allied Airborne Army

- **Commanding General**: Lieutenant General LH Brereton *(USA)*
- **Deputy Commander, commanding I British Airborne Corps**:
Lieutenant General FAM Browning [1]
- **1st British Airborne Division**: Major General RE Urquart
- **6th British Airborne Division**: Major General RN Gale [2]
- **SAS Elements**
- **1st Polish Independent Parachute Brigade Group**: *Gen. Brygady S. Sosabowski* [3]
- **XVIIIth US Airborne Corps**: Major General MB Ridgway
- **82nd US Airborne Division**: Major General JM Gavin
- **101st US Airborne Division**: Major General M. Taylor

1. Took command of all Allied airborne forces engaged in operation 'Market Garden.'
2. Not committed in 'Market Garden.'
3. Under command of the 1st British Airborne Div. as of 10 August 1944.

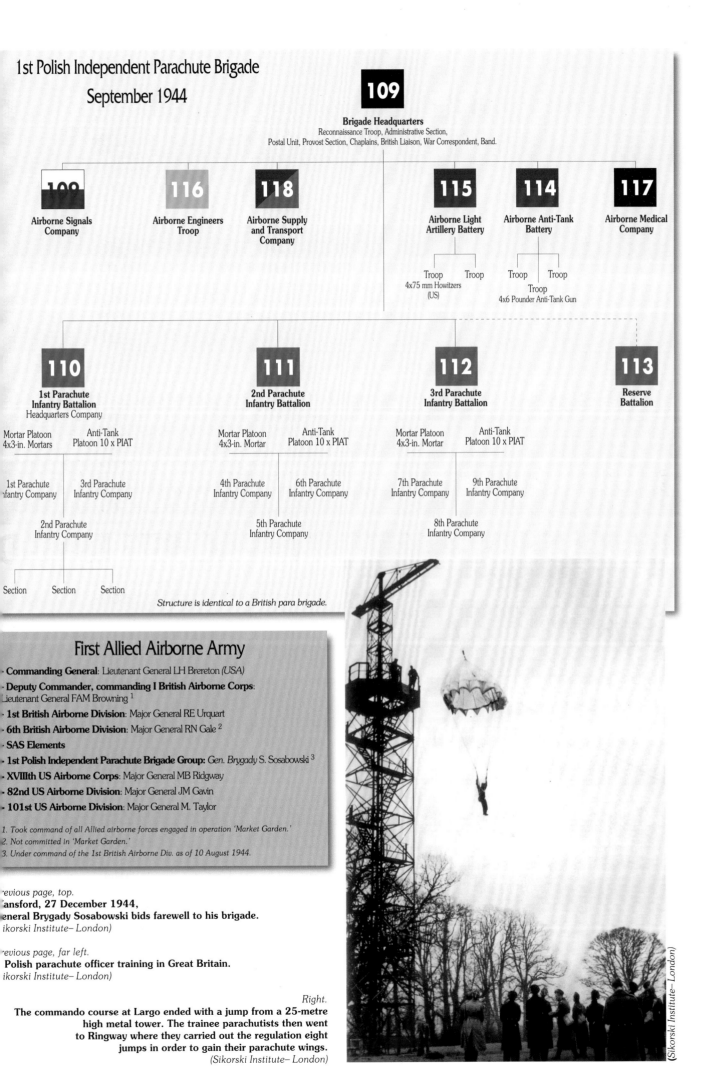

Previous page, top.
Lansford, 27 December 1944,
General Brygady Sosabowski bids farewell to his brigade.
(Sikorski Institute– London)

Previous page, far left.
Polish parachute officer training in Great Britain.
(Sikorski Institute– London)

Right.
The commando course at Largo ended with a jump from a 25-metre high metal tower. The trainee parachutists then went to Ringway where they carried out the regulation eight jumps in order to gain their parachute wings.
(Sikorski Institute– London)

(Sikorski Institute– London)

Strength of the 1st Polish Indep. Para. Brigade

NOMINAL STRENGTH	LOSSES		
2,198 OF/OR		Killed	Wounded	Missing

NOMINAL STRENGTH

2,198 OF/OR
Number committed during 'Market
Garden': 1,689

Allocation:
— Brigade Headquarters
(+ 9 British Liaison Officers) 104
— 1st Parachute Inf. Battalion
354
— 2nd Parachute Inf. Battalion
351
— 3rd Parachute Inf. Battalion
374
— Anti-Tank Battery 132
— Engineers Company 133
— Signals Company 93
— Medical Company 90
— Transport and
Supply Coy 43

*The Light Artillery Battery was not
engaged. Only 5 Junior Officers and
1 Liaison Officer took part in the
operation within the 1st British Airborne
Division.*

LOSSES

	Killed	Wounded	Missing
Brigade Headquarters	5	16	15
1st Para Battalion	11	28	4
2nd Para Battalion	11	33	7
3rd Para Battalion	30	48	39
Anti-Tank Battery	20	30	29
Engineers Company	2	20	1
Signals Company	8	16	10
Medical Company	2	13	10
Transport/Supply Coy	8	13	8
Light Artillery Battery		2	
Total	97	219	128[1]

Amounting to 23% of strength deployed
1. *Many prisoners later escaped bringing
the number of missing to 81.*

1st Polish Independent Parachute Brigade
Operation 'Market Garden', September 1944

COMMAND STRUCTURE

Brigade Commander General
Brygady Stanislas Sosabowski
● **Brigade Headquarters**
— **Assistant**
Podpulkownik Stanislas Jachnik
— **Operations Officer:**
Kapitan Wladislaw Stasiak
— **HQ Section**
Major Ryszard Malaszkiewicz
— **Tactical Officer**
Kapitan Jan Lorys
— **Signal Officer**
Major Jozef Morkowski
— **Reconnaissance**
Kapitan Ludwik Zwolanski
— **Medical Officer**
Major Jan Golba
— **Supply Section**
Podpulkownik Marcin Rotter
— **Chaplain**
Kapitan Franciszek Mienki

*Pulkownik S. Sosabowski was promoted
to General Brygady on 14 June 1944*

PARACHUTE BRIGADE

● **1st Para Battalion**
Podpulkownik Marian Tonn
● **2nd Para Battalion**
Podpulkownik Waclaw Ploszewski
● **3rd Para Battalion**
Podpulkownik Waclaw Sobocinski

BRIGADE TROOPS

● **Light Artillery Battery**
Major Jan Bielecki
● **Anti-Tank Battery**
Kapitan JK Warzdala
● **Signal Company**
Kapitan Joseph Burzawa
● **Engineers Company**
Kapitan Piotr Budziszewski
● **Transport/Supply Company**
Kapitan A. Siudzinski
● **Medical Company**
Porucznik Janusz Mozdzierz
● **Provost Section**
Podporucznik Ignacy Zaja
● **War Correspondents**
Marek Zwicicki, Engenius Romiszewski

Origins and war record

The 1st Polish Independent Parachute Brigade originated in Great Britain as early as September 1940 with volunteer personnel of the 4th Rifle Brigade that had been evacuated from France in June 1940. During the winter of 1940-41, training began under the command of Pulkownik Stanislas Sosabowski at a camp in Largo, county Angus, North-east Scotland.

The establishment of a brigade was made official on 23 September 1941, with the future objective of being able to intervene in Polish territory. However, in March 1944, the Polish and British authorities agreed that the Brigade could be committed on a different front and on 10 August 1944 it was attached to the 1st Allied Airborne Army.

During the course of Operation 'Market Garden,' the Brigade was und the command of the 1st British Airborne division. After the battle it w tasked with guarding bridges and airfields in Holland then, in Octobe the Brigade was sent back to Great Britain for reorganisation and to brought up to strength.

General-Brygady Sosabowski was relieved of his command on 27 D cember and replaced by Podpulkownik S. Jachnik. After 8 May, 1945, th Brigade joined the 1st Polish Armoured Division in its occupation zone Germany before being disbanded in 1947.

In September 1944, the Sten Machine Carbine Mk II (as seen her or Mk III were replaced by the Mk V for airborne troop

Awards ceremony, 4 September 1943. On the left is Brygady Sosabowski.
(Sikorski Institute, London)

Below.
September 1943. The Brigade is inspected by General Stanislaw Kopanski, chief-of-staff of the Polish army in Great Britain.
(Sikorski Institute, London)

Organisation and equipment

These elements were determined by the War Office according to personnel availability.

During 'Market Garden,' available air transport capacity meant that only approximately two thirds of the Brigade was sent into action.

Equipment and armament did not differ from that used by British airborne units, as described in 'D-Day Paratroopers, the British, Canadians and French' written by this author in September 2004.

In this chapter we will only look at the badges, various markings and head dress used by the Polish unit.

HELMET MARKINGS
(left hand side only, in a 5 cm square, as stipulated in July 1944).

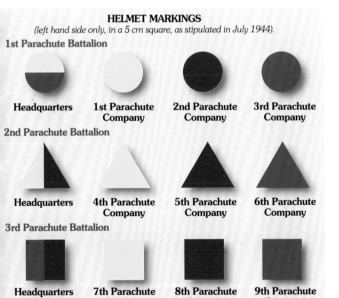

1st Parachute Battalion

Headquarters | 1st Parachute Company | 2nd Parachute Company | 3rd Parachute Company

2nd Parachute Battalion

Headquarters | 4th Parachute Company | 5th Parachute Company | 6th Parachute Company

3rd Parachute Battalion

Headquarters | 7th Parachute Company | 8th Parachute Company | 9th Parachute Company

Parachute Engineers Sqn | Parachute Medical Coy | Parachute Signals Coy

(From Military Illustrated, April-May 1988)

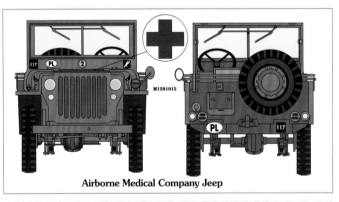

Airborne Medical Company Jeep

TRANSPORT AND ARMAMENT

Transport
- Bicycles, Folding (Airborne)
- Bicycles
- Motorcycles, Solo 125 cm³, 350 cm³
- Motorcycles, Solo Welbike
- Cars, 2 Seater 4 x 2,
- Cars, 4 Seater 4 x 2,
- Cars, 5-cwt, 4 x 4 Jeep (Airborne-modified)
- Trucks 15-cwt 4 x 2 GS, Water
- Lorries 3-Ton 4 x 2 GS

Signals
- W. Set No 18,
- W. Set No 38,
- W. Set No 46,
- W. Set No 76

Armament
- Pistols, 45, Automatic
- Rifles, 303 in. No 4 Sniper's and No 4 Mk I*
- Sten SMG, 9-mm Mk V
- Bren 303 in. LMG
- . 303 in. Medium Machine Gun
- PIAT
- Mortars 2-in. (Airborne)
- Mortars 3-in.
- 6-Pounder Anti-Tank Gun
- 75-mm Howitzer, Pack M1A1 Carriage M8

1940 Pattern Battledress blouse belonging to a soldier of the Medical Service who took part in Operation 'Market Garden.'
(D. Blanchard collection)

Close-up of the Medical Service collar tabs with metallic parachute insignia.
(D. Blanchard collection)

Parachutist medical services collar tabs.

POLISH PARATROOPERS COLLAR TABS

1. White cotton embroidered parachute placed in the centre of the tab.
1A. Metallic version usually reserved for officers. It was sometimes replaced by a silver wire embroidered version.
2. Parachute, Infantry.
3. Artillery.

4. Engineers.
5. Provost.
6. Transport and Supply.
7. Medical Services.
8. Chaplains.

This type of collar tab was not just used by the Polish Para Brigade. Some units of General Anders' army in action in Ital also wore collar tabs, such as dark blue with a yellow infantry soutache, for example.

Polish paratroopers
collar tabs

Placement on the Battledress blouse collar.

40
40
50
50

The British Airborne Forces 'Pegasus' badge was not worn as a formation badge by the Poles, and only appeared on Brigade pennants and flags.

The Polish airborne troops beret. Grey-blue in colour, it replaced a lighter coloured beret worn before June 1943. It was identical in shape to the maroon beret used by the British Airborne, as the manufacturer was one of the main suppliers of the Army Air Corps. It was worn with the badge over the centre of the forehead and pulled towards the back of the head; this was true for all Polish soldiers wearing berets.
(Yves Sacleux collection)

...ztwo I.Korpusu | SZTAB NACZELNEGO WODZA

LEGITYMACJA
...class PICARD AUGUSTIN

BOJOWY ZNAK SPADOCHRONOWY
nadany
rozkazem
z dnia

na nadany
...NYKŁY ZNAK SPADOCHRONOWY
No... 1208

SZEF SZTABU N.W.

...DTas I Korpusu L.3909/V/42

...25.XI.1942r.

dnia

SZTAB NACZELNEGO WODZA

LEGITYMACJA
upoważniająca do noszenia
ZNAKU SPADOCHRONOWEGO
No 1208

...diploma awarded
...ong with the Polish
...arachute qualification
...dge. The one seen
...re was awarded to a
...ench parachutist who
...nderwent training at
...upar camp, Angus
...raining Centre in
...cotland. 468 non-
...olish soldiers qualified
...Cupar, of whom 238
...ere French.
...Bonnefoux collection)

...and 2. Parachute qualification badge. The diving eagle design was drawn by illustrator
...larian Walentyonwicz. It was approved by the commander-in-chief of Polish forces in Great
...ritain and the minister of defence on 20 June 1941. The badge was worn on the left breast
...ove any medal ribbons (if worn). The badge could be worn by all personnel who passed the
...ll parachute training course. No badge could be awarded in an honorary fashion.
...The reverse of the badge bears the motto 'Tobie Ojczyno' ('For you, my Motherland') and
...he badge number. Seen here is number 103 awarded to Kapitan Wujek Boleslav of the
...rigade Headquarters. The badge was affixed with a threaded pin and brass bolt bearing the
...anufacturer's name of Kirkwood and Sons, Edinburgh.
...author's collection)
...Badge with golden laurel wreath awarded for a combat jump (Arnhem), created in Great
...ritain on 20 September 1944 upon the orders of the commander-in-chief and the minister
...r national defence. On post-war variants, the wreath and eagle were one-piece.
...Blanchard collection)
..., 5, 6 and 7. Other versions of the parachute qualification badge placed on a black leather
...acking. Made by CR. Techn. London.
...Blanchard collection)
...Commemorative badge for glider borne troops created on 15 February 1945. Made by
...irkwood and Son, Edinburgh.
...Blanchard collection)
...Commemorative badge for glider borne troops having landed in enemy territory (Arnhem).
...lade by Kirkwood and Son, Edinburgh.
...Blanchard collection)

*...ote: during operation 'Market Garden', glider pilots who flew in elements of the Polish Parachute Brigade were
...ritish personnel of the Glider Pilot Regiment (Army Air Corps).*

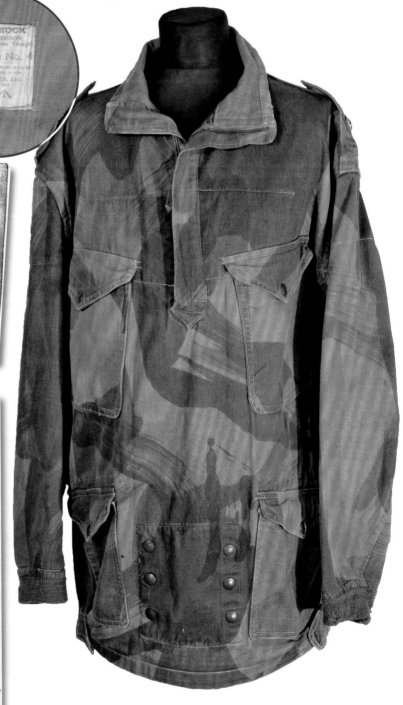

The camouflage Denison Smock worn by British airborne units.

Operation *'Market Garden,'* 17-26 September 1944

The operation was the brainchild of Field Marshal Montgomery and was authorised by General Eisenhower. The objective was to create a corridor some 102 km in length through Holland in order to open the way to the Ruhr, Germany's industrial heartland. Two American and one British airborne division would seize bridges over various water obstacles, allowing a British army corps to pass through.

The real strength of enemy forces in the sector was underestimated, as was the ability to keep open the lines of communications, thus leading to the failure of the operation.

Above.
Medical personnel in front of a Douglas C-47 of the American 315th Troop Carrier Group.

Air transport to Arnhem

Following several cancellations due to bad weather, air transport of the Polish brigade was carried out in the following way:

Tuesday 19 September, 45 Horsa gliders towed by the Albemarle and Stirling aircraft of the RAF 38 Group, carrying the Anti-Tank Bat-

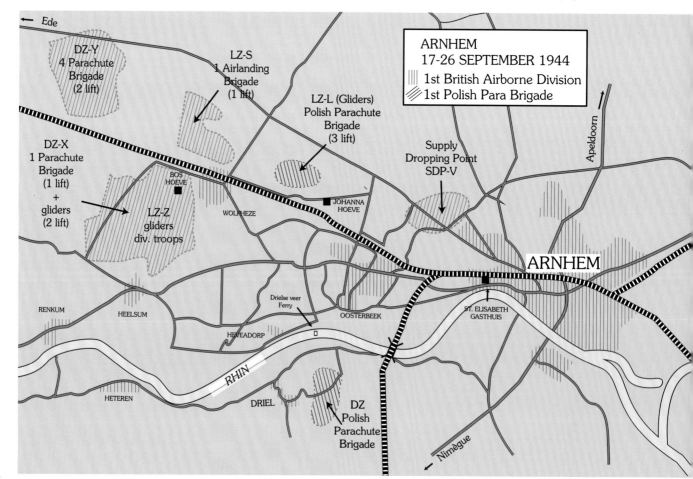

This photo, taken at Oosterbeek on the right bank of the Rhine, shows the width of the river (appx. 400 m) One can see, in the distance, the metal arches of the railway bridge. The Drop Zone of the 1st Polish Para Brigade was situated east of Driel on the left bank, practically opposite Oosterbeek.

tery, Medical Company (elements) and various support units. Landing Zone 'L' was situated on the right bank of the Rhine 4 km west of Arnhem.

Thursday 21 September, 1st Group: 114 Dakotas, of which 90 were assigned to the 3rd Para Battalion for a total of 1,568 men; Drop Zone situated on the southern bank of the Rhine near town of Driel. During the course of the flight the weather conditions worsened and following a misunderstanding concerning a radio message, forty-one aircraft turned back. In all, only 1,003 parachutists were dropped, including General Brygady Sosabowski, on the planned DZ.

Finally, the remaining 565 parachutists jumped on the 24th near Grave in the 82nd US Airborne sector and made their way to Driel by road.

Thursday 28 September, 3rd Group: due to lack of available air transport, the transfer was planned to go ahead by sea to Arromanches. This included the Light Artillery Battery and various heavy equipment. Strength: 332 OF/OR. As the battle was progressing badly, they did not link up with the bulk of the Brigade until the fighting was over.

Above.
September 1944. Men preparing to leave for Holland. These are elements of the Medical Parachute Section with one of the unit's Jeeps.

Below.
September 1944. A radio operator equipped with a Set No 38 in action at Driel.

Douglas C-47 of the 52nd Troop Carrier Wing

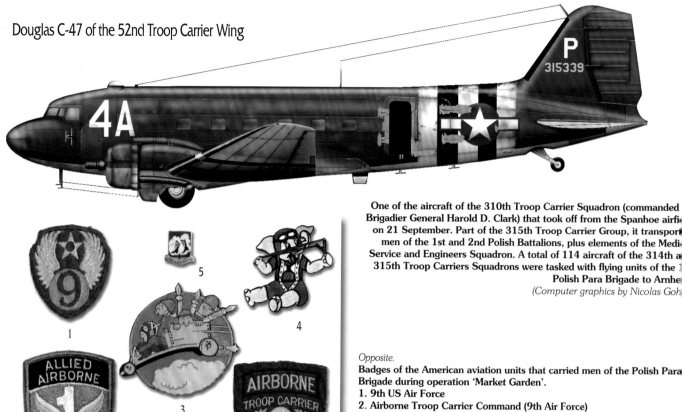

One of the aircraft of the 310th Troop Carrier Squadron (commanded Brigadier General Harold D. Clark) that took off from the Spanhoe airfie on 21 September. Part of the 315th Troop Carrier Group, it transport men of the 1st and 2nd Polish Battalions, plus elements of the Medi Service and Engineers Squadron. A total of 114 aircraft of the 314th a 315th Troop Carriers Squadrons were tasked with flying units of the Polish Para Brigade to Arnhe

(Computer graphics by Nicolas Goh

Opposite.
Badges of the American aviation units that carried men of the Polish Para Brigade during operation 'Market Garden'.
1. 9th US Air Force
2. Airborne Troop Carrier Command (9th Air Force)
3. 310th Troop Carrier Squadron
4. 43rd Troop Carrier Squadron
5. 314th Group Carrier Group
6. Shoulder Patch worn by personnel attached to the Headquarters of the 1st Allied Airborne Army (left sleeve). This only concerned Americans and attached Polish personnel.
(Pierre Besnard documentation and collection)

Typical profiles of Polish airborne personnel

Sierzant
walking out dress

Szeregowiec
combat uniform

Kapral
Bren Group Leader

Kapral
combat uniform

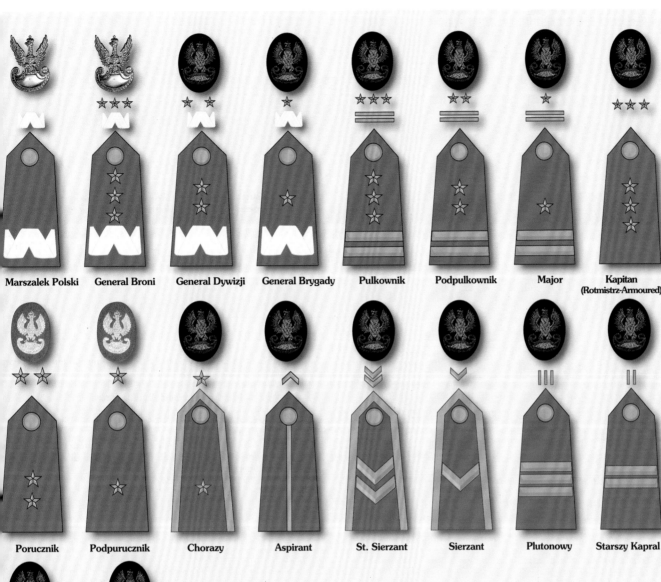

Marszalek Polski	General Broni	General Dywizji	General Brygady	Pulkownik	Podpulkownik	Major	Kapitan (Rotmistrz-Armoured)

Porucznik	Podpurucznik	Chorazy	Aspirant	St. Sierzant	Sierzant	Plutonowy	Starszy Kapral

Starszy Szeregowiec   Szeregowiec

RANK INSIGNIA, 1st POLISH ARMOURED DIVISION

Marszalek Polski	Field Marshall	**Podpurucznik**	2nd Lieutenant
General Broni	General	**Chorazy**	Warrant Officer
General Dywizji	Major General	**Aspirant**	Aspirant
General Brygady	Brigadier	**St. Sierzant**	Staff Sergeant
Pulkownik	Colonel	**Sierzant**	Sergeant
Podpulkownik	Lieutenant Colonel	**Plutonowy**	Lance Sergeant
Major	Major	**Kapral**	Corporal
Kapitan (Rotmistrz Armoured)	Captain	**Starszy Szeregowiec**	Lance Corporal
Porucznik	Lieutenant	**Szeregowiec**	Private

Rank insignia on the shoulder straps for a Porucznik of the 1st Polish Armoured Division. The Battledress blouse is private purchase and the tailor has placed the stars and shoulder title upon a non-regulation black backing.

Rank badges were seen on the front of the beret and on shoulder straps. They were made with silver wire for officers and senior NCOs and in white cotton for lesser ranks. The shoulder straps in the table are for the right side, the left hand strap was black from the rank of General Dywzji under for the entire division.

Within the 1st Polish independent Parachute Brigade, on the Denison smock, rank badges were displayed on black or brown cloth shoulder strap slip-ons.

The Polish national emblem represents a white crowned eagle on a red background and dates from the 13th century. The red and white were adopted as national colours in 1831 and the flag was officially created in 1919. The eagle upon a shield seen here was the emblem of the armed forces.

The Polish eagle

The white Polish eagle with a golden crown is the symbol of Poland[1]. In the armed forces it was worn on head dress:
- as a silver metal or silver bullion badge for officers,[2]
- for other ranks, the grey cotton embroidered eagle could be replaced by a silver plastic British made badge.

The Polish army fighting within the Soviet army (1943-45) wore the eagle less its crown, as did by Polish infantry groups in France, numbering approximately 3,000 volunteers from the Communist maquis that joined the 1st French army at the end of 1944. As long as Poland was part of the Eastern Bloc, the crown was deleted from official symbols, but came back into use when the regime crumbled in 1989. It was sometimes worn in a non-regulation fashion by senior NCOs.

The 1st Polish Armoured Division badge

This badge was worn on the left sleeve of the Battledress blouse and greatcoat, between the armhole and the elbow. Embroidered onto a rectangular piece of khaki cloth, it was issued to units in this form but was most often cut out around the shape of the motif. British made at the outset, it was later manufactured in Belgium, Holland and even Germany during the period of occupation of 1945 to 1947.

Authorized on 11 August 1942, the badge was designed by Captain Glasser who took his inspiration from the Cape-

1. Eagle of Wladyslaw Jagellon, King of Poland, 1386-1434, who vanquished the Teutonic Knights at the Battle of Tannenberg in 1410.

Variants of the eagle worn on head dress. Top: Embroidered bullion wire cotton, bottom, metallic badges.
(D. Blanchard collection)

line lobster tail helmet that was worn by the 17th century cavalry, plac upon a shield in the black and orange colours of Polish armoured un

Positioned vertically above this was a large wing, the symbol the cavalry, evoking a glorious chapter of the nation's milit history: in 1683, King Jan Sobieski III cut to pieces a Tu ish army laying siege to the city of Vienna. At the decis battle of Kalenberg, the Polish Hussars attached two la wings to their backs, made from wooden framework w leather feathers. When the Hussars charged, the wir made a strange noise, terrifying the horses of the Turki cavalry and thus provoking its rout.

The black shoulder strap

The black shoulder strap, always worn on the left side of the Battledre blouse, was characteristic of the 1st Polish Armoured Division and wc by all personnel.

It symbolised the 10th Armoured Cavalry Brigade that formed the moured element of the division. Its origins went back to the 1936 mo black leather jackets worn by tank crews during the 1939 campaign. T unit's fighting spirit was recognised by the Wehrmacht who dubbed it t 'Schwarze Brigade.'

The black shoulder strap was adopted in Great Britain when the Divisi was formed and officialised in February 1945.

Variants of the divisional insignia either worn on the rectangular backing, or cut out in the shape of the emblem.
(D. Blanchard collection)

1 and 1bis. Embroidered eagles.
2. British made plastic cap badge, manufactured by Stanleys & Sons.
(Jacques Sacleux collection)
3. Bullion wire model usually reserved for officers.
4. Silk woven badge, of French or German manufacture, 1944-47.
5. British made embroidered shoulder title.
6. British printed version.
7. Silk woven insignia. French or German manufacture (although typical of SEVO type German military insignia, this type of weave had been used in France long before WW2 in the Lyon region).
(Blanchard collection)

Nationality shoulder titles

Based on the British pattern, they were worn on both sleeves of the battledress blouse and greatcoat.

Metallic unit badges

Illustrated on the page overleaf, these were worn on the left blouse pocket and attached by a threaded post and flat round nut. Original Polish made badges can be seen on the early volunteers who had made their way to Great Britain. British made badges replaced ones that were lost or for men who joined after 1940. This was also the case for units that did not have badges when they were formed. Note that such badges were also made after the war until 1947, some in Germany.

During the north-west Europe campaign, many Polish military personnel did not wear any particular breast insignia. Some were only issued after May 1945 and generally, the generic armoured units badge could be worn, having been introduced in 1932 (fig. 1 on the plate).

Manufacture: there were silver badges with enamelled motifs for officers (private purchase). Issue insignia was in silvered or gilt metal.

Collar flashes (Pennants)

Characteristic of the Polish army, the cloth, painted metal or plastic collar flashes were in the traditional of arm of service colours. Their shape followed that of the 'Pennor,' the pennants flown by the knights of old. A silver Polish eagle attached to the collar pennants designated a staff officer. Worn on the blouse, greatcoat (or service dress tunic for officers remaining in Great Britain), they permitted the ready identification of the wearer.

Lanyards

This is a basic cord or braided cord worn on the right shoulder by personnel of certain units in the colours determined by unit tradition.
– **Black**: HQ Squadron, 1st Polish Armoured Division, 24th Uhlans, 10th Dragoons, 10th Mounted Rifles, 1st Motorised Artillery Regt
– **Orange**: HQ Squadron of the

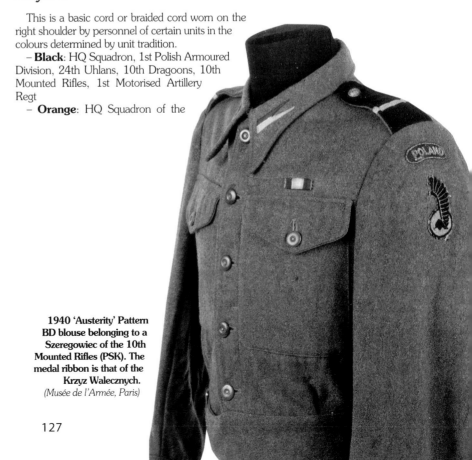

1940 'Austerity' Pattern BD blouse belonging to a Szeregowiec of the 10th Mounted Rifles (PSK). The medal ribbon is that of the Krzyz Walecznych.
(Musée de l'Armée, Paris)

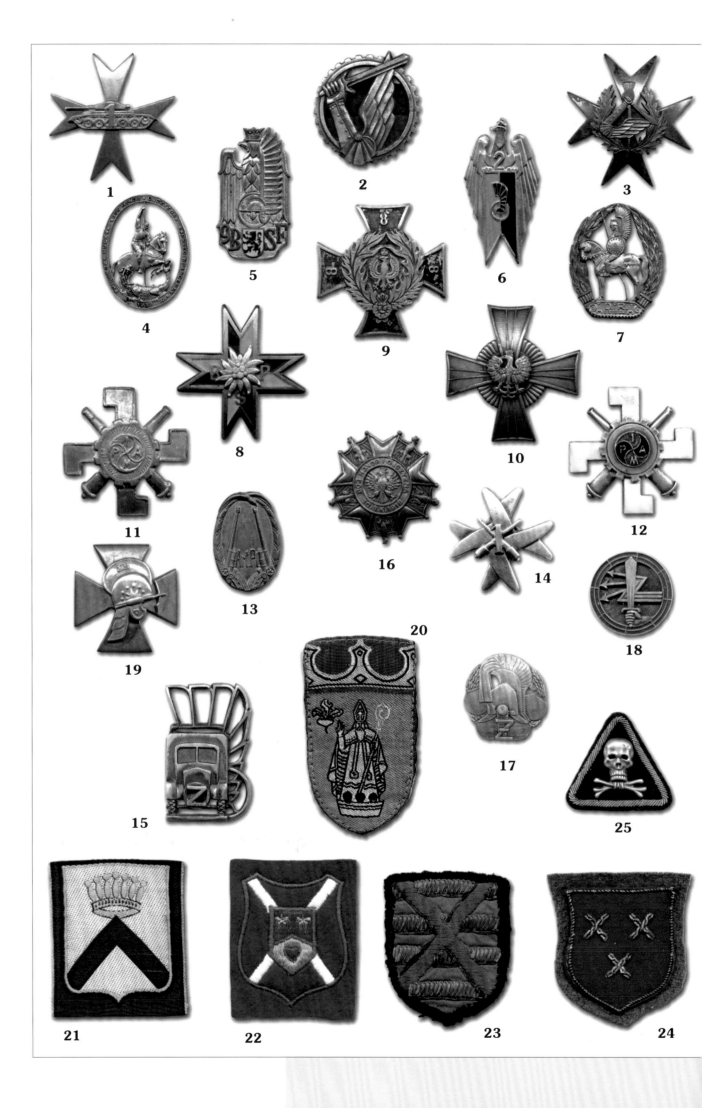

th Armoured Cavalry Brigade, 1st Armoured Regt, 2nd Armoured gt, Workshop unit
- **Maroon**: 1st Medium Machine Gun Squadron (upholding the traditions of the 1st Reconnaissance Regt, from whence it came).

urragères

Polish personnel were entitled to wear the following foreign awards:
- Fourragère of the Norwegian war cross: Podhale Rifle Battalion. Awarded by King Haakon VII of Norway on 25 January 1941 when in le in Great Britain, for their role in the fighting at Narvik. The fourragère e the shield of Norway with the rampant lion brandishing an axe. (see ow, right)
- The Fourragère of the Belgian Croix de Guerre was awarded to the Rifle Battalion on 7 December 1946 by a decree signed by Prince gent Charles, earl of Flanders. This was in recognition for its role in the ting in Belgium in September and October 1944.

Pulkownick Franciszeck Skibinski, commanding officer of the 3rd Rifle Brigade.

Left.
Norwegian fourragère for the Podhale Rifles.

METALLIC UNIT BADGES
(Worn on the left blouse pocket)

There were silver variants for officers or private purchase. Approval ates (in brackets) do not mean the badge had not been worn beforeand. No more than three badges could be worn at the same time, whether or not they were cloth or metallic.

. **1st Armoured Regiment (1943).**
. **Generic armoured troops insignia (1932).**
. **2nd Armoured Regiment (1943).**
. **1st Anti-Tank Artillery Regiment (1943).**
. **9th Rifle Battalion. Flanders Rifles (1946).**
. **2nd Motorized Artillery Regiment (1945).**
. **10th Dragoons Motor Battalions (created before 1939)**
. **Podhale Rifle Battalion (1946).**
. **8th Rifle Battalion. Brabant Rifles (1946).**
0. **24th Uhlans, Armoured Regiment (1921).**
1, 12. **1st Motorized Artillery Regiment, variants (1931).**
3. **Anti-aircraft Artillery (created before 1939).**
4. **1st Light Anti-Aircraft Artillery Regiment, replaced n° 13 (1945).**
5. **Supply and Transport (1946).**
6. **10th Mounted Rifles, PSK. Created before 1939.**
7. **Provost Units (created before 1939).**
8. **Corps of Signals (created before 1939)**
9. **Medium Machine Gun Squadron. Support unit armed with mortars and machine-guns. Used the former insignia of the 1st Reconnaissance Regiment from which it came (1942).**
Some units did not wear insignia during this period: Engineers, Medical Service, Workshops, Ordnance.

HONORARY BADGES
(cloth badges, worn at the top of the right arm)

0. **1st Armoured Regiment. Shield of the Belgian town of Sint Niklaas, liberated by the unit in October 1944 (1945).**
1. **1st Light Anti-Aircraft Artillery Regiment. Shield of the Belgian town of Exarde in memory of the fighting of October 1944 (1946)**
2. **10th Dragoons. Heraldic shield of the Scottish earl of Lanarkshire, where the unit was stationed in 1942.**
3. **2nd Armoured Regiment. Shield of the Belgian town of Beveren. Commemorating the fighting of October 1944. (1946).**
4. **8th Rifle Battalion. Shield of the town of Breda, in Holland. Commemorating the fighting in October 1944. (1946).**
5. **1st Motorized Artillery Regiment, 1st Battery 'The battery of death' (winter 1944).**

Research and translation of original Polish documents by Daniel Blanchard, nsignia Stéphane Brière collection, photographs by S. Jonot, Mémorial de Mont Ormel)

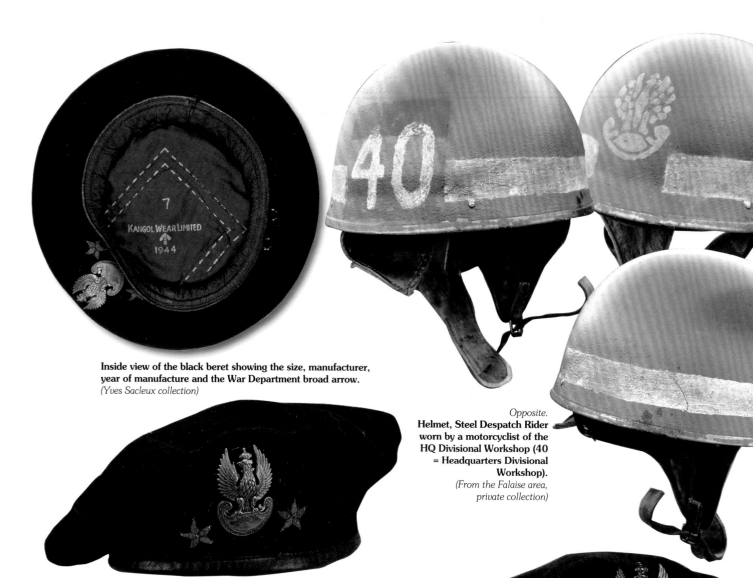

Inside view of the black beret showing the size, manufacturer, year of manufacture and the War Department broad arrow.
(Yves Sacleux collection)

Opposite.
Helmet, Steel Despatch Rider worn by a motorcyclist of the HQ Divisional Workshop (40 = Headquarters Divisional Workshop).
(From the Falaise area, private collection)

Above.
Porucznik rank insignia on the Royal Armoured Corps black beret adopted by all personnel of the Division, except for the Podhale Rifle Battalion that retained the khaki beret of French fortress troops (below).

Metallic eagle on a RAC black beret.
(Yves Sacleux collection)

Belo[w]
Helmet, Steel, Royal Armoured Corps, Mark I (helmet for tank and A[...] crews) bearing the crowned Polish eag[le]
(Collection François Cybuls[ki])

Above.
The eagle on khaki backing is placed here on the khaki beret used by French fortress troops, issued to the Polish Podhale mountain troops engaged in the Norway operations of April-May 1940. Before embarking at Brest, the Brigade was entirely armed and clothed along the lines of the 13e Demi-Brigade de la Légion Etrangère (Foreign Legion) with whom it served in Norway. Regrouped in Great Britain, the survivors of the Brigade formed the core of the Podhale Rifle Battalion (3rd Rifle Brigade) and the khaki beret was retained in memory of their service in Norway. At the beginning of 1945, however, Brygodny General Maczek ordered the unit to wear the RAC black beret.
(Le Poilu collection)

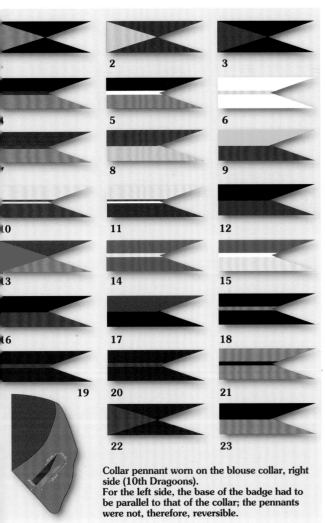

1st POLISH ARMOURED DIVISION COLLAR TABS

1. Divisional HQ and 10th Armoured Brigade
(orange and black).

2. HQ 3rd Rifle Brigade
(navy blue and dark green).

3. Divisional Artillery HQ
(black and dark green).

4. 1st Armoured Regiment
(black-orange-maroon).

5. 2nd Armoured Regiment
(black-orange-white).

6. 24th Lancers (white and yellow).

7. 10th Dragoons
(maroon-orange-green).

8. Podhale Rifle Battalion (navy blue and yellow).

9. 8th Rifle Battalion
(pale green and navy blue).

10. 9th Rifle Battalion
(navy blue and yellow).

11. Independent HMG Squadron
(yellow-maroon-navy blue and white).

12. 1st and 2nd Motorized Artillery regiments (black and dark green).

13. 1st Anti-Tank Regiment
(red-orange-black).

14. 1st Anti-Aircraft Regiment
(green and yellow).

15. 10th Mounted Rifle Regiment
(green-yellow-white).

16. 1st Transport Battalion
(black and blue).

17. Divisional Engineers
(red and black).

18. Repair Workshops (black and Orange).

19. Quartermaster (claret and green).

20. Medical Services (claret and blue).

21. 1st Road Traffic Control Squadron (orange and black).

22. 1st Materiel Park
(claret and blue).

23. 1st Reserve Tank Squadron (orange and black).

Collar pennant worn on the blouse collar, right side (10th Dragoons).
For the left side, the base of the badge had to be parallel to that of the collar; the pennants were not, therefore, reversible.

A Kapral of the 10th Dragoons (Motor Battalion) in 1946 during the occupation of Germany in the British zone. He wears the medal ribbons of the Odznaka Honorowa za Rany Kontuze (on top), the Krzyz Walencznych and the Odrodzenia Polski (with silver swords). Also present are the British campaign medals awarded later.
(Reconstruction, Laurent Taveau collection)

...lemen lifted on a Challenger of the 10th PSK. The tank model was ...livered to the regiment in November 1944 in Holland. At the rear, the ...ite square indicates B Squadron and the oval PL, the nationality.
...ivate Collection, RR)

Decorations awarded to Polish ground forces from 1939 to 1945

Left side of a Kapitan Chaplain's service dress tunic. The three five-pointed stars are made in silver bullion and the black shoulder strap is attached with a button bearing the Polish eagle. The shoulder title letters are also in bullion. The formation sign is embroidered onto khaki cloth and worn here as supplied by the manufacturer. It was only displayed on the left sleeve.
(Overlord collection)

Right and above.
Close up on the medal ribbons: Top rwo: O*dznaka Honorowa za Rany i Kontuzze* (wound badge with one star for one wound). Middle and bottom, from left to right: *Krzyz Walecznych* (Cross of Valor, 2 awards), *Order Odrodzenia Polski V Klassy* (Cross of Merit, 5th class). British ribbons: 39/45 star, France and Germany star, Defence Medal.

(Damien Cierpisz and Stéphane Brière documentation and collection)

...ecorations for bravery, ...mpaign medals and ...eritorious service

... Order of *Virtuti Militari* V ...asy (silver). Existed in five ...asses. (1. great cross, 2. ...mmander, 3. knight, 4. gold, ... silver) awarded to officers ...d other ranks for exceptional ...llantry under enemy fire.

***Krzyz Waleznich.* Cross of ...lour** (London model).

***Brazowy Krzyz Zastugi z ...ieczami.* Cross of merit.** ...isted in three classes (see ...low) A. *Brazowy* (bronze), ... *Krzyz* (silver), C. *Zastugi z.* ...old).

***Medal Wojska.* Created in** ...945 for 12 months of non-...erational service or 6 months ...' operational service.

Krzyz Czynu Bojowego ...olskich Sik Zbrohnych na ...achdzie.
...ar cross for Polish forces in ...e West.

...ote. *The 9th Rifle Battalion was ...arded the Belgian Croix de Guerre ... 1 July 1945 by Prince Regent ...harles (also see page 36)*

Right.
***Brazowy Krzyz Zastugi z ...ieczami.* Cross of merit in its presentation box from Spink & Son, Saint, James Street, London.**
(Damien Cierpisz collection).

3A **3B** **3C** **3**

5 - WAR CROSS (COMMEMORATIVE) OF POLISH FORCES IN THE WEST

As stipulated by the law concerning orders and decorations dated 16 October 1992 for decorations instituted by the People's Republic of Poland, the cut-off date retained for the award of medals was set for 8 May 1995, but was then extended to 8 May 1999.

The commemorative War Cross was part of the list of decorations affected by this law. The medal was created by a law dated 17 May 1989 and ceased to be awarded on 8 May 1999. It was awarded to former personnel of the Polish forces in the west who had fought under the authority of the Polish government in exile in London. This is the only Polish medal that has campaign bars on the ribbon. There are fifteen of these bars, thirteen for battle honours.

Bar	Date of the battle	Awarded to
Narvik	May 1940	Podhale Ind. Rifle Brigade (SBSP)
Lagarde	June 1940	1st Grenadier (F/1 Dgren.)
Maiche-St. Hippolyte	June 1940	2nd Rifles (2 DSP)
Bitwa O Anglie	August/October 1940	
Tobrouk	August/October 1941	Carpathian Ind. Rifle Brigade (SBSK)
Monte Cassino	May 1944	2nd Corps (2 KP)
Ankona	July 1944	2nd Corps (2 KP)
Falaise-Chambois	August 1944	1st Podhale Ind. Rifle Brigade (1 DPanc. + SBSP)
Axel	September 1944	1st Armoured Div. (1 DPanc.)
Arnhem	September 1944	1st Ind. Para. Bde. (SBSP)
Breda	October 1944	1st Armoured Div. (1 DPanc.)
Bolonia	April 1945	2nd Corps (2 KP)
Wilhelmshaven	May 1945	1st Armoured Div. (1 DPanc.)
Dzialania Bojowe Lotnictwa		Aerial operations and combat
Bitwy I Konwoje Morskie		Naval battles and convoys

Abou...
**Czech soldiers patrol the flooded zon...
around Festung Dunkerque on boa...
Mk III Stormboat...**
(HIM archive...

THE 1st CZECH INDEPENDENT

On 15 March 1939 and in violation of the agreements signed at Munich on 29 September 1938, the German army invaded Czechoslovakia. The country then became the Protectorate of Bohemia and Moravia and Slovakia, thus becoming a vassal state of the Reich (obligatory conscription into the Wehrmacht would later be decreed).

Unable to resist, the Czech army was disbanded and many of its personnel found refuge in France by travelling via Romania.

After 3 September 1939 and the declaration of war against Germany by France and Great Britain, the Czechs and Slovaks were gathered in Southern France near Agde and formed into the 1st Czechoslovakian infantry division. In May and June 1940, two of the regiments saw action at Coulommiers and on the Marne. Following the armistice, 3,500 men were evacuated via Sète and set sail for Great Britain. President Eduard Benès, who had set up a Czech government in exile, made an appeal from London to his fellow countrymen, exhorting them to join him and carry on the fight.

As early as September 1940, a thousand men travelled via the USSR and Romania, reaching the Middle East where they were incorporated into the British Army. Their contingent fought in Syria and at Tobruk.

In August 1943, the contingent was transferred to Great Britain where it was incorporated into the Czech Independent Armoured Brigade Group (CIABG) that was officially formed on 1 September 1943 and placed under the command of Brigadny-General Alois Liska. Following a period of training and out-

Left.
Czechoslovakia in 1938 before the Munich agreements of September the same year.

fitting, the Czech Brigade was designated to take part in the invasion due ... begin in the spring of 1944.

On 31 August 1944, the CIABG landed at Graye-sur-Mer near Courseulle... It concentrated at 21st Army Group transit camp No 60 north of Falaise in th... Epaney, Fontaine and Breuil sector.

Attached to the 1st Canadian Army on 2 October, the Brigade Group r... ceived orders to advance towards the Dunkirk sector, and on the 6th, relieve... the 51st (Highland) Division whose 154th Brigade was covering the town.

The brigade headquarters of Brigadny-General Liska was situated in Worn... hout.

Festung Dunkerque was strongly fortified and had a garrison of 12,000 men... it was almost entirely surrounded by flooded land which meant that it was in... possible to launch an operation with a unit the size of the CIABG.

From October 1944 to May 1945, it was tasked initially with preventin... any break out by the German forces, although the latter did launch several vio... lent counter-attacks, notably at the end of October/early November, as well a... March and April 1945 when eight Cromwell tanks were destroyed.

On 8 May 1945, rear-admiral Frisius, commander of Festung Dunkerque... declared that he was ready to lay down his arms and the following day, Brigad...

---

1. Despite the active participation of French units placed under the command of the CIABG, the British authorities, for reasons that remain unknown, refused to fly the French tricolour. Only a few officers were allowed to take part in the ceremony. The flag was, however, flown from the bell tower by French officers.

Strength of the Czech Independent Armoured Brigade Group

At the beginning of operations on 8 October 1944 there were **246** officers and **4,134** NCOs and men.

On 22 April 1945 were **326** officers and **5,437** NCOs and men.

The increase in manpower was due to the arrival of the 3rd Armoured Regiment in March 1945, as well as Czech volunteers who had previously served with the German army where they had been forcibly enrolled.

Losses by 8 May 1945 [1]

189 killed, 214 wounded and 25 prisoners from the following units:
– 1st Armoured Regt: 21 killed.
– 2nd Armoured Reg: 31 killed.
– 3th Armoured Regt: 11 killed.
– Motor Battalion Regt: 66 killed.
– Anti-Tank Battery: 14 killed.
– Engineers Squadron: 10 killed.

Strength per unit (October 1944)	OF	OR
Headquarters		
Armoured Brigade [2]	30	196
Brigade Signals	5	182
Recce Squadron	91	58
Armoured Regiments	36	580
Motor Battalion	31	575
Field Artillery Battery	27	436
Anti Tank Battery	8	158
Anti-Aircraft Battery	3	81
Engineers Squadron and Bridging Troop	7	196
Supply and Transport Coy.	14	426
Ordnance Field Park	22	2
Brigade Workshop	7	154
Light Field Ambulance	12	167

1. Many Czech soldiers killed at Dunkirk rest at nearby Leffincbrouke cemetary.
2. Including attached elements.

liberation parade was organised in Prague. The Brigade was disbanded at the end of 1945.

Organisation and structure

The bulk of the Brigade Group's fire power consisted of three tank regiments. A Motor Battalion was adjoined to them and ensured the role of support infantry, carried by M5/M9 half-tracks. These armoured regiments were equipped with Cruiser and Cromwell tanks reinforced with Sherman IC 'Fireflies' in each regimental Headquarters (as a replacement, Challenger Mk VII tanks were issued in May 1945 but did not take part in operations).

Support fire was provided by the reinforced Field Artillery Battery, with twelve 25-pounder guns. There was also an Engineer Squadron accompanied by a Bridging Troop for the detection of mines and booby traps and crossing the flooded sectors around Festung Dunkerque. Well endowed in manpower and vehicles, these units undertook support missions that allowed the Brigade Group to meet its own needs.

Below.
At the end of the fighting in May 1945, 80% of the town of Dunkirk was destroyed. This was due to the fighting of 1940 and 1944-45, but also to Allied bombing raids. On the left is the bell tower of the town hall where the Czech and British flags were flown on 9 May 1945.

In insert.
The national flag in red and white was created in 1918. An official emblem was created in 1920 with the addition of a blue triangle representing the Slovak population.

General Liska accepted the surrender of the town. The Czech and British flags were flown from the steeple of the bell tower. [1]
Following negotiations by President Benès with the Allied command, the CIABG was authorised to return to Czechoslovakia on 30 May and a great

...RMOURED BRIGADE GROUP

générale   Edition P. L, Lille

The CIABG commander, Brigadier General Alois Liska (right) in conversation with Field Marshal B. Montgomery.
(IHM archives)

CIABG Order of Battle

- ● **Headquarters Armd. Brigade**
- — Liaison Staff and British Liaison
- — Headquarters Coy.
- — Field Cash Office, Chaplain
- — Welfare Section
- — Court Martial
- — Disciplinary Company
- — Reconnaissance Squadron
- — Replacement Squadron
- — Traffic Control MP Coy.
- — Postal Unit
- ● Brigade Signals Forward Headquarters Armoured Brigade
- ● Anti Tank Battery
- ● Engineers Field Coy.
- ● Supply and Transport Coy.
- ● Ordnance Field Park
- ● Brigade Workshop
- ● Light Field Ambulance
- ● **1st Armoured Regt**
- ● Field Artillery Battery
- ● Bridging Troop
- ● **2nd Armoured Regt**
- ● Light Anti-Aircraft Battery
- ● **3rd Armoured Regt**
(March 1945)
- ● **Motor Battalion**

COMMAND STRUCTURE

- **Brigade Commander**
Brigadni General Alois Liska
- **Chief of Staff**
Plukovnik Karel Ondracek
- **Second in Command**
Plukovnik Antonin Barovsky

- **Provost**
Major Frantisek Divoky
- **Postal Unit**
Stabni Kapitan Joseph Sommer
- **Court Martial, Prosecutor**
Nadporucik Joseph Mrazek
- **Reconnaissance Troop**
Stabni Kapitan Jaromir Petzold
- **Anti-Aircraft Battery**
Kapitan Jiri Pujman
- **Engineer Squadron**
Podplukovnik Jiri Souhrada
- **Signal Company**
Stabni Kapitan Vaclav Reitinger
- **Train/Supply**
Podplukovnik Vladimir Bartosek
- **Ordnance Field Park**
Nadporucik Leopold Skulina
- **Light Field Ambulance**
Major Zdrav Vladimir Janca
- **Light Aid Detachment (Armd)**
Kapitan Jiri Cimrhaki
- **Delivery Squadron**
Kapitan Oldrich Zacek
- **1st Armoured Regiment**
Major Frantisek Rezabek
- **2nd Armoured Regiment**
Plukovnik Ferdinand Seda
- **3rd Armoured Regiment**
Major Jaromir Petzold
- **Motor Battalion**
Plukovnik Joseph Chvalovsky
- **Field Artillery Regiment**
Podplukovnik Lubor Marek
- **Anti Tank Regiment**
Podplukovnik Alois Sitek

Reinforcements under CIABG command

- ● **21st Army Group** *(up to February 1945)*
- — 7th RTR, detached from the 31st Army Tank Brigade (Churchill tanks)
- — 2 Field Artillery Regiments restructured as infantry units.
- — 133rd Light Anti-Aircraft Regiment (RA)
- — 2nd Heavy Anti-Aircraft Regiment (Canada), du 30 Sept. 44 to 06 Feb. 45
- — 150th Field Regt (RA)
- — 109th Heavy Anti-Aircraft Regt (RA)
- — 32nd Light Anti-Aircraft Regt (RA)

- ● **French fighting forces**
[men from the former Forces Françaises de l'Intérieur (FFI, FTP)] [1]
- — 33e régiment d'infanterie
- — 51e régiment d'infanterie
- — 67e régiment d'infanterie
- — 110e régiment d'infanterie
- — Groupe Franc Marine Dunkerque
- — 2 batteries of captured 155 m/M1917 guns

1. See details in France chapter.

Rifleman

Machine-gunner

Mortar operator

Radio operator

Motorised artillery

Mechanic armourer

Musician

Baker, butcher

Postman

Pioneer

Speciality and trade badges
Worn at the top of the left sleeve of the Battledress blouse

At the end of August 1944, the CIABG left its billets at Bridmington (Yorkshire) and made its way to the embarkation zones in the south of England. The men here are seen receiving last instructions on a troopship waiting to cast off.

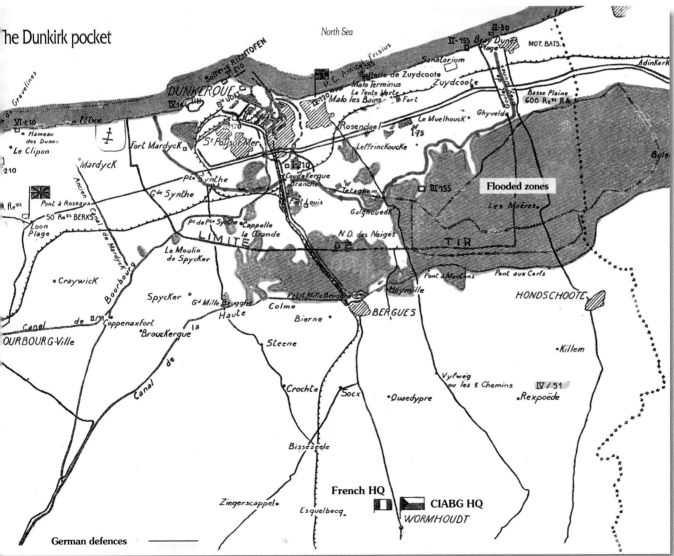

The Dunkirk pocket

North Sea

Gravelines
Battery RICHTOFEN
P.C. Amiral Frisius
Sanatorium
Batterie de Zuydcoote
II.50 Bray Dunes Plage
MOT. BATS.
AdinKerK

DUNKERQUE
St. UDE
Malo Terminus
La Tente Verte
Malo les Bains
Fort
Zuydcoote
Basse Plaine 600 Reg RA
Bysl

VI 10
Hameau des Dunes
Le Clipon
Fort Mardyck
St. Pol sur Mer
Rosendael
Le Muelhouck
Ghyveld

Mardyck
Pte Synthe
CoudeKergue Branche
LeffrincKoucKe
I.75

210
Gde Synthe
Fort Louis
Teteghem
III.155
Flooded zones
Les Moëres

Ancien Canal de Mardyck
Pont à Roseaux
50 Reg BERKS
Galghouedk
TIR

Reg
Loon Plage
Pt de Pte Synthe
Cappelle la Grande
N. D. des Neiges

Le Moulin de Spycker
LIMITE DE

Craywick
Bourbourg
Spycker
Gd Mille Brugghe
Petit Mille Brugghe
Hoymille
Pont à Mousons
Pont aux Cerfs
HONDSCHOOTE

Canal de II.51 Coppenaxfort
Colme
Haute
Bierne
BERGUES

OURBOURG-Ville
BrouckerQue
Steene
Killem

Canal de la
Crochte
Socx
Quaedypre
Vyfweg ou les 5 Chemins
IV/51
Rexpoëde

Canal
Bissezeele

Ziegerscappel
French HQ
CIABG HQ
Esquelbecq
WORMHOUDT

German defences ———

Left.

The cap badges were attached to the black beret or General Service Cap with metal prongs. Symbols used were the crossed swords and crowned lion of the Czech armed forces.

1. Gilded metal version for officers.
2. White metal version for other ranks.
3. Cap badge worn on the Field Service Cap (OR) befor the adoption of the General Service Cap.
4. Embroidered nationality shoulder title (British made)
5. Variant on Battledress cloth (British made)
6. Printed version approved in October 1942 by the British Chief Inspectorate of Clothing with the contract being awarded in October 1943. Accompanied by the formation sign of the Czech Brigade Group, the title wa sewn beforehand to a piece of cloth being sewn onto th uniform sleeves. Created in Great Britain in 1943, this shield became the badge of the 1st Czech Independent Armoured Brigade Group (CIABG, the regulation Britis abbreviation).

The white crowned lion of Bohemia bears the shield of Slovakia with the patriarchal cross and the Carpathian hills. According to heraldic rules, a lion on a town's shi faces left. In the case of the Czech Armd. Brigade, the looks to the front when on the left sleeve and to the rea when on the right sleeve.

Below, left.

8. A small commemorative veteran's badge with a Fren Adrian helmet, that was worn by the Czechs in the Grea War and in 1940.
9. Tank crew badge worn on the left pocket of the blou
10. Souvenir badge of the Czech army presence in Grea Britain. Made by M.W. Miller B'Ham.

Bel
Shoulder straps taken from a Battledr
blouse belonging to an infantry Podplukovr

CZECH INDEPENDENT ARMOURED BRIGADE GROUP RANK INSIGNIA

COMMAND STRUCTURE OF THE ARMOURED REGIMENT

Officer Commanding	*Padplukovnik*	Reconnaissance Troop	*Nadporucik*
Second in Command	*Major*	Intercommunication Troop	*Kapitan*
Technical Officer	*Kapitan*	Administrative Troop	*Porucik*
Medical Officer	*Kapitan*	Squadron	*Major*
Squadron HQ	*Major*	Administrative Troop	*Nadporucik*
Anti-Aircraft Troop	*Nadporucik*	Troop	*Porucik*

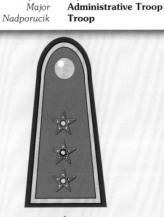

1

2

3

4

5

6

7

8

9

10

11

12

13

14

15

16

17

18

19

Infantry

Armoured

Signals

Medical

Artillery

Engineers

Star of rank marks

The crossed two-edged swords are the symbols of the Czec army. We find them on uniforms and later equipments in 1945

1. Divizni general	(General)	6. Stabni Kapitan	(Staff Captain)	11. Stabni Praporcik	(Staff Warrant Officer)
2. Brigadni general	(Brigadier)	7. Kapitan	(Captain)	12. Praporcik	(Warrant Officer)
3. Plukovnik	(Colonel)	8. Nadporucik	(Senior Lieutenant)	13. Stabni Rotmistr	(Staff Sergeant)
4. Podplukovnik	(Lieutenant-colonel)	9. Porucik	(Lieutenant)	14. Rotmistr	(Sergeant)
5. Major	(Major)	10. Podporucik	(Junior Lieutenant)	15. Rotny	(Senior Platoon Sergeant)

16. Cetar	(Platoon Sergeant)
17. Desatnik	(Corporal)
18. Svobodnik	(Lance Corporal)
19. Vojin	(Private)
Officers	Gold
O/R	silver

General Service Cap issued to Brigade personnel (except armoured units). Cap badge for other ranks.

RAC black beret worn by armoured regiment and reconnaissance squadron personnel (officer's cap badge).

Left.
Mk II helmet bearing the Czechoslovakian flag.

1. *Pametni medaile K20 Wyroci Osvoionzeni Ceskoslovenska.* Commemorative medal for the 20th anniversary of the liberation of Czechoslovakia.
2. *C-S Valecny Kriz z roku 1939.* WW2 war cross, instituted in 1939.
3. *C-S Medaile za Chabrost pred Nepticelem.* Medal of valour in the presence of the enemy, 1940.
4. *C-S Vojenska Medaile za Zasluny Stribrna.* Military merit medal instituted in 1943 by the Czech government.
5. *C-S Vojenska Pametni Medaile.* Commemorative medal with the bars SV (Middle East), VB (Great Britain), F (France).
The bronze lime tree leaves indicate the various classes. British Campaign Stars and War Medal (in non regulation order here).

'Austerity' Battledress blouse.
The rank insignia is that of an artillery
Svobodnik. The blackened cap badge
was often worn by other ranks during
the campaign.

1937/40 Pattern Battledress blouse for an infantry major. Note that
the British medal ribbons are not worn in regulation fashion. According
to these, the owner was one of the early members of the contingent at
Gedera camp near Tel Aviv in September 1940.
The British approved the formation of this 11th Field Bn (Eastern) in
December. It fought in Syria against the French Vichy forces before taking
up garrison duties in North Syria. It then went to Tobruk on 21 October
1941 to take part in the defence of the latter, where it was incorporated
into the Polish Carpathian Independent Brigade. The battalion saw action
in Tobruk before being evacuated and was then reorganised into a LAA
battalion in May 1942. It defended Alexandria and Haifa before going to
Great Britain in August 1943.

This photo was taken on 9 May 1945 after the surrender of Festung Dunkerque and shows General Liska on his way to raising the Czechoslovakian and British flag on the town hall tower. The local British commander refused to fly the French flag and only a few French officers were allowed to take part in the ceremony, an event that was widely captured on film by the Allied war correspondents. It was not until the next day that Lieutenant-Colonel Lehagre ordered the French flag to be flown. *(IHM archives)*

9 May 1945 after the surrender of Festung Dunkerque. A group of Czech, British and French officers pose for posterity. *(IHM archives)*

ow.

Above.

y 1945, the road home. A Motor Battalion Bren Carrier has halted in front
a 3 Ton 4x4 Chevrolet and the crew are chatting with a GI of the 3rd US
my that controlled this part of German and Czechoslovakian territory.
M archives)

The five man crew of this Cromwell tank wear the Tank Suit (Winter)
and rubber boots that were standard issue in some Royal Engineers units.
The issue of these boots was due to the presence of marshlands
in the zone of operations.

Men of the armoured regiments with their specific RAC helmet and Denim Tank Suit in the role of riflemen. Given the nature of the terrain, the tanks were more often used as fire support.

Below, left.
Cruiser tank Cromwell Mk IV. The '52' code number indicates that it belongs to the 2nd Armoured Regiment.

Below.

These Cromwell Mk IV tanks of the 1st Armoured Regiment (code number 51) patrol around the flooded zones. The formation badge is painted on the front left-hand side. *(Below).*

Another group of tank crew in the role of riflemen.
(IHM archives)

CIABG TRANSPORT AND ARMAMENT [1]

(Note WO 106/4186. 1st October 1944)

BRIGADE HEADQUARTERS
– 9 Motorcycles
– 5 Cars 4-seater
– 4 Cars 2-seater
– 2 Cars 4-seater 4 x 4
– 10 Jeep
– 4 Trucks 15-cwt (Including 1 water)
– 2 Half-Tracks M 14
– 1 White Scout car
– 14 Lorries 3-Ton 4 x 2 GS

BRIGADE SIGNALS
– 9 Motorcycles
– 10 Jeeps
– 1 Car 4-seater
– 10 Truck 15-cwt
– 9 Truck 15-cwt Wireless
– 1 Truck 15-cwt Office
– 6 White Scout Cars
– 14 Lorries 3-Ton 4 x 4 GS

RECONNAISSANCE SQUADRON
– 3 Motorcycles
– 1 Jeep
– 2 Trucks 15-cwt
– 2 Half-Tracks M-14
– 12 Lorry 3-Ton 4 x 4 GS
– 1 Lorry 3-Ton 6 x 4 Store
– 3 Daimler Scout
– 11 Cruiser Tanks Cromwell
– 2 Close Support Tanks
– 1 Light Tank, M5A1

– 1 Armoured Recovery Vehicle

MOTOR BATTALION
– 36 Motorcycles
– 7 Jeeps
– 1 Car 4-seater
– 11 Trucks 15-cwt GS 4 x 2
– 39 Half-Tracks IHC M5-M14
– 20 Lorries 3-Ton GS 4 x 4
– 24 Universal and Loyd Carriers
(16 MMG + 4 x 3-inch Mortar)
– 6 x 6-pdr Anti-Tank guns

FIELD ARTILLERY BATTERY
– 19 Motorcycles
– 12 Jeep
– 2 Cars 4-seater 4 x 4
– 31 15-cwt 4 x 2 GS
– 2 Half-Tracks IHC M-14
– 16 Lorries 3-Ton 4 x 4 GS
– 24 Artillery Tractors 4 x 4
– 24 Limbers
– 12 25-Pounder Field gun
– 4 Advanced Observation Post

LIGHT ANTI-AIRCRAFT BATTERY
– 5 Motorcycles
– 1 Jeep
– 3 Truck 15-cwt
– 1 Lorry 3-Ton 4 x 2 GS
– 3 Lorries 3-Ton 4 x 4 GS
– 6 Tractors 6 x 4
– 6 40 mm AA guns

ANTI-TANK BATTERY
– 3 Motorcycles
– 6 Jeeps
– 8 Trucks 15-cwt 4 x 2 GS
– 8 Lorries 3-Ton 4 x 4 GS
– 12 Artillery Tractor 4 x 4
– 6 canons 17-Pounder AT

ENGINEERS SQUADRON AND BRIDGING TROOP
– 16 Motorcycles
– 3 Jeep
– 1 Car 4-seater
– 2 Cars Light Recce
– 4 x 4 Humber Mk III
– 6 Trucks 15-cwt 4 x 2 GS
– 2 Trucks 15-cwt Compressor
– 5 Half-Tracks IHC M-14
– 30 Lorries 3-Ton 4 x 4 GS
– 3 Lorries 3-Ton 4 x 4 Winch

SUPPLY AND TRANSPORT COMPANY
– 37 Motorcycles
– 8 Car 2-seater 4 x 2,
– 1 Car 4-seater 4 x 2,
– 15 Trucks 15-cwt 4 x 2 GS,
– 14 Lorries 3-Ton 4 x 2 GS,
– 4 Lorries 3-Ton 4 x 2 Stores,
– 2 Lorries 3-Ton 6 x 2 Stores

LIGHT FIELD AMBULANCE
– 14 Motorcycles
– 6 Cars 2-seater 4 x 2,

– 1 Car 4-seater 4 x 2,
– 2 Trucks 15-cwt 4 x 2,
– 13 Lorries 3-Ton 4 x 2 GS,
– 18 Ambulance 4 stretcher 4 x 2

ORDNANCE FIELD PARK
– 2 Motorcycles
– 1 Jeeps
– 1 Truck 15-cwt GS 4 x 2
– 6 Lorries 3-Ton 4 x 2 GS
– 6 Lorries 3-Ton 4 x 4 Stores

BRIGADE WORKSHOP [2]
– 9 Motorcycles
– 2 Cars 2-seater 4 x 2
– 9 Trucks 15-cwt 4 x 2 GS
– 2 Trucks 15-cwt Machinery
– 1 Trucks 8-cwt Type T
– 24 Lorries 3-Ton 4 x 2 Stores
– 14 Lorries 3-Ton 4 x 4 Stores
– 6 Lorries 3-Ton 4 x 4 Machinery
– 1 Lorry 6 x 4 Breakdown
– 3 Tractors 6 x 4
– 4 Tank Transporters 30-Ton

Abbreviations:
AT *Anti-Tank*
AA *Anti-Aircraft*
GS *General Service*

_____
1. For the armoured regiments see the table on page 146-147
2. Strength and materiel in the armoured and artillery regiments

AN ARMOURED REGIMENT, CZECHOSLOVAK FORCES (War Office Note WO 106/4186) dated 1 October 1944)

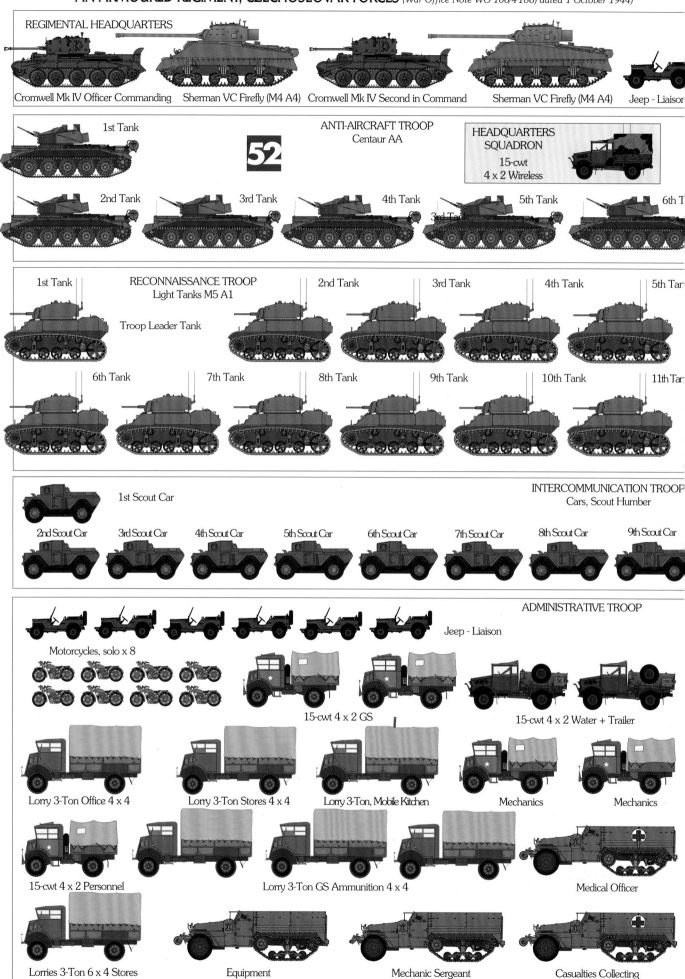

REGIMENTAL HEADQUARTERS

Cromwell Mk IV Officer Commanding   Sherman VC Firefly (M4 A4)   Cromwell Mk IV Second in Command   Sherman VC Firefly (M4 A4)   Jeep - Liaison

1st Tank

ANTI-AIRCRAFT TROOP
Centaur AA

52

HEADQUARTERS SQUADRON
15-cwt
4 x 2 Wireless

2nd Tank   3rd Tank   4th Tank   5th Tank   6th T
3rd Tank

RECONNAISSANCE TROOP
Light Tanks M5 A1

1st Tank   2nd Tank   3rd Tank   4th Tank   5th Tar

Troop Leader Tank

6th Tank   7th Tank   8th Tank   9th Tank   10th Tank   11th Tar

INTERCOMMUNICATION TROOP
Cars, Scout Humber

1st Scout Car

2nd Scout Car   3rd Scout Car   4th Scout Car   5th Scout Car   6th Scout Car   7th Scout Car   8th Scout Car   9th Scout Car

ADMINISTRATIVE TROOP

Jeep - Liaison

Motorcycles, solo x 8

15-cwt 4 x 2 GS   15-cwt 4 x 2 Water + Trailer

Lorry 3-Ton Office 4 x 4   Lorry 3-Ton Stores 4 x 4   Lorry 3-Ton, Mobile Kitchen   Mechanics   Mechanics

15-cwt 4 x 2 Personnel   Lorry 3-Ton GS Ammunition 4 x 4   Medical Officer

Lorries 3-Ton 6 x 4 Stores   Equipment   Mechanic Sergeant   Casualties Collecting

ARMOURED SQUADRON [the example shown here is of three squadrons (A, B and C) in the Regiment]

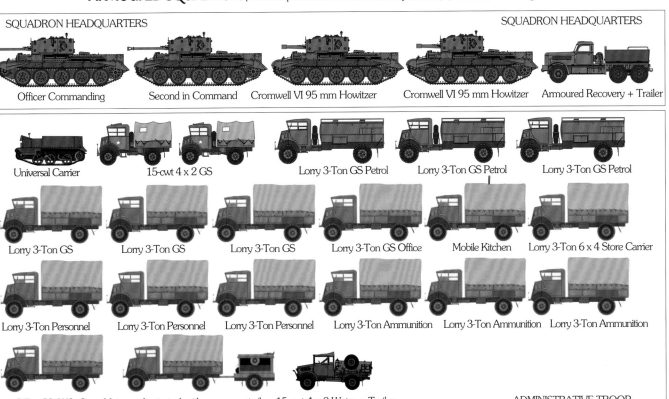

SQUADRON HEADQUARTERS

Officer Commanding

Second in Command

Cromwell VI 95 mm Howitzer

Cromwell VI 95 mm Howitzer

Armoured Recovery + Trailer

SQUADRON HEADQUARTERS

Universal Carrier

15-cwt 4 x 2 GS

Lorry 3-Ton GS Petrol

Lorry 3-Ton GS Petrol

Lorry 3-Ton GS Petrol

Lorry 3-Ton GS

Lorry 3-Ton GS

Lorry 3-Ton GS

Lorry 3-Ton GS Office

Mobile Kitchen

Lorry 3-Ton 6 x 4 Store Carrier

Lorry 3-Ton Personnel

Lorry 3-Ton Personnel

Lorry 3-Ton Personnel

Lorry 3-Ton Ammunition

Lorry 3-Ton Ammunition

Lorry 3-Ton Ammunition

Lorry 3-Ton GS 6 Wh, Store, Motor mechanics tools with compressor trailer

15-cwt 4 x 2 Water + Trailer

ADMINISTRATIVE TROOP

The three armoured regiments were organised in an identical fashion. The 2nd Armoured Regt. is shown here as an example.

STRENGTH
(Officers, ORs)

Regimental HQ	21
Squadron HQ	6
Anti-Aircraft Troop	24
Reconnaissance Troop	44
Intercommunication Troop	18
Administrative Troop	96
Squadron HQ (x 3)	23
Administrative Troop	51
Troop (x 4)	15
Total Squadron	**134**
Total Regiment	**611**
Attached	29
Total	**= 640**

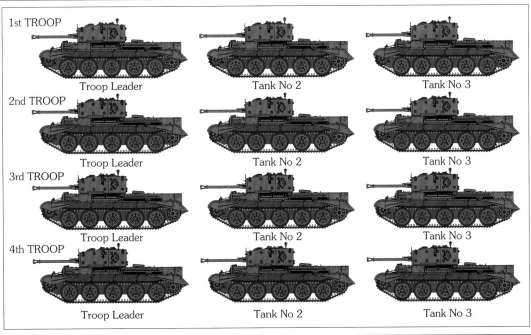

1st TROOP

Troop Leader · Tank No 2 · Tank No 3

2nd TROOP

Troop Leader · Tank No 2 · Tank No 3

3rd TROOP

Troop Leader · Tank No 2 · Tank No 3

4th TROOP

Troop Leader · Tank No 2 · Tank No 3

ATTACHED TO REGIMENT

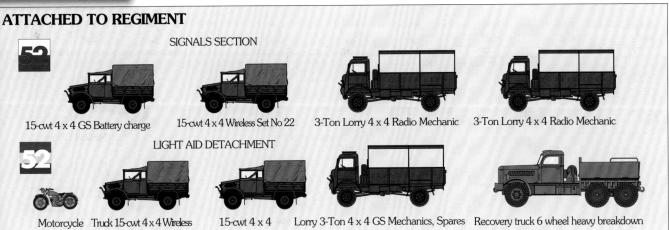

SIGNALS SECTION

15-cwt 4 x 4 GS Battery charge

15-cwt 4 x 4 Wireless Set No 22

3-Ton Lorry 4 x 4 Radio Mechanic

3-Ton Lorry 4 x 4 Radio Mechanic

LIGHT AID DETACHMENT

Motorcycle

Truck 15-cwt 4 x 4 Wireless

15-cwt 4 x 4

Lorry 3-Ton 4 x 4 GS Mechanics, Spares

Recovery truck 6 wheel heavy breakdown

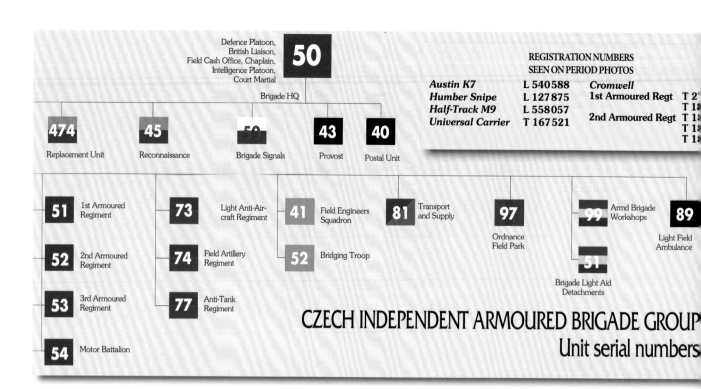

Defence Platoon, British Liaison, Field Cash Office, Chaplain, Intelligence Platoon, Court Martial

50

Brigade HQ

REGISTRATION NUMBERS
SEEN ON PERIOD PHOTOS

Austin K7	L 540588	*Cromwell*	
Humber Snipe	L 127875	**1st Armoured Regt**	T 2
Half-Track M9	L 558057		T 18
Universal Carrier	T 167521	**2nd Armoured Regt**	T 18
			T 18
			T 18

474 Replacement Unit

45 Reconnaissance

50 Brigade Signals

43 Provost

40 Postal Unit

51 1st Armoured Regiment

52 2nd Armoured Regiment

53 3rd Armoured Regiment

54 Motor Battalion

73 Light Anti-Aircraft Regiment

74 Field Artillery Regiment

77 Anti-Tank Regiment

41 Field Engineers Squadron

52 Bridging Troop

81 Transport and Supply

97 Ordnance Field Park

99 Armd Brigade Workshops

51 Brigade Light Aid Detachments

89 Light Field Ambulance

CZECH INDEPENDENT ARMOURED BRIGADE GROUP
Unit serial numbers

Brigadni General Alois Liska, 1895-1977

Mobilised in 1915, he underwent training as an officer cadet in the Austro-Hungarian army. Promoted to Aspirant then Porucik in May 1919, he was an artillery Kapitan in 1920. He then went to the war academy, graduating in 1929. Promoted to Padpulkovnik, he was sent to the 51st artillery regiment where he became commanding officer in October 1938 with the rank of Pulkovnik. After the occupation of Czechoslovakia by the German army in March 1939 and the disbanding of his regiment, Pulkovnik Liska began organising a resistance movement. Threatened with arrest, he reached France in 1940 where he found the Czechoslovakian army undergoing ref-

ormation. After the fighting of May-June 1940, he followed the survivors to Great Britain. It was there, on 21 March 1943, that the 1st Czech Independent Armoured Brigade Group was officially formed under his command, with the rank of General Brigadny. The formation landed in Normandy at the end of August 1944. The CIABG assembled around the Dunkirk pocket in October and General Liska now had British, French and Canadian units under his command in order to reduce the pocket of resistance. On 9 May 1945, he accepted the surrender of rear-admiral Frisius, commander of 'Festung Dünkirchen.' Following the return to Czechoslovakia, Alois Liska was pro-

moted to General Divizy then General Armada in 1946. With the change in political regime in February 1948, he was forcibly retired and chose to go into exile in London where he died on 7 February 1977.

Main decorations:
– Czechoslovakian war cross 1918
– Czechoslovakian war cross 1939
– Medal for bravery against the enemy
– Order of MR Stefanik in Memoriam
– French Légion d'Honneur
– French Croix de guerre 1939 with palm
– Commander of the British Empire
– Distinguished Service Order
– Legion of Merit (USA)

2nd Armoured Regiment 'A' Squadron

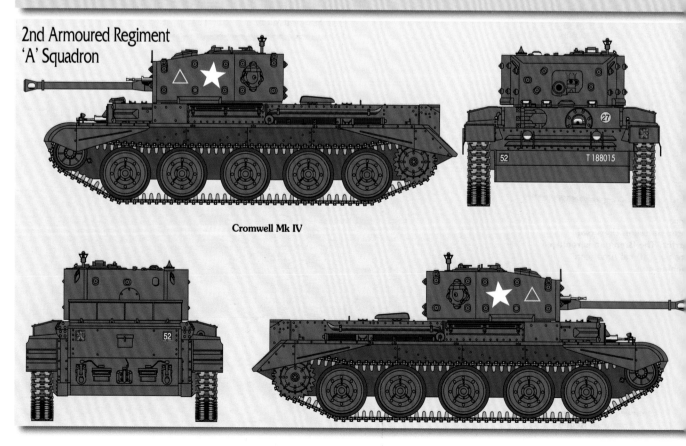

Cromwell Mk IV

Prague 30 May 1945.
~e victory and liberation parade
took place in the presence
President Benès returned from
exile in Great Britain where
~ led the Free Czechoslovakian
government.

Right.
**Motorcyclists
preceding the parade.**

té I. čsl. obrněné brigády na pražských ulicích.

MAIN VEHICLES AND TANKS
USED BY CZECH ARMOURED REGIMENTS. *(October 1944)*

VEHICLES			
- Motorcycle	213	- Close support Tank	14
- Car, 2 str. 4x2	23	- Cruiser Tank,	
- Car 5-cwt 4x4 Jeep	79	Sherman IC "Firefly"	4
- Truck 15-cwt 4x2	157	- Light Tank, Stuart M5A1	35
- Lorry 3-Ton 4x2 GS	218	- Carrier, Universal	24
- Lorry 3-Ton 4x4 GS	245	- Carrier, Loyd	16
- Ambulance 4x2	18	- 15-cwt, Half Track	64
- Tractor, C-8 Field Artillery	36	- 25-pounder, Field gun	12
- Tank Transporter 30-Ton	4		
COMBAT MATERIEL [1]			
- Car, scout Humber	34		
- Cruiser, Tank			
Cromwell Mk IV	127		

1. Situation at the start of the campaign. Does not include vehicles of the 3rd Armoured Regiment arriving in March 1945.

Těžký tank I. čsl. obrněné brigády se svým velitelem.

~ove.
~tor Battalion Universal
~rrier. The Bren gun is replaced
~re by a.30 cal American
~chine-gun.

Těžké tanky I. čsl. obrněné brigády na Příkopech

Right.
**Cromwell tanks of the 1st
Armoured Regiment.**

BIBLIOGRAPHY

The Battle of Normandy

For the reader particularly interested in the Battle of Normandy, the fighting undertaken from August 1944 onwards by the 1st Polish Armoured Division, the Royal Netherlands Brigade, the Belgian Brigade Group and the 1er Bataillon de Fusiliers-Marins Commando attached to the 1st Special Service Brigade, the author recommends five books by historian Eddy Florentin that cover these units in detail. These books are still in print, also in English:

— *Stalingrad en Normandie*. Perrin, 2003.
— *Opération Paddle, la bataille pour la Seine*. Perrin 2006.
— *Der Ruckmarsch. La retraite de Normandie*. Presses de la cité, 1991.
— *Montgomery franchit la Seine*. Presses de la cité, 1987.
— *Le Havre à feu et à sang, 12 septembre 1944* Presses de la Cité 1985.

French units

— *Mémoires de Guerre*. Tome III. Général de Gaulle. Plon 1959.
— *Les Insignes du Train*. SHAT. 1988.
— *Les Grandes Unités françaises – Guerre 1939-1945, Forces Françaises de l'Intérieur*. SHAT. 1980.
— *Le Réarmement et la réorganisation de l'Armée de Terre Française 1943-1946*. Chef de bataillon J. Vernet. SHAT. 1980.
— *Dictionnaire d'identification des insignes de la Résistance Française*. B. Fourage. R. Gerdil.
— *Qui ose gagne. Les parachutistes du 2e RCP (4th SAS)*. Henry Corta. Service Historique de l'Armée de Terre. 1997.
— *Les parachutistes SAS de la France Libre 1940-1945*. David Portier. Édition d'auteur 2004. Infofflsas@clubinternet.fr
— *Fire From the Forest. The SAS Brigade in France, 1944*. Roger Ford. Cassel. 2003.
— *Les dossiers de la 2e Guerre mondiale. La France en guerre*. Magazine No 4, avril 2006.
— *Paras de la France Libre*. Colonel Roger Flamand. Presses de la Cité. 1976.

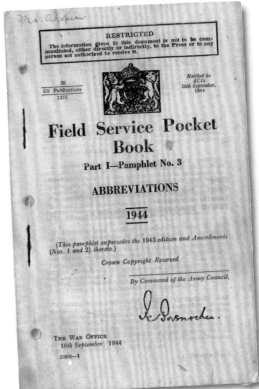

— *Un béret rouge*. Jean Dupontel. Édition d'auteur 1950.
— *Commandos du ciel*. DI Harrison. Plon 1957.
— *Les Parachutistes des FFL*. Denis Lassus. *Militaria Magazine* No 51, novembre 1989.
— *Béret vert*. Capitaine de corvette Philippe Kieffer, Éditions France Empire.
— *Commando de la France Libre*. Gwenn-Aël Bolloré, Éditions France Empire 1983.
— *Mille et un jours pour le Jour J*. Maurice Chauvet, Éditions Michel Lafon 1994.
— *Commandos and Rangers of World War II*. James Ladd, Macdonald and Jane's Publishers 1978.
— *Jour J avec le 1er BFM Commando*. Joël Tanter, Éditions Charles Corlet 1983.
— *Lancelot, soldat de la France Libre*. Maurice Chauvet, 1964.
— *Guide des plages du Débarquement et de la bataille de Normandie*. Eddy Florentin, Éditions Perrin 2003.
— *Le Commando du 6 juin*. Raymond La Sierra, Presses de la Cité 1983.
— *Opération Paddle*. Eddy Florentin, Presses de la Cité 1983.
— *Foreign Volunteers of the Allied Forces*. Nigel Thomas, Simon Mc Couaig. Men at Arms Series, 1998.
— *D-Day – 1er BFM Commando*. Maurice Chauvet, 1974.
— *La participation de la Marine française aux débarquements de Normandie, Corse et Provence*. Historique des Forces Navales Françaises Libres. Service Historique de la Marine Nationale, Vincennes, 1969-1992.
— *Les Français Libres et leurs emblèmes*. B. Le Marec, C. Lavauzelle 1964.

— *Commando Kieffer, Free French N° 10 & N° 4 Commando*. Éric Le Penven. Éditions Heimdal 2006 (complément du Tome I paru en 2004).
Ouvrages abondamment illustrés.

BIBLIOGRAPHY

Belgian units

La Brigade belge en Normandie.
litions du Sablon, 1945.
Des hommes oubliés. Guy Weber. Louis
usin Éditeur, 1978.
Les parachutistes belges 1942-1945 7.
an Temmerman. Éditions DVB, 1999.
Historique des bataillons de fusiliers belges
)44-1945 – Henry de Pinchart – Bruxelles.
Au galop de nos blindés. Lieutenant-Général
Dewandre. Éditions Dieu-Brichart, 1981.
L'artillerie belge en Grande-Bretagne et dans
combats de la Libération. Lieutenant-colonel J.
lard. Éditions Cabay, 1986.
Les volontaires de guerre belges et leurs
signes. Jacques P. Champagne. Éditions
Everling, 1990.
La Brigade Piron. Henri Demaret. 39/45
agazine No 71.
Les para-commandos belges. J.-
Chantrain – René Smeets – AMI 1981.
Militaria-Belgica 2004, provided by Pierre
erneux, Musée Royal de l'armée, Bruxelles.
Opération Paddle. Eddy Florentin,
rrin, 2005.
Montgomery franchit la Seine. Eddy
orentin, Presses de la Cité, 1987.
La Ruckmarsch. Eddy Florentin, Presses
la Cité, 1991.
Le Havre à feu et à sang. Eddy Florentin,
esses de la Cité, 1985.
elgian and Dutch units also mentioned in:
Seine de Guerre. Thierry Chion. Ysec
litions, 2011.

Dutch units

Geschiedenis van de Koninklijke
ederlandse Brigade Prinses Irène.
Gravenhage 1959.
Montgomery franchit la Seine. Eddy
orentin, Presses de la Cité 1987.
La Rückmarsch. Eddy Florentin, Presses de
Cité 1991.

— *Opération Paddle.* Eddy Florentin, Éditions
Perrin 1999.
— *Militaria magazine* No 214. Article by Mike
van Dobbelsteen.

Norwegian and Danish units
— *Foreign Volunteers of Allied Forces 1939-*
1945. Nigel Thomas, Men at Arms Series
1998.
— *No 10 Inter-Allied Commando 1942-1945.*
Nick van der Bijl Bem. Osprey Elite 2006.
— *National Geographic Magazine.*
November 1945.

Polish units

The odyssey of the 1st Polish Armoured
Division, from Normandy to Wilhemshaven,
has been told in numerous books and articles,
and especially the battle at Mont Ormel
and for the Dutch town of Breda, two of its
prominent battle honours,.
— *L'épopée de la 1re DB polonaise.*
S. Brière & M. Pépin, Ysec Éditions, 2004.
— *La Massue.* Didier Lodieu, Ysec Éditions,
2004.
— *Avec mes blindés.* Général Stanislas
Macek, Presse de la Cité, 1967.
— *The Black Devils' March.* E. McGilvray,
Elion & Company, 2005.
— *1 Dywizja Pancerna 1944-1945.*
Volume II. Jacek Solarz, Wydawnictwo,
Militaria, Warszawa 2004 (some english text).
— *Wojsko Polskie 1939-1945.* Warsawa,
1990 (badges, uniforms).
— *Stalingrad en Normandie.* Eddy
Florentin, Nouvelle édition, Perrin, 2002.
— *La 1re division blindée polonaise.* Jordan
Gaspin, Stéphane Brière et Laurent Taveau,
Militaria Magazine No 253, Histoire & Collections.
— *La 1re division blindée polonaise.*
Philippe Naud, *SteelMasters* No 77, Histoire
& Collections.
— *La contribution des Polonais dans les*

combats de 1939-1945. Z. Wyderkiewicz,
Print Forum, Lille, 2002.
— *Un pont trop loin.* Cornelius Ryan,
Éditions Robert Laffont, 1974.
— *Les Bérets rouges à Arnhem.* Fabien
Reberac, Histoire de Guerre No 5,
mai 2005.
— *La 1re Brigade Parachutiste*
indépendante polonaise. Daniel Blanchard,
Uniformes No 167, 2007.
— *Poles Apart.* GF Cholewczynski, Greenhill
Books, London, 1993.
— *Arnhem, a tragedy of errors.*
P. Harclerode, Arms and Armour Press,
1994.
— *Arnhem 1944 – The Airborne Battle 17-*
26 September 1944. Martin Middlebrook,
Penguin Books, 1994.
— *Les Paras polonais, Militaria Magazine*
No 267, Histoire & Collections
— *Arnhem, la bataille des Paras.*
Christopher Hibbert, *Historia Magazine* No
77, Tallandier, 1969.
— *Opération Market Garden.* Yves
Buffetaut, *Militaria Magazine Hors-Série* No
23, Histoire & Collections – 1996.
— *Military Illustrated* No 12 (avril-mai
1988). Article by Krzysztof Barbarski.

Czech units

— *Journal du Vice-Amiral Friedrich Frisius,*
Commandant de la Forteresse de Dunkerque,
3 septembre 1944 — 9 mai 1945.
2002-Punch Éditions, ZI La Trésorerie, 62126
Wimille.
— *39/45 Magazine* No 87 (1944) Éditions
Heimdal: *1945 Poche de Dunkerque.*
— *Dunkerque 1944-1945* par Serge
Blanckaert, Éditions La Voix du Nord, 1995.
— *Dunkerque, Valecny denick*
Ceskoslovenske, Samostatne obrnene brigady
1944-45 par Ivan Prochazka, Praha 2006.
— *Ceskoslovenska armada ve Velke Britanii*
by Vilem Fencl & Martin Riha, Praha 2002.

Design and layout Jean-Marie & Jean-Baptiste Mongin © *Histoire & Collections 2012*

ISBN: 978-2-35250-191-6
Publisher's number: 35250
© *Histoire & Collections* 2012

Book edited by
HISTOIRE & COLLECTIONS
5, avenue de la République
F-75541 Paris Cedex 11 - FRANCE
Tel: +33-1 40 21 18 20
Fax: +33-1 47 00 51 11
www.histoireetcollections.com

This book has been designed, type
laid-out and processed by *Histoire & Collectio*
on fully integrated computer equipme

Color separation: Studio A &

Print by Calidad Grafi
European Union, December 20